Critical Reading in Language Educatio

Other titles by the same author

ADVANCED READING SKILLS (with P. Barr & J. Clegg)

LEARNING TO READ IN A MULTICULTURAL SOCIETY: The Social Context of Second Language Reading

READING

Critical Reading in Language Education

Catherine Wallace

Institute of Education, University of London

First published in hardcover 2003
First published in paperback 2005 by
PALGRAVE MACMILLAN
Houndmills, Basingstoke, Hampshire RG21 6XS and
175 Fifth Avenue, New York, N.Y. 10010
Companies and representatives throughout the world

PALGRAVE MACMILLAN is the global academic imprint of the Palgrave Macmillan division of St. Martin's Press, LLC and of Palgrave Macmillan Ltd. Macmillan® is a registered trademark in the United States, United Kingdom and other countries. Palgrave is a registered trademark in the European Union and other countries.

ISBN-13: 978–0–333–98579–3 hardback
ISBN-10: 0–333–98579–6 hardback
ISBN-13: 978–1–4039–9339–7 paperback
ISBN-10: 1–4039–9339–4 paperback

This book is printed on paper suitable for recycling and made from fully managed and sustained forest sources.

A catalogue record for this book is available from the British Library.

Library of Congress Cataloging-in-Publication Data
Wallace, Catherine.
    Critical reading in language education / Catherine Wallace.
        p.   cm.
    Includes bibliographical references and index.
    ISBN 0–333–98579–6 (cloth)
    1. Language and languages—Study and teaching.   2. Reading.   I. Title.

P53.75.W35 2003
418'.4'071—dc21   2003046917

10   9   8   7   6   5   4   3   2   1
14   13   12   11   10   09   08   07   06   05

Printed and bound in Great Britain by
Antony Rowe Ltd, Chippenham and Eastbourne

For my mother and in memory of my father

Contents

Acknowledgements

This book is the outcome of many conversations with students and colleagues over the years. I should like to thank all those who have contributed to it, in particular the students who are at the centre of the study and kindly gave their permission for me to use their words. I should also like to thank a number of people who have read and commented on parts of this book and earlier drafts. They include: Alison Appleby, Elsa Auerbach, David Block, Shoshana Blum-Kulka, Colin Lankshear, Lindsay Mair, Carolyn McKinney, John O'Regan and Henry Widdowson.

Finally thanks are due both to my current colleagues in the School of Culture, Language and Communication, at the Institute of Education, University of London, in particular Professor Deborah Cameron who offered strong support for this project, and my former colleagues and students at Thames Valley University, formerly Ealing College of Higher Education. One of these, Monica Hermerschmidt made a special contribution to the classroom study which underpins the book, giving up many hours of her time to discuss aspects of critical reading and critical pedagogy. I am very much indebted to her.

Points of Departure

This book investigates reading as a social, critical process. It is addressed to language teachers and researchers, and is based on studies of reading and readers, as well as on classroom interactions around text. My point of departure is the text: what do texts have to tell us about contemporary social life? How can we make use of them in the language classroom for critical reading?

I taught my first 'critical reading' class to a group of intermediate foreign language students from various European and Far Eastern countries in the Autumn of 1989. In Europe it was a time of change, typified most memorably by the fall of the Berlin Wall. I recall discussing with students the image of Germany in one newspaper report 'striding like a colossus across Europe', an image which, in the view of the German students in the class, conveyed a menacing and false impression. Later that academic year, in February 1990, came the release of Nelson Mandela. The texts recording this occasion remain defining texts of their era – we all recall the clenched fist salute of Winnie and Nelson Mandela, which featured on the front pages of newspapers worldwide. The following year brought the Gulf War and a fresh set of newspaper reports, which as I revisit them now in the Summer of 2003, take on a new resonance in the context of further conflict in the Gulf. During that first course and those in subsequent years, students and I went to work critically on a wide range of texts, not just newspaper report texts, but brochures, posters, advertisements and magazine articles, drawn largely from everyday life. I shall follow Luke *et al.* in calling these 'community texts'. These texts of everyday life may seem, as Luke *et al.* put it, 'innocuous, neutral texts requiring simple decoding and response' (Luke *et al.* 2001: 113 in Fehring and Green eds), but cumulatively they document and shape social and cultural life.

My experience of working with community texts, largely with foreign language learners, over several years ultimately fed into the rationale for the particular course which is at the centre of this book. The class I shall describe took place in 1993, and consisted of first year university students, those preparing

1

for the Cambridge Proficiency examination and, in addition, several students doing a Master's degree in English language teaching (ELT). The students were mainly in their early twenties and came from France, Spain, Germany, Japan, China, Indonesia, and Argentina.

In looking for some analytical tools to present to students in their work with texts, I turned to critical discourse analysis (CDA), and the work of Norman Fairclough, whose influential book *Language and Power* appeared in 1989, and I have since continued to develop frameworks based broadly on the systemic/functional grammar of Michael Halliday (e.g. 1970, 1994), which Fairclough in turn drew on. I will describe more fully in Chapter 2 the varying accounts of this work and the nature of its impact. Suffice it to say for the moment that CDA is concerned with critiquing the ideology of texts, the way discourses serve to privilege those with power. A discourse, as Kress describes it, 'provides a set of possible statements about a given area and organises and gives structure to the manner in which a particular topic, object, or process is to be talked about' (Kress 1985: 7). Here Kress is drawing on a Foucauldian view of discourses as deriving from the major institutional bases of society. Foucault (1972) downplays the role of individual agency in the manipulation of power, seeing it as mediated through social institutions, such as education, the military establishment and the law, rather than being consciously exercised by the authors of specific written or spoken texts. Discourses are implicated in power relations in the sense that they tend to reaffirm the largely taken-for-granted dominance of particular social practices and social groups.

While critical discourse analysts such as Kress and Fairclough offer detailed textual analyses of the manner in which power operates through language, as an educational procedure a further step is needed, one which can translate some of the principles of CDA into pedagogic action. This became the role of critical language awareness (henceforth CLA), more fully described in Chapter 3, which saw its goal as raising students' awareness of how the uses of language in all its realisations serve to perpetuate dominant discourses and the ideologies they encode. For the moment I shall use the term CDA generically to include the pedagogic strand represented by CLA.

Some might say that, both in educational and popular texts, greater care is now taken to avoid the discriminatory language of earlier times. Yet, I would argue that, while grosser, more visible forms of sexist and racist language are relatively rare, discourses continually regroup around new issues and social groups, in a manner which privileges dominant members of societies, and is prejudicial to others. A current example might be discourses of islamophobia (cf. Sarwar 2002). To be alert to these, and to invite students' attention to them, is part of our project as educators. A key principle of this book then is that texts matter, what they say and how they say it. At the World Congress of Reading in 2002, Vincent Greaney, lead education specialist for the World Bank in Washington DC, made this the theme of his keynote lecture, with particular reference to school textbooks. He talked of how school textbooks can promote ideology by omission, imbalance and distortion; that far from serving an educational role, they can actually promote intolerance of other nations, ways of life and beliefs. Certainly the idea of 'critical thinking' has been around for sometime, but not, as Greaney pointed out, thinking critically about difficult political issues. A comment after the lecture by one of the course participants was along the lines of 'well that's just history texts; it does not relate to the texts we use for teaching reading'. My answer would be that *all* the texts we use in teaching are history texts – they are historically situated and embody the ideology of their day. They therefore repay critical analysis. And while a key principle in much contemporary reading theory is intertextuality across contemporary texts, it is also salutary to look at the history of discourses, their shifting articulations, even within recent times.

The focus on critical reading

I see critical reading as one strand within the wider project of CLA, and one which has been relatively neglected. Fairclough (1992a: 28) notes: 'In critical linguistics there tends to be too much emphasis upon the text as product and too little emphasis upon the processes of producing and interpreting texts.' It is largely, perhaps, because of the relative neglect of the interpretation of texts, within their contexts of use, that critical discourse analysts have been accused of merely 'reading off' effects from texts (cf. e.g. Stubbs 1994; Widdowson 1995). At the same time, within ELT, while reading is well covered in the psycholinguistic and general methodology literature (cf. e.g. Davies 1995; Nuttall 1996; Urquhart and Weir 1998), there is little on critical reading in the second or foreign language classroom. Many models of second language (L2) reading have been ultimately reductive in their effects. For early learners, reading may be seen as decoding texts, pronouncing the words correctly or practising language structure. For more advanced learners a comprehension view remains the dominant model. Indeed it is assumed that the eventual and unique goal of reading *is* comprehension of text, even though recent writers in the field of reading research make a plea for the development of a model of reading as interpretation (cf. e.g. Urquhart and Weir *op. cit.*). I do not want to deny that understanding a text conceptually and linguistically must be a starting point for all reading positions; merely to point out that readers may want and need to respond to texts in more diverse and complex ways than is generally acknowledged. All learners, whether reading in a first, second or other language, are, from the earliest stages, potentially both making meaning from texts, and engaging in critique. I would want too to challenge the dominant 'four skills' view, which is common in the discourse of foreign language teaching, by which we mean 'speaking, listening, reading and writing'. Even though integrated approaches to teaching the skills are argued for, it continues to be assumed in ELT methodology that there is an underlying discrete set of abilities which can be sequentially taught and learned. Broadly I want to argue not just for an integrated approach in teaching, but that language abilities are holistically acquired – in helping learners to be better readers one is necessarily enhancing overall knowledge and use. When I say 'better', I mean more critical, more powerful users of a language, in this case of a second language. Terms such as 'powerful' and 'critical' are much used and abused, so I hope that I may be permitted to use them provisionally for the moment, in advance of arguments which I will flesh out in future chapters.

In short, one of the aims of this book is to present a view of reading as a social, critical and interpretative process rather than as a skill or set of skills.

The focus on language learning

The learners whom I have taught, as mainly non-native or L2 speakers of English, are language learners. Of course *all* learners, both first as well as second language learners, are continuing learners of language. However, the learners of English as a second or foreign language are enrolling in something that they expect to look like a language class. Language classes are generally seen as transmitting knowledge about language in some way. Contemporary approaches are no different in this respect from traditional ones. Attention has shifted methodologically over the years to what is broadly known as the 'communicative' approach. However, knowledge about language, in particular about English, tends still to be enshrined in authoritative texts and the – usually native speaker – teacher. Many language classrooms will see growth in knowledge or competence in terms of knowledge about or mastery of linguistic structure. In my study, the concern is with development of a particular kind of language awareness – CLA. Unlike those in second language acquisition (SLA) studies (e.g. Ellis 1996, 1997), who are interested in language awareness as facilitative of language learning, my interest here is in enhanced language awareness as a goal in itself. This raises issues concerning the second language learners who have enrolled on the kind of reading course I describe here. For, it might be argued, how can they engage in language critique when, even though some of them are very proficient users of English, they are all still in the process of acquiring aspects of the language system? I shall return to this question in the final chapter.

In language teaching theory and practice, notions of fluency and accuracy have been widely drawn upon since Brumfit's original conceptualisation of those terms (Brumfit 1984). Here, however, my discussion will centre neither on fluency nor accuracy, which favour the native speaker but on criticality which, I will argue, does not. The notion of criticality cannot be linked to innate linguistic competence but is socially and educationally learned.

It does not make reference to native speaker norms in the way that fluency and accuracy typically does. Rampton (1990) in an oft-quoted paper favours the term 'expert user' of English, over native versus non-native speaker, and I shall follow Rampton and talk about expert speakers and readers. Many have drawn on Rampton's argument in a liberal spirit, seeing in it the consequence that a whole range of users of English can now more readily lay claim to the language. While this is true in principle, the implications are that using English well – as an expert – is achieved only by some effort. It is learned rather than acquired. While the native speaker qua native speaker is no longer seen to be privileged, in order to make serious claim to expertise in the use of English across a range of domains, speakers and writers need to develop the language in cognitively and critically challenging ways.

The focus on the classroom

Finally this book centres on the classroom as what I call an 'interpretative community'. I have adapted the term from Fish (1980) who applies the term to schools of literary critics. But we can use it in a broader sense, as Carter and Walker (1989: 3) do, when they talk of an interpretative community 'within which readers grow up and are educated'. Extending the term still further, 'interpretative community' can refer to the classroom itself, the way in which the respective members of the class, as they come to know each other, make sense of texts and their interpretations of those texts collectively. And, as I note in Wallace (1992a), the longer the class is together, the more of a community it becomes and the more it begins to share and exchange interpretative resources.

Organisation of book

My book is in two parts: the first section deals with critical reading and critical pedagogy; the second section focuses on a particular Critical Reading course. The issues I address, both in the general discussion and through the account of the specific course, relate to texts, reading and society, and are underpinned by these assumptions, namely:

- There is a need, in educational settings, to address social and political issues through text study.
- Reading is a public and social act as much as it is individual and private.
- Texts and our readings of those texts relate to the wider society; they do not just reflect but are constitutive of contemporary social life.

Later chapters link these issues to readers in the classroom, in particular within language teaching, where my discussion is largely located. But I aim too to draw some wider implications for readings beyond the classroom context.

My overall question is: what does it mean to be a critical reader in a foreign language, both within and beyond the language classroom? Connected to this broad question is: how can we, as teachers or researchers, look critically not just at texts in the classroom but at the classroom itself? For CDA lends itself to two types of analysis, as Pennycook (2001: 81) points out: analysis of texts and, secondly, analysis of interactions between participants. In the research reported here, which was originally part of my PhD thesis (Wallace 1998), I aimed to investigate the classroom discourse within which text analysis was embedded. I also wanted to gain a view of how students interpreted the value of critical language study beyond the classroom. More specifically my questions were:

- What ways of reading texts can be described as critical?
- How far is it possible or desirable to address social and political issues in the language classroom through text analysis?
- What kinds of language analysis procedures promote critical reading?
- What sense do students make of CDA approaches in the classroom context?

Different parts of the book address these questions from different angles. Thus, Chapter 1 considers reading as a social process, and argues that interpretations are negotiated within communities of readers. Chapter 2 looks more specifically at views of text and reading within a CDA perspective, and at how this perspective might be realised in a teaching sequence. Chapter 3 locates the discussion of texts and reading within critical pedagogy more widely. The overriding principle here is that critical language study addresses social and political issues, is transformative, is interventive in outcome and dialogic in process or means towards outcome. Chapter 4 describes the methodology of the empirical classroom-based part of my study. Chapter 5 offers an account of the particular Critical Reading class and thus, together with Chapter 6, aims to address the issue of how one addresses social and political issues within pedagogic practice. Finally Chapter 7 turns to the students themselves, to determine what they make of the experience of attending the course, and what themes emerge from their narratives.

It should be emphasised that the study I present here is not offered as a model of good practice. It is exploratory rather than explanatory; raising issues as opposed to settling them. Also, because this is a retrospective study, it should be emphasised that some views and underlying principles I acknowledged to myself at the start. Others became more available to me as the study progressed. Yet other perspectives came into view later, when I analysed the classroom data. Indeed at each revisiting of the material new insights and adjustments to previous interpretations have emerged.

1
Reading as a Social Process

Reading in a social context

The reading process has tended to be characterised primarily as psychological, cognitive and individual. Baynham presents this understanding of literacy as typified by 'the solitary writer struggling to create meanings...which can be recreated by the solitary reader' (Baynham 1995: 4). This is a view which I aim to challenge in this book, through examination of the ways in which readers collaborate to derive meaning from text. We see the mediation of social and cultural factors, not just at the micro level of negotiated interpretation of texts but more widely. First, at a macro-societal level there are culturally different understandings of what it means to 'do schooling', of which literacy instruction is a major part. Alexander (2000) in his extensive study of schooling in five countries, talks of the 'web of inherited ideas and values, habits and customs, institutions and world views which make one country, or one region or one group, distinct from another' (Alexander 2000: 5). There are also, more specifically, differing understandings of what it means to be a reader and writer, as Brice-Heath's famous (1983) study of two socioeconomically different communities in the United States showed. Brice-Heath describes the different 'ways with words' of a black and white working class community, Trackton and Roadville, respectively. In addition she compares the verbal repertoires and styles of these groups with a third group, the 'mainstreamers', or middle-class townspeople. 'Ways with words' are linked to a whole range of identities. I recall recently talking to Jamila, a nine-year-old Muslim girl, whose family came from Afghanistan, about the books she read at home. When I asked if she could bring something in Arabic to read the following week she replied, clearly alluding to the Koran: 'You're supposed to take lots of care of it. It's supposed to be above you, above your legs. I have to go somewhere else to read. I go to this lady's house.' Further conversations confirmed that Jamila's ways of reading were context specific and closely linked to the salience of different identities in different social settings. She felt it inappropriate to bring religious texts to school.

Jamila's case recalls Street's well-known conceptualisation of literacy as autonomous or ideological (Street 1984). The autonomous model assumes a universal-skills basis to literacy, while the ideological model sees literacy as inherently variable and culturally mediated. Street's emphasis on literacy as situated social and cultural practice, reflected in its typically favoured pluralisation as 'literacies', set the scene for rich debate about the variability and culture dependency of literacy and has evolved into extensive studies of literacy practices cross-culturally, under the auspices of the New Literacies Studies (e.g. Street 1995; Barton and Hamilton 1998; Barton *et al.* 2000). In these studies there is a preference for the study of vernacular literacies which move beyond the confines of schooling, although notable exceptions to this tendency are seen in the work of Baynham (1995), Gregory (1996), Gregory and Williams (2000) and Baker and Freebody (2001), all of whom in different ways, locate their accounts of reading behaviour within classroom studies of literacy instruction or report the interrelationships of home and school.

My aim here is to look less at practices than processes, or rather to point to the ways in which they interact. I will also focus largely on print literacy and the continued value of sustained reading of linear text. This is in the light of a current preference for the new modalities, where the emphasis is rather on multimodality and the increasing importance of visual literacy and the new technologies, which involve different, non-linear ways, of drawing from text (cf. e.g. Cope and Kalantzis 2000). My plea however, is that orthodox reading and writing should maintain its place centre stage in literacy instruction for a number of reasons. First, many of the new modalities are to a large extent parasitic on the old. Arguably, for instance, using e-mail communication means carefully balancing the features which make it a mixture of spoken and written discourse. Skill in orthodox writing and reading is a prerequisite for effective handling of this relatively new medium. Second, there are clear advantages in terms of critical language study for maintaining a place for print literacy. One is that knowledge of the grammar of written language, best gained from extensive exposure to print, constitutes a resource not only to analyse texts but, as Halliday points out (1996: 350), is 'a critical resource for asking questions about (texts): why is the grammar organized as it is? Why has written language evolved in this way?' As a more stable medium than ephemeral modalities such as bodily communication or visual signalling systems, it makes aspects of the grammar more accessible to learners. Moreover, the new literacy has not seen the demise of the old: within Britain, more books are published than ever before. Along with a whole range of other printed material they remain easily obtainable, reproducible, relatively cheap, and, uniquely, pleasurable. So, in their different ways, are newspapers and magazines. We need not scorn the modest, familiar and accessible world of print, at the same time as we welcome the worlds of hypernet, e-mail and text messaging.

Whether we are talking of the new literacies or the longer established ones, we need to hold to the overall view of reading as social: social in the sense that readers and writers enact their roles as members of communities; social in that it unfolds in a social context, both an immediate and wider social context. The kind of social process I want to argue for here is one which posits a shifting and dynamic relationship between text producers, text receivers and the text itself. Any one of the participants in this inter-action may assert greater power, depending on a number of variables in the reading situation. Within classrooms it involves, in addition, the teacher as mediator between text producer or author, the text and the students. Whether in a public setting like a classroom or alone, reading is a three way interaction between the writer, the text and the reader, each of which, I wish to argue, is socially constrained and directed if not socially constructed. Below, I set out ways in which authors, texts and readers can be seen as social phenomena.

The role of the author

Writers have different relationships to the texts they produce. Casual ephemeral notes suggest a lower degree of investment than carefully reworked and crafted texts, which may lay claim to aesthetic or intellectual significance; notions of authorship are crucial both for learners entering literacy worlds and for critical reading in particular. Good young readers read authors not just books: they are likely to have favourite writers even though the notion of authorship is still insecure. Any curious or critical reader will seek out the author: who wrote this, where is it from? As a reader, who perhaps eccentrically often plunges into the middle of texts such as magazine or news articles, I usually eventually turn to the beginning of the article to confirm my sense of its authorship, especially in terms of gender and ethnicity. Some texts are authorless. Olson (1977) refers to the necessarily decontextualised nature of written language, the very fact that it can stand on its own, as a strength of written language. However, some years later Olson (1990) comes to question his earlier stance on authorship, noting that the autonomy of texts is an assertion of unwarranted power rather than legitimate authority. The anonymity of formal written texts, such as for instance, school textbooks, may deny readers the space to ques-tion the grounds or sources of statements, effectively precluding challenge. The deletion of the author, as Olson puts it, 'hides the fact that statements are, after all, only someone's beliefs, which, like all beliefs, are open to ques-tion' (Olson 1990: 21).

Of course, a named author may be a smokescreen and the idea of author-ial ownership, an illusion. Barthes (1977) famously talked of 'the death of the author'. Those who argue for a diminished role for the individual author will tend to question the extent to which authors can claim any ownership at all of the meanings of their texts; they will challenge the view that any dispute over a text's meaning can be resolved by reference to the author's communicative intent (Lodge 1987). Or texts may be abandoned, disowned by their authors. Bourdieu scholar Derek Robbins observed to me that his exegesis of Bourdieu's texts was made more difficult by the fact that Bourdieu claimed that he no longer remembered what he meant by what were considered to be key passages in the work, and seemed to care even less! And of course with his recent death, further opportunities to establish authentic authorial intent are lost. Other writers will reluctantly acknowledge that in spite of their original intentions when writing a piece, counter-interpretations will be made of their work by new generations of readers. This is the case with Herman Hesse's 'author's note' which was added to the second edition of his famous novel *Steppenwolf*, where he challenges the interpretations made by younger readers of his book. He says: 'of all my books *Steppenwolf* is the one that was more often and more violently misunderstood than any other, and frequently it is actually the affirmative and enthusiastic readers...who have reacted to it oddly' (Hesse 1965). Hesse's attempt to assert some intentionality would be dismissed by those, such as Pennycook (1994a), who take the Foucauldian inspired view that all social subjects, whether writers or readers, have their positions largely determined for them, through the prevailing dominant discourses which circulate below the level of individual consciousness. They doubt the feasibility of consciously executed authorial choices, on the grounds that 'the discourse speaks us'. Such is the effect, claims Eagleton (1991: 219), of the views of those who elide all distinctions between material reality and discourse so that discourse becomes all.

In spite of the fragility of the notion of authorship, authorial intentionality is frequently invoked in discussions of reading and especially in comprehension tests for learner or apprentice readers; it continues to be assumed that writers have fixed sets of beliefs and views, and that these are clearly conceptualised and articulated, and for all time. On a comprehension model of reading at least, our task as readers is 'to know what the writer really meant'.

Social authorship

Just how then does the author fit into the picture, whether we see authorship in terms of actual, named individuals or are concerned with the principle of authorship more generally? While some kinds of communication are readily seen to be personally authored, such as simple requests, far more are socially mediated in complex ways. 'Each utterance is filled with echoes and reverberations of other utterances' (Bakhtin 1986: 91). This is why talk of the ownership of texts, especially in the case of novice writers, can be naive. All our texts contain echoes of other texts, raising the issue alluded to by Pennycook: 'on what grounds do we see certain acts of textual borrowing as acceptable and others as unacceptable?' Pennycook

(1998: 266). In the case of public texts which have passed through many hands, it is particularly difficult to attribute individual responsibility. Institutional texts such as official documents are likely to be multiply produced, with a frequent absence of named authors. However, even apparently single authored texts are jointly constructed both in a literal sense, as texts – certainly published texts go through editing processes which may involve participation by many different individuals – and also because we inevitably plagiarise; the voices heard in our texts are the influential social and personal forces in our lives, some consciously appropriated, the majority unconsciously so, in what Bakhtin calls a more or less creative process of assimilation (Bakhtin 1986: 89).

The loss – or at least equivocality – of the notion of individual ownership of texts is liberating but also problematic for critical reading. It is liberating in the sense that the text once created becomes a resource for the construction of fresh interpretations for all readers including a text's original author or authors. The text's natural parent need not feel the burden of responsibility too keenly. However, a weakening of individual authorial agency means that writers can, disingenuously some would say, disclaim responsibility for the discourse they have produced. Critical Discourse Analysts would not wish to exclude authorial agency from the whole process of text production. It is particularly important, as Olson (*op. cit.*) notes, to identify authorial sources in powerful public texts, whose very anonymity masks responsibility and enhances the collective and complex power of invisible text producers.

The role of the text

Historically the text was seen as a self-contained macrostructure consisting of sequences of sentences (cf. e.g. Van Dijk 1977: 4) viewed propositionally and frequently represented by abstract networks. More recently, social theories of language and literacy have conceptualised text in social rather than cognitive ways. A contemporary view of text and text production emphasises the functioning of the text in a societal whole. This needs to include an adequate understanding of the conditions in which a text is produced and consumed. These conditions can be captured by the general term *context*. And context must be understood as more than the immediate and visible circumstances of production and consumption. Implicit conditions can be understood only if we take account of the wider perspective of social power. This view resonates with that of Fairclough who accounts for 'text in context' by proposing three layers of context, the immediate, the institutional and wider societal context (Fairclough 1989). These contextual layers interact with each other and are mutually influential and reinforcing, with, for instance, the recurrence of certain texts and text types continually bolstering institutional and wider social orders. The notion of 'text in context' is central to critical reading, as will be demonstrated in the course of this book.

In spite of earlier work in cognitive psychology, such as that by Van Dijk noted above, recent conceptualisations of reading in the cognitive psychology literature pay scant attention to the role of text in reading instruction. There tends to be a preoccupation with micro elements of textual patterning, mainly at word level (cf. e.g. Adams 1990; Gough 1995). Issues of textual variability of style, content or structure are little addressed. As Meek (1988: 5) puts it: 'The reading experts, for all their understanding about "the reading process" treat all text as the neutral substance on which the process works.' On the other hand, reading educators such as Meek herself and Kenneth and Yetta Goodman (e.g. Goodman 1984; Goodman 1996) give a central role to texts on the grounds that linguistic and sociolinguistic features of texts can frustrate or facilitate reading acquisition. This is particularly the case with second language readers (hereafter L2 readers), who by definition have fewer resources to predict their way through texts. If we draw on the Vygotskyan principle of the zone of proximal development (Vygotsky 1986), just as teachers can support learners to achieve what, unaided, would elude them, so can texts perform a comparable scaffolding role, where they are selected so as to be just in advance of the second language learners' (L2 learners) current proficiency.

While texts are largely ignored by researchers with a cognitive psychological bias, linguists and applied linguists place the text centre stage. Halliday, as a grammarian, takes the text as the starting point for his functional grammar, seeing it both as product and process. It is a product as an output, something that can be 'recorded and studied' (cf. Halliday and Hasan 1985: 10), but with the social semiotic perspective which Halliday simultaneously adopts, the text is also process, as an interactive event, a social exchange of meanings. He links text to situation through a conceptual framework which uses the terms 'field', 'tenor' and 'mode'. For Halliday these are components of the context of situation, looked at semiotically as the construction of meanings and serve to interpret the social context of a text. The field of discourse refers to what is happening, the nature of the social action that is taking place; the tenor refers to the participants in the action and the nature of their relationship, and the mode of discourse to the part played by language, how stretches of language have cohesion as socially recognisable texts, such as a lecture or a lesson (cf. Halliday and Hasan 1985).

In looking at Halliday's second, dynamic sense of text as process, we perhaps need to consider where that leaves the status of the text qua text, as product. The notion of the indeterminacy of the text is strong in literary theory. For instance, Iser claims 'the study of a literary work should concern not only the actual text but the actions involved in responding to the text' (Iser 1978: 21). In many conceptualisations of reading, however, the notion that texts might be, in some manner or other, recreated by readers is barely acknowledged. The text is seen exclusively as artefact or product, often, as noted earlier, being elided with the author. Certainly in comprehension tests for children, 'what does the author/text mean' tend to be indiscriminate questions. Can we ultimately divorce the text from writer intention or reader interpretation? If we wish to challenge the view of texts as mere products or containers of meaning and we prefer, as has now become commonplace, to talk of 'negotiating meaning', we still need to ask: where exactly is meaning initially located, where does our search begin? In general, as Lodge (1987: 90) notes, there is scepticism about 'the possibility of recuperating a fixed or stable meaning from discourse'. Lodge is talking of literary texts but the same point might be made of non-literary discourse.

Eco (1992) appears to wish to hold to some kind of stable meaning in texts, talking of the 'transparent intention of the text' (Eco 1992: 78), which may be different from the intention of the author and which it is perverse to disregard. Others such as Rorty (cf. Collini in Eco *et al.* 1992: 11) urge us to forget the quest to discover 'what the text is really like' – to use it merely for our own purposes. Rorty's sanguine disregard for any inherent meaning or value within texts, whether intended by authors or not or whether ideologically, conceptually or aesthetically based, may seem to take an extreme deconstructionist position. In principle, his is a position which is available for classroom teachers and students and indeed is widely accepted in reader response views. My view, however, is closer to Eco's, namely that the text in itself does carry meanings, apart from writer intention (and indeed apart from reader interpretation), at a number of levels signalled, in complex ways, by the nature and combining of the formal features selected. In other words, texts carry significance in and for themselves. Eco (ibid.) gives the example of the text in a bottle found at sea. Not knowing who sent it, or where it came from, we are nonetheless likely to be able to make some sort of sense of it, provided we know the language. It can be very important in some instances to return to the text qua text. This is what two British Muslim women did, forced into marriages, by family members in the name of cultural and religious tradition. They found that the Koran was unequivocal in its condemnation of forced marriages, that indeed such marriages were invalid.

In short, we can retrace and recreate a sense of the production of the text, and these contextual roots must be part of its meaning. Nonetheless the text must be allowed some autonomy as a product. The text retains its status as an artefact. At the least texts serve as documents of their time and place. Some, such as religious texts have longer term and, as the example of the Koran shows, potentially emancipatory as well as conservative effects.

The social text

The view that texts are social constructs is a key principle of the group of genre theorists, such as Martin *et al.* (1987), which strongly influenced by Hallidayan systemic functional grammar, arose as an educational movement in the mid-eighties in Australia, although much earlier, social theorists such as Bakhtin drew extensively on the term. Indeed Bakhtin introduces the notion, adapted by others such as Gee (1990), of primary and secondary genres. Primary or everyday speech genres may evolve into secondary genres such as novels, or scientific works which arise out of more complex and relatively highly developed cultural communication (Bakhtin 1986: 62). While the notion of primary and secondary genre types has not been widely followed by the contemporary genre theorists, what they share with Bakhtin is the view that genres are socially and culturally recognisable language events, both spoken and written. Examples might be medical consultation, poem, joke or cartoon. Swales similarly emphasises the socially determined nature of genres, describing them as 'communicative events which are socioculturally recognisable' (1990: 53). On this definition, genres are social categories rather than rhetorical types of texts such as exposition, narrative or argument (cf. Urquhart 1996: 29). However, the conceptualisation of *genre* is open to some confusion as the categories tend to look more rhetorical than social when translated into educational practice. Thus Deriawianka (1990), closely following Martin's (1989) categories, talks of *recounts, narratives* and *instructions* and *exposition* which cut across socially recognisable categories such as *personal letter, editorial, recipe*. For foreign language learners, it may be helpful to note how the links between the rhetorical shape of texts and their social function is culturally variable. For instance, in British newspaper editorials a typical rhetorical move is for a concession to precede the major argument of the piece, not the case it seems with newspaper editorials in other cultural contexts, at least as observed by students of mine (cf. Wallace 1992a).

The genre movement has lain itself open to accusations of rigidity or essentialism. The boundaries between genres are not always clearly demarcated and Kress, for instance, as one of the early advocates of the Australian genre movement, was taken to task for proposing a finite number of genres (Kress 1982). Any text is constructed as a mosaic of quotations; any text is the absorption and transformation of another (Kristeva 1986). Kristeva, drawing on Bakhtin, uses the concept of intertextuality to account for the way in which texts need to be read against other texts within or across genres. Intertextuality is used to describe the range of ways in which texts make reference to other texts, to 'focus on the interdependence between texts rather than their discreteness or uniqueness' (Montgomery *et al.* 1992: 174). This kind of interdependence is closely linked to the notion of hybridity, which becomes a theme in the later work of Fairclough and his collaborators (e.g. Chouliaraki and Fairclough 1999). Moreover hybridity has the effect of dissipating the autonomy of genres in the case, for instance, of politically powerful texts, such as advertisements which colonise other fields through appropriation of their characteristic discourses, sometimes with the intention of disguise. It is important, however, for CDA purposes, as Chouliaraki and Fairclough caution, not to see textual hybridity as the loss of *all* social constraint on the nature of texts and interpretation, and to bear in mind that 'the concept of intertextuality must be combined with a theory of power' (Chouliaraki and Fairclough 1999: 119). This means that hybridity should not be seen as innocently playful and inventive, open to a myriad of interpretations but that real and malign forms of power continue to be exerted by certain genres, which need in turn to be responded to in powerful and critical ways. Readers will, of course, come to texts with their own agendas as well as with a whole range of socially and culturally shaped identities and resources which we turn to next, in considering the role of the reader. While wishing to hold to some notion of the autonomy of the text, for reasons argued earlier, texts are nonetheless continually reshaped and reinterpreted by readers in different contexts of use and for different purposes.

The role of the reader

The reader or text 'receiver'

We can talk about roles in two rather different ways: first, we can envisage the role relationship between reader, author and text. How do these parameters of any reading event interact with each other? Secondly, and more dynamically, what kind of role does the reader adopt in the course of reading itself? I shall consider both questions here.

Structuralist views which emphasised the autonomy of the text left the role assigned to the reader a relatively straightforward one – namely the gaining of meaning which, it was assumed, was intact and whole within texts. Some of the early work in critical linguistics (cf. e.g. Trew 1979) took this position. The reader was active in the pursuit of meaning, as opposed to earlier accounts of the reading process which talked of reading, along with listening, as a 'passive skill'. It was assumed that meaning was there within the text for the taking. The shift in emphasis from a passive, acquiescent reader to an active one led to the use of rather aggressive metaphors. The reader was described as 'extracting' meaning from texts – rather like teeth! Just and Carpenter express it thus: 'the main goal of a comprehender, of course, is to extract information from the prose he is listening to or reading' (Just and Carpenter 1977: ix). While even relatively recent accounts of the reading process continue to draw on this and similar metaphors (Nuttall (1996), for instance talks of 'text attack' skills), the ground has shifted in L2 as in L1 (first language) reading theory to talk of reading as interactive rather than active. What the readers bring to the text is as important as what they gain from it.

In short, most contemporary accounts of the role of readers see them as interacting with the text or writer. However, the nature of this interaction is differently characterised. Widdowson (1984), for instance, talks of the reader choosing to take up either an assertive or submissive position depending on purpose. Widdowson gives weight to individual choice in this matter, arguing that the reader is 'free to take up whatever position suits his purpose on the dominance/dependence scale' (Widdowson 1984: 91). Others argue for less individual choice (e.g. Kress 1985); some people in some situations are less at liberty to exercise individual preference. This may be because of contextual factors which operate at different levels of specificity. For instance, the immediate situation in which the event takes place may be uncongenial to the exercise of assertion. Within the particular setting, features of the 'field', 'tenor' or 'mode' – to draw on Halliday's character-isation of the context of situation – that is, for example, the manner in which a text is presented or framed, and the content of the text and the surrounding discussion may not invite ready participation and may effect-ively preclude critique. Or institutional factors beyond the immediate setting may work against an equal encounter between text and reader. This brings us to consider less the individually selected stance of the reader, as a matter of personal choice, than the social role of the reader.

The social role of the reader

Bakhtin talks of the 'hierarchical position of the addressee' (Bakhtin 1986: 151), in considering what kind of role relationship pertains between writer and reader, such as son, student, defendant, parent and so on. We need to consider in what relation is the addressee to the producer of any text. We are all aware of a shift of reader role, once we know that the producer of a piece of writing, previously considered to be of indifferent quality, is in fact of some status and reputation. This is even more the case with many genres which have no named authors, masking, as noted earlier, authorial responsibility.

Moreover, characteristics of the text itself as well as authorship or the context of situation may marginalise readers in their access to texts – may skew the interaction. The degree to which information, values and attitudes are assumed to be shared is signalled by the language of the text, in particu-lar the degree of elaboration and clarification provided. For this reason, unexpanded texts with little modality may exercise greater power simply because assumptions are implicit. There is a higher degree of taken-for-grantedness. If you are not part of the writers' imagined readership, the effect is of eavesdropping on a dialogue between the writers and their readership. Arguing from a Foucauldian perspective, we might say that the discourses within a text construct what are called preferred readings – that is, certain interpretations of the events or phenomena described are privileged over others. By extension one can talk of 'preferred', 'implied' or – the term I shall use here – 'model readers' (cf. Eco 1979) to characterise the way in which a reader is written into a text. The notion that it is useful to distinguish a text's actual or real reader from an ideal one constructed by the text has a long history in literary history (cf. e.g. Culler 1983); a rather shorter one as applied to non-literary texts. Olson (1994: 136) extends the idea of model or ideal reader in useful ways for critical reading purposes, by introducing the term 'putative' readers and writers. The putative reader captures the idea of a reader other than oneself, and, at the same time, the key notion that there are ways of reading texts other than the one currently adopted by oneself. Olson quotes one study (Wineburg 1991) in which professional historians were able to make a distinction – more readily than knowledge-able students – between what the author was trying to get them to believe and what, in fact, they as actual readers, were prepared to believe. However, a preparedness to take up such a stance to text initially is likely to depend on our having a hierarchical role vis-à-vis the text, which, as with the case of the professional historians, gives one some authority. Such an authoritative role may not be readily available to some readers, who are marginalised for various reasons. I turn to this point next.

Marginalised readers: the reader as overhearer

Writers may indicate in a number of ways, in particular by the interpersonal choices selected, which kind of reader in terms of social group membership is envisaged. And, as Mills (1992) notes, certain social groups faced with certain types of texts may habitually be in a position of 'overhearing' rather than of being directly addressed. She relates this to gender identity: 'gender is a crucial element for determining whether readers consider they are being directly addressed or whether they are in a position of over-hearing' (Mills 1992: 188). Many other groups can be perpetual overhearers of texts. Smith (1983) famously talked about reading as 'joining the literacy club', a club to which many children are denied ready entry. One is struck, for instance, by the social class bias of many discourses in children's books (terms such as 'elevenses' and 'linen cupboards' come to mind from my recent reading with children). They are heavily lexicalised in areas such as to reflect the middle-class preoccupations of writers and the children they know best. We might add that other kinds of reader identities such as that of 'foreigner' may lead to marginalisation, may, that is, offer readers roles as mere overhearers rather than as participators in the interaction. L2 readers are frequently expected to forgo or suspend the normal range of social identities which can potentially be brought into play in the reading of texts.

Identities and roles: the L2 reader

With what kind of identity does the L2 reader approach the foreign language text? Is it not over-deterministic to represent the L2 reader as inevitably an outsider, one who is marginalised and disempowered, destined never to be a fully proficient reader in the foreign language? L2 readers are, through the materials and methods we offer them, frequently constructed as marginal to mainstream social life, offered competency based survival literacy or the vapid contentless language of the EFL (English as a foreign language) textbook, typified in one recent course book, whose author shall be nameless, by the question: 'how many calories has an orange'? Textbook writers – and I include myself here – envisage a model reader with the same life style, tastes and preoccupations as themselves. As teachers too we mediate in the establishment of learner identities. Do we, for instance, wish L2 readers to submit as novices or to lay claim to kinds of expertise which can in fact offer them advantages over the indigenous, model reader, and even the opportunities to develop *new* identities as foreign or L2 readers? This issue is central to the interpretation of critical reading offered here. L2 readers do not simply approach texts as foreigners. As with all readers, their identities are complex and interwoven. They come to texts with different identities and different reader roles which shift in the course of reading. Nonetheless, in a whole range of ways L2 readers tend to be perceived by teachers and positioned by materials writers as incompetent, not just because of inadequate linguistic proficiency but because of assumed lack of cultural competence in the reading of texts written for native speakers of English. It is true that the issue of accessibility of cultural meanings in texts needs to be addressed, and I discuss this in Chapter 5. However, I would like to reiterate the claim made earlier that, drawing again on Rampton's term of 'expert', the native speaker/reader does not have exclusive rights to expertise, particularly if we interpret this to include criticality.

Nonetheless, it may be hard for the L2 reader to claim equality of status with the model L1 reader, a disadvantage which may be compounded by a number of factors. By way of illustration, Janks and Ivanic (1992) quote the case of the visiting scholar spending a period of time at a British university who had difficulties in adjusting to his new identity as a student rather than a fellow colleague of the university's academic staff. On confronting one of these with his sense of disempowerment, she gave him one of her papers to read – one she was still in the process of working on. In doing so, claim Janks and Ivanic (*op. cit.*: 310), 'she constructed a new position for them both: collaborative colleagues'. One may doubt the ability of individuals to counter institutionalised disadvantage in such ad hoc ways. Nonetheless the anecdote draws attention to the taken-for-granted circulation of power; it highlights the manner in which readers can be offered a disadvantaged reading position not just through the text itself or even the contextual circumstances of its reading, but through the way in which various people – often of higher status than the reader – can mediate in the event, acting as gatekeepers or additional filters between text and original reader.

The role of the reader in the ongoing interaction with text

Once we have considered the positions which readers, writers and the physical text itself take vis-à-vis each other, we can look at the ongoing interaction. Here we are talking less of social roles or identities of readers and writers – as determined for example, by gender, nationality or class and status – and more of how those initial identities come into play in the course of processing written text.

Much of the current literature on the reading process, centres around the strategies used by effective and less effective readers. It coexists with research on reading skills which has a longer history. As Urquhart notes (1996: 24): 'skills may be seen as an attempt to breakdown the monolithic aspects of "comprehension" into more manageable, more teachable, more testable components'. However, as Urquhart points out, as far back as 1979, Lunzer and Gardner (1979) in an extensive research project were unable to provide evidence for the psycholinguistic reality of the skills taxonomy which they initially proposed. A skills orientation in more recent reading research is characterised by an emphasis on the value of developing automaticity in text processing (cf. e.g. Grabe 1991; Paran 1996), while other researchers have shifted attention to empirical examination of the strategies which readers use or claim to use. There is now a substantial body of research which aims to identify what kinds of thinking processes readers are drawing on in the course of reading. Some of these can be captured in verbal protocols, used for example, by Cavalcanti (1987) who asked her students in silent reading to 'think aloud' and therefore verbalise when they noticed a pause in their reading process which indicated a potential problem situation. Other studies have involved asking students to consider their strategies retrospectively. For example, Kletzien (1991 in Davies 1995: 50) asked students after they had completed a cloze exercise to explain their thinking processes as they had tried to overcome problems with identifying the missing word.

One study which centred specifically on L2 readers was that by Block (1986), who investigated the range and nature of strategies used by relatively successful and less successful L2 readers; she identified different modes of response, including what she called *extensive* and *reflexive* modes. In the former, the reader attempted to deal with the message conveyed by the author. In the latter, reflexive mode readers related affectively and personally to the text content, focusing on their own train of thought. The group of readers which Block called 'integrators', judged in the study as the better readers, were exclusively extensive. Block takes it for granted that a convergent reading which is integrated with the writer's line of enquiry is a qualitatively better reading than a divergent one which, in reflexive mode, pursues the reader's own train of thought.

In earlier studies of L2 readers, Hosenfield (1977, 1984) also compared the strategies used by good readers, as identified by standardised tests, with less successful readers. Hosenfield notes that successful readers, asked to report their own strategies, used a wide range of strategies: they skipped inessential words, guessed from context, read in broad phrases and continued reading the text when they were unsuccessful in decoding a word or phrase. Other studies however, claim that good readers do not in fact skip, but read nearly every word on the page. Thus research in eye movement has been drawn on to show that in laboratory conditions good readers apparently fixate over 80 per cent of content words and over 40 per cent of function words (Harrison 1992).

One difficulty with some of these studies of characteristics of good readers, as Urquhart (1996) points out, is that the tests used initially to identify supposedly good readers may firstly be very crude and secondly select just those readers who will score well on the particular measures used in the research. In other words, the full range of effective reading behaviour may simply not be captured by the particular research procedures used. Moreover, the experimental conditions of many of these studies are different in striking ways from the whole range of real life settings, including classroom ones, in which readers engage with written texts for different purposes. In fact more recent eye movement research, conducted with more extended, whole texts, rather than text extracts, and in different languages seems to reaffirm the highly selective nature of the reading process (Freeman 2002).

Overall in the strategies literature there is an emphasis on the location of problems; reader strategies are seen as the varying ways of dealing with problems confronted in the course of reading. Moreover, problems tend to be seen as linked to reader inadequacy or shortcoming in some way or another, rather than as being triggered by features of the language or content of the text or by situational constraints. A further difficulty is with identifying the status of strategy. How can strategies be satisfactorily discriminated from each other and, more importantly, how do they interrelate or link to some overarching kind of position or stance on the reader's part? Moreover, how can the critical examination of ideological aspects of texts, the focus of this study, fit into a strategy framework? Indeed, frequently, no framework is provided in the research studies; rather, we are offered open-ended lists of strategies, sometimes as many as fifty being identified, as described in the studies reported by Davies (1995). What are described as 'socio affective strategies' (cf. e.g. O'Malley and Chamot 1990), of potential relevance to a critical orientation to reading, are seen not as permeating the reading process, but as discrete strategies. In short, the strategies literature (as Koo notes 1998: 65) makes only minimal concessions to social dimensions in the reading process.

Finally the notion of strategy itself is reductive. As Kramsch says (1995: 48), 'it focuses on local problem-solving, not on contemplation or reflection.' Kramsch contrasts the strategy scholars' preoccupation with procedural knowledge and automaticity with what she calls declarative forms of knowledge, more emphasised in some European countries such as France. It is this kind of declarative, explicit knowledge, rather than automaticity of processing which, as I hope to demonstrate in the classroom study, characterises reading as a social, critical process.

Because of the problems involved in identifying specific strategies or even, so Urquhart (*op. cit.*) claims, the ability of the strategies research ultimately to distinguish in ways initially hypothesised between so-called good and poor readers, other researchers studying the interaction between L2 readers and texts are concerned less with attempts to identify good readers in terms of the deployment of sets of strategies than with exploring in greater depth the kinds of online responses made by readers confronted by different genres in different situations (cf. e.g. Koo 1998). The encounter with written texts is seen less in terms of strategies for gaining meaning by the reader from text than a dialogue between reader and writer, mediated by text and context and guided by reader purpose (cf. Wallace 1992b; Widdowson 1979). This account of reading, as opposed to those studies which take a cognitive psychology orientation, offers us a more socioculturally based view of the process in that it acknowledges contextual factors in the reading event, such as the role of reader identity. On this view, the relatively stable identities we start out with will influence the fluid and changing responses we make in the course of processing written texts.

This dialogic view of reading also has the potential to build in a critical orientation. In acknowledging the social identity of the reader, it takes note of the way in which online reader responses make reference, directly or indirectly, to the reader's own ethnic or gender identity. An example may make the point: Yuko, a Japanese student, was asked to do a verbal report on a text about Singapore. I provide the full protocol in Chapter 7, but will offer a brief preview here. After some minutes of reading the article, following an ongoing summary of the main points of content, Yuko said: 'Ah, I don't like this article so much...or other European article...seem like they're looking at Far East people in some different way...like people who's mad or who act beyond their comprehension.' Here Yuko was bringing to bear her identity as an Eastern woman on a text written for Western readers. Even though Yuko does not explicitly identify 'they' and 'their' in this response, she is clearly distancing herself from the preferred reading of the text. She is commenting not on the propositional content but on the discourses embedded within the text; not on what is said but how it is said. In many ways she is not behaving like 'the good reader' identified by studies such as Block's (*op. cit.*). A British student, William, on the other hand provided a convergent reading of the same text in that he appeared to accept the content of the text as unproblematic, with comments such as: 'OK, first paragraph on how hard and harsh the rules are'. The point I wish to make is not that William is an uncritical reader; merely that, asked as he was to 'just comment on the text', he opted for a convergent reading, which focused on content and structure rather than ideological aspects of textual meaning, characterised in terms of discourse and genre, that is related to the nature of the text socio/culturally and how social institutions and phenomena were represented within it.

In short, we may want to think of critical reading as less to do with specific strategies than with an overall stance or position, an orientation to the reading task. If asked to verbalise their responses to texts, readers may reveal not just their strategies as readers at the micro level of response to individual utterances, but their stance both critically, conceptually and affectively, influenced by their personal and social histories as readers. One goal of my research was to explore not the exercise of strategies but to take a wider perspective on the sociocultural as well as individual resources which readers bring with them to a reading task. One way in which reader experiential and knowledge resources have been built into a model of the reading process is through the literature on Schema Theory which I turn to next.

Schema theory

Schema theory, a notion deriving originally from Bartlett (1932), is concerned with the way readers match up incoming data from the text with existing mental representations of situations, events or phenomena. It is presented as primarily a cognitive construct. Widdowson (1983: 34), for instance, describes schemas as 'cognitive constructs which allow for the organisation of information in long term memory'. However schematic knowledge is also socially based. For instance, D'Andrade (D'Andrade and Strauss 1992 in Richardson 1995: 76) argues that cognitive schemas are learned in specific social contexts. If we take a construct like 'mother' for instance, while there are clear core universals cognitively speaking to be attached to the concept, what it means to be a mother, the responsibilities and social advantages which accrue to the role and so on, will clearly differ. One can make the link between the Foucauldian sense of discourse and the notion of schema to claim that in different social milieus different discourses about motherhood will be in circulation. It follows that members of different social groups will have different 'motherhood' schemas.

Cook (1994) discusses the manner in which schemas reinforce stereotypes. Certainly much if not most of our day-to-day processing of texts proceeds on the basis of confirmation of existing knowledge and attitudes. Cook argues that because of their stereotypical nature, schemas serve to reinforce preju-dices, unexamined judgements about everyday reality, kinds of behaviour, and stock responses to the unfamiliar. For this reason, claims Cook, we should value texts which have a schema breaking function. He talks particu-larly of literature as serving this role. But, as Cook concedes, literature does not hold the premium on schema disruption. The intellectual quality, the integrity of non-literary texts, such as expository pieces, can be judged – as much as aesthetic value with literary texts – on their ability to challenge conformity. It is partly for this reason that the view taken in this book is that texts are not equally ideologically pernicious. In intellectual terms, texts variably challenge their readers to question conformity to stereotypical views. Moreover, the 'stock response' nature of schemas suggests that we see its role as key in first impression reading, the nature of which I discuss in the next section of this chapter. One goal of critical reading, as discussed more fully in Chapter 2, is to throw open to question such initial unanalysed readings.

It follows too that in a social setting such as a classroom a diversity of responses to the same text is healthy in that it challenges the 'common sense' of unified schema-based stock reactions. This is, incidentally, much more readily achieved in a multicultural classroom, such as the one at the centre of my study. As teachers we might aim for a diversity of interpretations which cuts across the grain of stale and routine responses. This does not mean that consensus will not emerge over time, but it will be rationally based, reflected upon and open to critique, not founded on a given, unanalysed 'common sense'. In short, schema changing rather than schema confirming is one of the key principles of critical reading.

We have seen that it is possible to draw on the valuable work done in reading theory in two fields: strategy use and schema theory, but by shifting them away from their usual territory in cognitive psychology and by relocating them as social/critical rather than mentalistic constructs. Thus strategies are in interplay with a variety of social factors. At the same time, schema activation involves bringing into play complex kinds of social identities. It allows readers to draw on the full range of their identities and to be agentive in their responses to texts. In Goffman's (1981) terms, readers are frequently 'animators' rather than 'authors' of their reading; in other words, the identities made available to them do not permit them to engage directly with textual meaning. Widdowson (1992: x) puts it thus: 'only as author does the reader provide an interpretation'. This begs the question as to what exactly is involved in interpretation, which I turn to next.

Response, interpretation, analysis and implication

At the same time as we have moved from a view of reading as extracting *from* to interacting *with*, discourse about reading has shifted from talk of comprehension to interpretation. However, 'interpretation' is itself a contested term. First, some account of the difference between the terms 'analysis' and 'interpretation' seems called for. Widdowson (1995) in fact claims that the notion of a CDA is inherently contradictory – that because critical analysts espouse a politically committed position and indeed deny the possibility of disinterestedness, analysis is precluded. It is possible to argue, however, that in the case of CDA, as with conventional discourse analysis, analysis and interpretation are both involved and that interpretation is an outcome of analysis. We are still left with the difficulty which Widdowson points to, namely that the analysis is motivated by the concerns of the analyst who is not and, certainly in the case of the critical discourse analyst, does not claim to be disinterested. It is true that analysis must always be partial – in both senses – as discussed more fully in the next chapter. However by separating analysis, that is the examination of features of texts – selective as it necessarily is – from interpretation, as a view of the overall intention and effect of a text in the light of such examination, judged in conjunction with a wide range of contextual factors, one can achieve a degree of distance or detachment. This is especially the case if one's own reading of a text is offered to the inspection of others in an interpretative community such as the classroom. In such a setting, it may be useful to see our reactions to written texts as moving from initial response, to analysis to interpretation. The key difference between our understanding of these terms is that: response is first-glance, schema activating and relatively unconsidered; analysis, a closer focusing on the language of the text; and interpretation, a revisiting of initial response in the light of textual scrutiny and peer group discussion. We might say that interpretation, even though socially shared and mediated in the classroom is still 'micro' in its centering on specific text. There is a further layer or level which is longer term, more dependent on intertextuality, which we might call 'social implication'. That is, what is the significance of this text, socially and ideologically, when read against other texts which circulate within particular social settings at particular historical moments?

In cases of our everyday reactions to texts for immediate functional purposes – that is, where there is simply inadequate time for much reflection – the process is short-circuited so that we move from response to interpretation, or the two phases become fused. An analytically mediated interpretation, however, provides some distance on first readings. Reading in educational settings, as opposed to everyday reading for pleasure or information for instance, involves revisiting texts. It might be objected, of course, that while aesthetically valuable texts may repay revisiting, this is less the case with media texts, such as newspaper reports or advertisements, the kind of community texts, such as those at the centre of my study. I return to this issue in Chapter 5. Hilary Janks poses a further dilemma here regarding our responses to such texts. Many advertising texts feature attractive images with which students wish to identify. Janks notes how in one classroom study, while students seemed able to gain some analytical distance on their readings of texts, they nonetheless still wished to identify with the arguably sexist images in some texts. Desire and identification, concludes Janks, works against reason (2001b: 4). And all of us might acknowledge that we can find pleasure in what we intellectually despise. One response to this dilemma might be to argue that we respond in pleasure and critique at leisure, maybe even moving in and out of conflicting reader stances. In other words, that we can both enjoy and deplore. Moreover, a range of interpretations may be derived from a text, even by the same reader, for texts mean in complex and even contradictory ways.

Finally we need to ask what is the status of interpretation: are all interpretations equally legitimate? My answer is no. I argue that some readers are in a stronger position than others to offer legitimate responses (Wallace 1992b). Readers may simply have more knowledge of the language itself. That is, they may have richer lexical knowledge or familiarity with the structure of the genre in question. And of course they may be more experienced and mature readers, through reading extensively in their first or other languages.

Even when we move from literal representations of textual meaning into more disputed territory relating to the deriving of inferences, some interpretations will be better based than others. And, of particular relevance to this book, and more controversially, ideologically based interpretations will not be of equal legitimacy. Careful and detailed textual support will need to be adduced and offered to the scrutiny of others. In other words, the shift from a text-oriented view of reading to a reader-oriented one certainly allows for multiple interpretations. However, this is not to suggest that any and all responses are permitted.

Conclusion

In this chapter, I have presented a case for the social nature of reading. Authoring is social in that we write as members of communities, whether religious, academic or professional. Texts that are the outcomes of these social collaborations are themselves social and cultural artefacts. Finally readers read not, ultimately, as private individuals but as members of interpretative communities. As the philosopher Habermas (1992: 152) puts it: 'the interpreter who understands meaning is experiencing fundamentally as a participant in communication, on the basis of a symbolically established intersubjective relationship with other individuals, even if he is actually alone with a book, a document or a work of art.'

However we need to ask how we can build on reading as a social interpretative process to offer opportunities for a wider than customary range of reader identities to be engaged. One of these is the reader as critic. If we wish to give, as Fowler (1996: 7) puts it, 'more power to the reader', then we need to think of ways of creating for readers opportunities for more specifically *critical* engagements with texts. This is addressed in the next chapter.

2
Critical Discourse Analysis and Critical Reading

How do we build on reading as a social practice and process to make a specific case for critical reading as a classroom project? *Critical* is a much overused term and so some account is needed of how I wish to use it here. As noted in the introduction, my account of critical reading is influenced by CDA. CDA has its genesis in Critical Linguistics which, concerned to theorise language as social practice, first formulated an analysis of public discourse which aimed to examine the ideological codings of texts (cf. Trew 1979). Drawing on this early work, subsequent generations of critical linguists, or critical discourse analysts such as, most notably, Norman Fairclough (1989, 1992b, 1995) and Gunther Kress (1985, 1996) have devised text-analytic procedures which can illuminate the power basis of the discourses embedded within texts. Discourses are, as noted earlier, linked to social institutions and are ways of talking about a whole range of associated phenomena, topics and relations, for instance, what it might mean to be a good wife, mother or teacher. In terms of reading, as Fowler (1996: 6) says, the aim is 'to equip readers for demystificatory readings of ideology-laden texts'.

As Fairclough notes (2001: 229), CDA has both wider and more specific aspirations. More widely, in the longer term, it is committed to social change, which, if one takes a Hallidayan perspective, is inextricably linked to language change. As Halliday claims: 'Every language is constantly renewing itself, changing in resonance with changes in its environment' (Halliday 1987: 138). To the extent that humans have agency over language and can therefore reshape the language for the better, CDA has emancipatory aspirations, holding to a notion of progress in human affairs. As an immediate means to this wider goal, critical discourse analysts examine interactions and indeed any type of semiotic material such as written texts, conversations, television programmes, and advertisements on billboards to show how language figures within relations of power. By scrutinising patterns of language choices, it is argued, one can uncover the ideological leanings of texts, that is, the manner in which discourses, ambivalent and contradictory as they frequently are, ultimately privilege the interests of certain social groups over others.

Critics of CDA, notably Widdowson (e.g. 1995, 2000) and Stubbs (1994, 1997), point to its unfeasibility and redundancy as a pedagogic or analytic procedure. Stubbs (1994) notes that whole texts in their contexts of use are not selected for analysis; that most critical analyses have been based on the analysis of short texts or fragments (although Fairclough (2001) offers more comprehensive analysis of longer texts than in previous work). Moreover, how is it possible to point readers' attention to textual features which are significant in critical interpretations, if, as Kress (1993: 174) argues, texts are ideologically saturated, permeated through and through. A second major criticism is ethical: critical reading, far from being emancipatory, may involve the analysts replacing the tyranny of the text with their own imposed interpretations. A final criticism has it that people are critical readers already, well equipped, as long as they are experienced readers and linguistically proficient in the language of the text, to notice the features which critical analysts are at such pains to point out to them. I will revisit these objections at the end of this chapter, and indeed throughout the book. Within the chapter, I shall first discuss some of the major issues and dilemmas which underpin the term *critical*. I shall proceed then to consider a second related question which deals with the kind of model of language which best fits the purpose of critical reading pedagogy. We will then be in a better position to consider a procedure for critical reading in the third section, before concluding with a summarising position on what we might understand by critical reading.

The critical project

One useful starting point is to distinguish initially between a weak view of critical as *critical thinking* and a strong one. A weak usage of the word *critical* would see it as close to the way it is used in discourse about 'critical thinking', where it usually means the ability to critique the logic of texts, to note inconsistencies and lack of clarity. A stronger view argued for here sees this understanding of critical as a staging post, albeit a crucial one, in the pursuit of an ultimately stronger sense of *critical*. The first, well established in liberal education, aims to help people see logical anomalies in texts and in arguments of all kinds, and to encourage independence of thought. The second is specifically concerned with issues of power and ideology, which I turn to discuss more fully below. Critical readers in this second sense are able and willing to critique not just micro features of specific texts but attend to wider implications which relate to the circulation of dominant discourses within texts and so ultimately to the power bases of society. Ideology, while an increasingly unfashionable term – one frequently hears talk of the 'post-ideology' age – remains a key concept in this stronger view of critical, which is the one linked to *critical reading* as used in this book. Eagleton (1991) usefully maps out the territory around this historically much disputed term by offering a list of popular definitions of ideology some of which I include here:

- a body of ideas characteristic of a particular social group or class;
- systematically distorted communication;
- ideas which help to legitimate a dominant political power;
- false ideas which help to legitimate a dominant political power (from Eagleton 1991: 1–2).

Most would agree that the first is too broad, all-encompassing a definition and may be closer to what we would understand by culture. Certainly the discourses within the texts critiqued in a critical reading pedagogy will be culturally inflected to varying degrees, featuring in overt and covert ways allusions to the practices and values of cultural groups. Understanding and discussion of these is a key feature of critical reading classes as discussed more fully in Chapters 3 and 5. However, in its concern with ideology as well as culture, critical reading needs to attend to the issues raised by Eagleton's second proposed definition which I turn to next.

Eagleton's second definition, *systematically distorted communication* would seem to be close to Habermas's (1984), for whom, as Eagleton (1991: 14) notes: 'ideology is a form of communication systematically distorted by power'. The possibility arises of 'an entire discursive system where the language is 'bent out of communicative shape' by the power interests invested in it. The introduction of the principle of distortion in language use suggests that there must be some norm of undistorted communication – if only at an idealised level – which we can set against distorted communication. The notion of what we might mean by distorted, or undistorted, communication is clearly a complex one but is at the heart of Habermas's Universal Pragmatics. Drawing on Speech Act literature and the work of Searle (1969) in particular, Habermas (1979) puts a case for sets of conditions which operate in all human communication and which are oriented to the reaching of understanding. I shall revisit these in detail in Chapter 3, when I discuss theories of critical pedagogy which might support critical reading. Suffice it to say at this point that Habermas's model of communication, in principle, offers a means of challenge to systematically distorted communication. It assumes that in rational discussion participants of goodwill make reference to shared underlying notions of what is true and truthful, although certain participants might opt to behave strategically. By this is meant that they have 'only *apparently* adopted an attitude orientated to reaching understanding' (Habermas 1984: 264).

Certainly not all of those who have engaged with the critical project accept the Habermasian position. Pennycook (1994a: 131) sees as problematic the view of Habermas that 'there can be a form of "communicative action" that is devoid of ideology', slightly missing the point, I believe that Habermas is not talking of forms of communicative action that might actually occur but an idealised form of ideology – free communication against which we can take our bearings in real-life settings. Eagleton appears, unlike Pennycook, to accept the key Habermasian principle of an underlying notion of communication which is not distorted by the unwitting or conscious intention to deceive, noting: 'in order to be able to decipher an ideological system of discourse, we must already be in possession of the normative, undistorted use of terms' (Eagleton 1991: 14).

Here I shall favour the Habermasian position on the grounds that there must be available to readers and all social subjects an idealised version of truth and justice embodied in undistorted communication for us to be aware of the *principle* of skewedness or distortion. I shall therefore argue for a model of critical reading, based on CDA, which is able to *pursue* claims of truth if not ultimately to arrive in the possession of an absolute truth of the kind proposed by the enlightenment philosophers of a more optimistic age. Without espousing a wholehearted Kantian transcendentalism, truth can still be pursued as an ideal. As Hammersley (1996) puts it: 'truth is a regulative ideal which we work towards'. This is a crucial underpinning to the view of critical reading which I am arguing for in this book.

Eagleton's third definition – *ideas which help to legitimate a dominant political power* – introduces the dimension of power which is central to most discussions of ideology. Here a conflict model of power is being emphasised, one which emphasises a relationship of domination/subjugation (cf. Reynolds 1990) rather than the more facilitative one offered by Giddens (in Cassell 1993) who provides a conceptualisation of power as mediating or stucturating all human affairs. In its broad sense it has transformative capacity, providing the capability of human beings to intervene in a series of events so as to alter their course. In allowing, indeed insisting on human agency, Giddens offers a model of power which fits better with CDA aspirations for social change, than does that of Foucault, for instance, who disallows agency in his account of power. As Giddens puts it: 'Human beings, in the theory of structuration, are always and everywhere regarded as knowledgeable agents, although acting within historically specific bounds of the unacknowledged conditions and unintended consequences of their acts' (Cassell 1993: 232).

In short, power can be facilitative of positive social change as well as restrictive or malign in effect. We need not see power as dominative, let alone as linked to false consciousness, as implied in Eagleton's fourth proposal – *false ideas which help to legitimate a dominant political power*.

Nonetheless, one can see how the idea of power and false ideas are liable to become linked, especially in some social or political circumstances. If a key aspect to ideology is the exercise of power of one group over another, a likely corollary will be to privilege some ways of thinking, and the language used to express those, over others and to have suppression of points of view which are inimicable to the interests of the dominant group. When ideas and belief systems and even everyday ways of doing things are not open to continued contestation, over time a skewedness will almost inevitably result. Certainly for Fairclough, language is ideological to the extent that it serves to establish or sustain relations of domination (Fairclough 1992b: 87).

However, we are still left with the question of ways of conceptualising domination, within the discussion of ideology. Fairclough (1989) and Chouliaraki and Fairclough (1999) draw on the work of the Italian philosopher Gramsci (1971) to offer a view of domination which is not necessarily related to force – or perceived as tyrannical. Indeed it is important that it should not be. Continued domination is exerted by those in power through the principle of what Gramsci calls hegemony, by which 'a ruling group, whether of the left or right must govern by a balance of force or persuasion'. As Easthope and McGowan (1992) put it (p. 43) 'a group, bloc or class must rule by winning consent in conjunction with the threat of force, the effectiveness of hegemony depending on how rarely, force, always present, has to be used.' Behind this principle is the view that people are in general not aware of the operation of power, especially as embedded in language. Fairclough argues that language conventions and language practices are invested with power relations which people are unaware of. He talks (1992b: 12) of the 'constructive effects discourse has upon social identities, social relations and systems of knowledge and belief' which are not 'normally apparent to discourse participants'.

This issue of consciousness is clearly crucial in the discussion of critical reading. We might link it at this point to the discussion of strategy and stance in Chapter 1. While conventional reading theorists have assumed that advances in reading are signalled by greater automaticity, critical reading means taking a stance which by definition, involves closer than customary attention to text, a heightened consciousness – the reverse of automaticity in short. We are talking not just of 'noticing' as it has been defined in some of the literature on SLA, but of a particular quality and depth of noticing. In order to activate such levels of consciousness we need ways of understanding what the language in texts is doing, especially when ideological effects are relatively disguised. We need a model of language, which I turn to next.

The language model

Critical discourse analysts and critical reading practitioners, attempting to develop critical perspectives to textual analysis, have looked to Halliday's systemic-functional grammar (Halliday 1994), and this book is no exception. There are understandable reasons for the choice of Hallidayan grammar. First, the grammar takes a wide view of context to move beyond the immediate textual environment in order to take account of the cultural landscape. Because functionally grounded, it sees all human language as 'shaped by the social functions it serves' (Chouliaraki and Fairclough 1999: 140). Halliday's is essentially a social grammar. This makes it compatible with a conceptualisation of reading as social practice and texts as social artefacts, in ways which have been further developed by the genre theorists, as noted in Chapter 1. The fact that, as Halliday puts it, linguistic choices are always socially motivated provides an understanding of language which clearly meshes with the CDA view, which takes as axiomatic that formal linguistic selections are not merely random, innocent matters of personal preference but are fundamentally shaped by social custom, deeply engrained and ideologically motivated. The Hallidayan influenced group of social semioticians in the New London Group (NLG) make a similar point: '(Grammatical) choices...need to be seen as not just a matter of individual style or intention, but as inherently connected to different discourses based on wider interests and relationships of power' (New London Group in Cope and Kalantzis 2000: 27).

Halliday takes the view that both syntactic and lexical choices are socially motivated in that they encode socially significant ways of looking at the world. 'Grammar creates the potential within which we act and enact our cultural being' (1990: 11). Such a view allows us to see the production and consumption of texts as not merely socially and culturally mediated but also that texts are ideologically permeated by power relations which underpin the whole of social structure.

Does this mean that language contains ideology; that ideology is embedded within texts? This certainly seems the view of Kress in his claim, noted earlier, that texts are 'saturated' with ideology, a view sharply at odds with that of Widdowson, for instance, who maintains (personal communication) that ideology is not an inherent feature of texts, but rather of interpretation. I want to argue that not only does text in itself carry meaning, as claimed in Chapter 1, but that ideological meaning necessarily accompanies, is embedded within what we normally think of as propositional or referential meaning. This would include the text in the bottle found at sea, referred to in Chapter 1. If the bottle contained a racist joke, say, that text would remain racist even if the bottle had been at sea for one hundred years, sent possibly from another continent and not intended to cause any offence. However, as noted in Wallace (1995), there is a case for saying that there is more at stake ideologically with some texts and genres than others. While texts are not ideologically empty, neither do they assert power, malevolently or benevolently, to the same degree. Secondly, it is important to emphasise that in taking up challenge to discriminatory meanings within texts, the challenge is not ultimately to individual text producers but to the institutional and wider societal circumstances which produce, facilitate and validate the circulation of discourses in particular historical periods.

If we look practically at reasons for the choice of Hallidayan grammar as a tool for text analysis in the classroom, it offers certain advantages over other models in that it moves from general to ever more specific features, allowing students of varying linguistic sophistication accessible entry points to the grammar. For instance, let us take a text such as the following: 'The brass rings, weighing about twenty pounds, hold the neck so stiffly that all movement is restricted. If the rings are removed, the head lolls forward, crushing the windpipe and causing suffocation' (from the 'Giraffe-Necked Women of Burma' by Linda Grant). Here students can readily see that the unmarked personal pronoun 'her' is replaced by the definite article in noun phrases such as: 'the neck' and 'the windpipe'. They are then able to speculate on what may motivate the linguistic selection here.

Systemic-functional grammar gives priority to breadth of analysis by invoking a simple conceptual framework of three contextual features, introduced in Chapter 1: field, tenor and mode which serve to interpret the social context of a text. The grammar thus offers the possibility of looking at whole texts in their social context: the ideational, interpersonal and textual functions of language, linked respectively to field, tenor and mode and exemplified by features of grammar such as transitivity, mood, modality and cohesion, are linked to features of the social situation in which the text arises, namely its content, the relationship between producer and receiver and the overall function or rhetorical mode of the text, whether descriptive, narrative or expository.

At the same time, Halliday (1990: 24/25) allows for depth as well as breadth of analysis. He proposes four levels of language use, the first most salient kind relating to the use of obvious logical anomalies such as 'eventually we will run out of food. We must learn to live with this'; the second to lexical effects, as observed, for example in ritualised collocations such as 'shedding jobs' or 'delivering the curriculum'; the third relates to what Halliday calls the 'outer layer' of grammar, as evidenced in function words such as pronouns, while the fourth is at the most concealed level of what Halliday calls the cryptogrammar (following Whorf (1971) who talks of 'cryptotypes'). The cryptogrammar is the hidden grammar, and the notion of 'the hidden grammar' is a potentially very useful one for critical reading. In other words, Halliday claims that while there are elements of grammar which we are conscious of, there are other, more concealed features of the grammar, less readily accessible to consciousness. One goal of critical reading pedagogy is to offer means of raising these more hidden elements to greater consciousness or kinds of noticing. Halliday (1987: 143) gives his own example to illustrate the process, which I quote in full here.

I selected a text – the headline of a news broadcast, which I had taken down verbatim from the radio; I read it aloud to a group of students and asked them to recall it. They gave me the motifs: death, disaster, violence and the like. I pressed them further: what was actually said? This time they gave me words: a list of the lexical items used, recalled with considerable accuracy although most of them had not figured in their first responses.... I pressed them for a more specific account (still without reading the passage again) and they gave me the more exposed parts of the grammar: the word, group and phrase classes, the derivational morphology and so on....I pressed them once more; and this time – since they were students of linguistics – they began to get to the hidden grammar: the transitivity patterns, the grammatical metaphors and so on.

Getting to the 'hidden grammar' is the ultimate goal of critical reading pedagogy, although the depth of that analysis will vary, depending on students' prior knowledge about language. The students in the Critical Reading class in my study were not, unlike Halliday's students, students of linguistics. However, many had studied English grammar, though not Hallidayan grammar, in some detail. One of the advantages which many foreign learners of English have over native speakers of the language is that they already possess explicit kinds of knowledge about language. As I note in Wallace (1992a: 69), they have a metalanguage, a way of talking about texts largely in terms of traditional categories such as 'pronoun', 'subject' and 'object'. It means that this knowledge can be put to use in looking not just at propositional content but at ideological assumptions. With a strong grammatical knowledge background, many of the students in my particular study quite readily accepted the introduction of the Hallidayan functions – ideational, interpersonal and textual – early on in the course, along with discussion of the more salient lexico/grammatical exponents of each function, that is the more 'exposed' parts of the grammar.

Critical literacy procedures

In this section I would like to bring together the discussion of criticality in section one, and the introduction of a language model in section two by offering an account of a framework or pedagogic procedure which illustrates how critical language study informs teaching and learning. As a heuristic then I should like to locate these two strands within some overall framework, that is offer some mapping out of the territory of critical literacy pedagogy.

One kind of framework which makes strong reference to criticality, although it is ostensibly concerned with what it calls the design of social futures more widely, is that offered by the NLG (Cope and Kalantzis 2000), whose work was introduced in Chapter 1. This model moves from *situated practice*, to *overt instruction*, to *critical framing* concluding with *transformed practice*. Although represented here sequentially, these four perspectives are not intended to indicate any teaching progression, with each phase proceeding to subsequent ones. By *situated practice* the NLG mean immersion in a community of learners engaged in authentic everyday literacy experiences. Kalantzis *et al.* have however argued elsewhere (e.g. 1990) the limitations of situated practice accounts of pedagogy which are typical of progressivist education which favours experiential modes of learning: mere immersion in practice, however authentic, will not always in itself promote learning. Situatedness or contextualisation needs to be supported by explicitness so that understandings can be raised to consciousness. This principle motivates the stage of *overt instruction* when aspects of texts and reading are made explicit and key terms introduced. However, neither immersion in experience nor explicit instruction will offer students the tools to critically assess the cultural locatedness of meanings, so a further necessary strand in the pedagogic theory must include what the NLG (*op. cit.*) call 'critical framing'. This involves students gaining some critical distance on texts which they have earlier engaged with experientially or analytically. The final strand is *transformed practice* which returns the learner to situated practice through what is called a 're-practice', 'where theory becomes reflected practice'. Students may be in a better position to put knowledge and understanding to work in different sites. In this sense it seems that there is some sense of a cycle or progression in the model, even though the NLG notes that these strands should not be seen as linear or as stages but may occur simultaneously or be variously emphasised at different moments of actual teaching and learning settings.

Lankshear (1994: 10) offers a simplified model which preceded that of the NLG but whose strands nonetheless have much in common with their theory of pedagogy. In his conceptualisation, a critical literacy might involve:

1. knowing literacy (or literacies) critically, that is having a critical perspective on literacy/literacies generally;
2. having a critical/evaluative perspective on particular texts;
3. having a critical perspective on – being able to make critical readings of – wider social practices, arrangements, relations, allocations, procedures and so on, which are mediated by, made possible and partially sustained through the reading of texts.

In Lankshear's instructional cycle, teachers might begin with situated practice, raising understanding of literacy events and artefacts, move on to explicit instruction based around analysis of specific texts, which has critical framing built into it, and conclude with a revisiting and transformation of practice. One difference between Lankshear's framework and the design of the NLG is that the latter attends to all modes of meaning, not only linguistic design. The NLG model embraces spatial, gestural and visual design, while Lankshear maintains a print literacy focus. However, both models share a preference for the term 'literacy' over 'reading'. It is, therefore, worth pausing to consider the relationship between the two terms, for critical reading purposes. The term *literacy*, as noted in Chapter 1, favours a social practice view of reading and writing and is a term consequently less used by researchers within the cognitive psychology tradition, who typically talk of 'reading' and 'writing'. When we come to consider critical reading, it is particularly important to build in both a literacy orientation and a reading and writing one – the first linked to a critical understanding of literacy practices within their sociocultural location; the second to sustained engagement with specific concrete texts. Both these aspects are built into Lankshear's framework. However, he gives more prominence to the second aspect, that is the sustained and close critique of specific texts. This is, in my view, at the heart of critical reading pedagogy and for this reason it better represents the rationale of the Critical Reading course I designed than the wider brief of the NLG. I shall therefore draw on Lankshear's three headings below to guide my account of the key phases of a critical literacy pedagogy.

Knowing literacies critically

A wider sociocultural perspective on literacy can be seen as preparatory and complementary to critical study of specific texts. Indeed a major point I wish to argue is that without a rich understanding of context, we are left with the version of CDA which consists of 'reading off the effects from texts', in the manner of the early critical linguists. One reason for favouring the term 'literacy' over 'reading' and 'writing' is to signal the social and cultural locatedness of what, following Brice-Heath (1983), are known as 'literacy events'. These refer to communicative events mediated by various kinds of reading and writing activities and can be broadly characterised as: who reads how, what, when, where and with or to whom; reading is seen as a social occasion involving for example, family members or friends or others in the community. However, being critically literate involves not just awareness of the micro-interactions between readers, writers and texts in immediate, specific social settings, but more macro-understandings of what it means to be a reader in the contemporary world, in particular knowledge of cross-cultural similarities and differences in literacy practices.

We need in short to relate critical reading to the wider project of critical literacy. While critical reading can be taught explicitly through classroom procedures, it also looks beyond the classroom to the way in which reading and writing practices are carried out and perceived in the wider society. As teachers, we need some understanding of what it means to be literate in contemporary societies if we are to be able to make any judgements about the kinds of social and personal identities available to our students in either L1 or L2 reading, both within and beyond the classroom. If we take an ideological view, in Street's terms, engagement with literacy does not just consist of the process of teaching and learning particular kinds of awareness and metalinguistic abilities in school settings. It also involves awareness of literacy practices, both within schools and in real life, which are mediated by wider sociocultural values and attitudes. Moreover, the aim is to make students aware not just of the existence of different forms of language in different settings, but of the implications of power involved in their use and circulation.

Language awareness at this macro level has been the concern of scholars in the fields of anthropology and ethnography. A recent application of this ethnography for CLA in an educational context is represented by the work of Barro *et al.* (1993) based at Thames Valley University and the University of Durham. In this project, first year university and secondary school students respectively were asked to carry out home ethnographies prior to doing similar observations of the foreign cultural setting during a period of study abroad. The aim was to achieve some critical distance on familiar cultural practices in order to better understand the unfamiliar ones which would confront them during their stay in another country. Morgan and Cain (2000) conducted a cross-cultural study of a rather different kind: this involved not actual visits to the foreign country but secondary school students from England and France taking part in an intercultural project by which they exchanged notes and commentary on selected cultural themes. Students chose their own means of expression for this exchange, which included questionnaires, role play scripts and drawings. The overall aim was to conduct an intertextual and inter-cultural dialogue.

One can draw on the ethnographic principles in these studies to encourage students to do more specific *literacy* ethnographies, by investigating the literacy practices of their own communities as well as those of other cultural groups and societies. I have begun critical reading courses with such investigations, asking students, for instance, to conduct observations of the literacy practices in homes where they are staying with British families. Across these families in contemporary multicultural Britain there will be considerable diversity. Students investigate and report back on the literacy practices of the families, that is who reads what, where and when; and, if possible, why. Or students may investigate the physical location of texts in particular kinds of public places, and what may motivate this. For instance, it was pointed out to me by Italian students in one class I taught that political advertising in Italy is only seen in specified limited settings, as opposed to Britain where, in the lead-up to general elections in particular, it occupies very prominent public spaces. These modest investigations can then form the basis for discussion and comparison within class. Cross-cultural differences may emerge between the values and attitudes represented by readers and texts observed in the foreign setting and those of the home setting. The overall aim is not just to 'make the strange familiar but the familiar strange', as they revisit and reflect on their existing taken-for-granted views of what it means to be literate.

Within the classroom itself investigations might take the form of tasks which have a cross-cultural emphasis. Thus I have on several occasions begun a Critical Reading course with a genre awareness task which involves students classifying sets of texts initially into categories that are socioculturally familiar to them, as for instance, advertisements, newspapers, women's magazines. A second stage involves learners devising new categories or rethinking the familiar ones, to account for what may be to them culturally unknown genres such as political leaflets, political manifestos or flyers which announce demonstrations or other kinds of public events.

Having a critical perspective on particular texts

When we turn to the analysis of specific texts, the challenge is to find a framework for close and specific text analysis which is compatible with the wider kinds of analysis of literacy practices which characterise the first phase of a Critical Reading course, *knowing literacies critically*, in Lankshear's framework. My choice of systemic-functional grammar was judged to provide such a link for the students on critical reading courses. It would provide a metalanguage for the description of both contextual and textual features, to include the introduction of terms such as 'genre', 'intertextuality', 'model reader' and the term 'context' itself as what I call 'contextual' metalanguage, as opposed to 'textual' metalanguage relating to the grammar of specific texts.

The provision of a grammatical framework which students are expected to draw on in their analyses presupposes the value of offering some kind of explicit metalanguage to sharpen awareness. Ellis (1997) notes the research by Alderson *et al.* (1995) which suggested that metalingual knowledge is not related to language proficiency. However, as Ellis (1997: 113) goes on to point out, this does not mean that explicit knowledge is unimportant; merely that the use of accompanying metalanguage is in doubt. Whatever the case, I initially developed pedagogic procedures on the assumption that metalinguistic knowledge would support awareness, and, while it might not facilitate language development in the first instance, might serve to stretch learners' language production in the longer term. Nonetheless it is possible to argue that students can reveal metalevel knowledge of various kinds without necessarily drawing on specific, taught terminology. Conversely, students may use metalinguistic terms unenlighteningly, largely for display purposes. This issue of the value of metalinguistic knowledge is raised in the discussion of individual learners in Chapter 7.

The degree to which it is possible to identify linguistic features as salient in particular genres can be related to the timing for the introduction of texts. Thus, certain genres such as advertisements will fairly consistently show a greater incidence of personal pronouns or strongly connotated vocabulary than genres, such as, for instance, arguments of various kinds, whose significant ideological effects will be observable only at clause level. It is one of the major principles of the genre school, informed by Hallidayan grammar, that certain text types will be typified and indeed made socioculturally recognisable by characteristic sets of linguistic features. Therefore, one might, on critical reading courses, link the phased introduction of particular kinds of texts with compatible linguistic features, salient in those texts. For instance, in critical reading courses I have taught, consistent with the introduction of 'interpersonal' texts has been an emphasis on key features of interpersonal language, such as personal pronouns and modality.

The Hallidayan framework

In this section, I include a description of the framework which I have designed to guide the analysis of particular texts on critical reading courses (Figure 2.1). Usually the framework is introduced gradually with key lexicogrammatical exponents of ideational, interpersonal and textual meanings presented within texts which make their social function relatively salient. The framework thus represents the outcome of a lengthy process of development and discussion of the terminology used. Only when its component parts have been fully discussed in context is the final framework made available as a point of reference for text analysis; it does not constitute the pedagogic material in itself, which I introduce in Chapter 5.

We might draw on this framework to attempt a preliminary analysis of the text about Singapore, which Yuko was responding to in Chapter 1 (p. 21) and which also features again in Chapter 7. I reproduce the opening section of the text here, and analyse it only from the point of view of selected aspects of the field of discourse: the major and minor participants and the material, mental or relational processes which collocate with them.

SINGAPORE

WHERE THE STATE CHOOSES YOUR PARTNER

Singapore's citizens are so law-abiding that many of them participate in state-run matchmaking schemes, which encourage intellectual equals to marry each other. Sophie Campbell reports from the country where failing to flush a toilet can be an offence.

Welcome to Singapore. Death to Drug Traffickers reads the immigration card on arrival at Changi Airport. Driving down a palm-bordered highway to the cluster of futuristic buildings that is downtown Singapore you find yourself on an island the size of the Isle of Wight, inhabited by three million of the most obedient people on earth. Singapore is famous for its Draconian laws. Gambling is banned, there are £185 fines for jaywalking within 50 metres of a pedestrian crossing or smoking in a public building and up to £370 fines for spitting, littering or failing to flush a public toilet. Even when the streets are empty, people wait patiently on the immaculate pavements until the lights indicate that they can cross (from *Marie Claire* 1992).

CRITICAL READING A framework for a critical analysis of texts, based on Hallidayan functional grammar **FIELD OF DISCOURSE** IDEATIONAL MEANINGS (how the writer describes what is going on in the text, i.e. what the text is <u>about</u>)	
PARTICIPANTS	WHAT/WHO is talked about? i.e. what or who are the major participants what or who are the minor participants what or who are the invisible participants HOW are the participants talked about, i.e. what adjectives or nouns collocate with them?
PROCESSES	What verbs (collocating with the major participants) describe what kind of processes, i.e. material, mental and relational processes?
CIRCUMSTANCES	How specifically are circumstances indicated, e.g. by adverbs or prepositional phrases?
CAUSATION	How is causation attributed? Is agency always made clear i.e. Who did what to whom? Are actors in subject position?
EFFECT OF THE WRITER'S CHOICES?	
TENOR OF DISCOURSE INTERPERSONAL MEANINGS (how the writer indicates his/her relationship with the reader and what his/her attitude to the subject matter of the text is)	
PERSON	What personal pronouns are selected? How does the writer refer to self, subjects and reader?
MOOD	What mood is most frequently selected – declarative, imperative or interrogative?
MODALITY	What role does modality play in, for example, expressing a degree of certainty or authority?
ADVERBS ADJECTIVES, NOUNS indicating writer attitude	Are there adjectives, nouns or adverbs which indicate writer attitude to his/her subject matter?
EFFECT OF THE WRITER'S CHOICES?	
MODE OF DISCOURSE TEXTUAL MEANINGS (how the content of the text is organised)	
SEMANTIC STRUCTURE	Is the text narrative, expository or descriptive, as indicated, for example, by the use of past or present tense?
OVERALL ORGANISATION	What larger structures does the text have, e.g. in terms of beginnings and endings? In what form is information represented?
THEME	What information is selected for first position, at clause level and at the level of the whole text?
COHESION	How does the text hang together as a text, for example what kinds of connectors are used (related to the semantic structure of the text)?
EFFECT OF THE WRITER'S CHOICES?	

Figure 2.1 The Hallidayan framework.

We might represent a preliminary analysis schematically as in Figure 2.2.

The text fragment is short and so open to the charge of lack of representativeness of the whole text from which it is extracted (cf. Stubbs *op. cit.*). However we do very frequently, especially as responders in daily life, read just the opening paragraphs of such texts. One can offer some defence therefore for examining this section of text. It should be added too that the word 'Singapore' in the original text makes a very striking impact, being reproduced within the magazine, *Marie Claire*, in heavy bold letters. The overall effect which can be derived even from this very partial analysis of the heading, sub-heading and opening paragraph is that Singapore is strongly thematised, not just graphically through the banner headline but through initial position in the opening lines of the text: Singapore – the State – Singapore's citizens. The coreferring nouns all suggest an authoritarian police state, if one connects: Singapore – The State – the country where failing to flush a toilet can be an offence and, within the body of the text itself which follows: 'the cluster of futuristic buildings that is down-town Singapore', 'Draconian laws' and 'immaculate pavements' (it needs to be understood that cleanliness is viewed with suspicion in the United Kingdom). On the other hand, Singapore's people are positioned as passive; they do not function, in this opening part of the text, as subjects of

PARTICIPANTS	PROCESSES		
Major participant:	*Strong material*	*Weak material*	*Relational*
Singapore			*is famous (for its Draconian laws)*
Coreferring and collocating noun phrases:			
The country where failing to flush a toilet can be an offence			
The State	*chooses*		
State-run match making schemes	*encourage*		
Minor participants:			
Singapore's citizens		*participate in*	*are law abiding*
Coreferring and collocating noun phrases:			
Three million of the most obedient people on earth		*inhabit*	
People		*wait patiently*	

Figure 2.2

sentences or as agents of material transitive verbs, that is who have goals or agency (for example, they 'participate in' rather than enact or effect change) and are generally linked with relational verbs or what one might call 'weak' material verbs: they are, they wait, they participate. The cumulative impression of passivity and helplessness and conformity is reinforced by the lexical cohesion which can be traced through this opening section: Your partner (the state chooses for you) – citizens are law-abiding – participate, all reinforced by later references within the text, as in 'the perfect Singaporean couple' and 'carefully selected singles'.

Having a critical perspective on wider social practices, arrangement, relations, allocations and procedures

This third phase of the cycle involves the revisiting of practices and values introduced in the first phase of the cycle at the start of a Critical Reading course. It offers the opportunity of a widening out of the parameters from the study of specific features of texts. At the same time there may be recontextualising and revisiting of specific texts studied either in phase one or two. This might take place in a number of ways. For instance, students might be asked to revisit a text which they looked at early in the course. A text which was read with a relatively shallow level of attention or noticing might be revisited with the purpose of looking at more of the hidden grammar, now available to the students because they have drawn more extensively on the Hallidayan framework in the analysis of other texts. Also texts may become, intertextually, points of reference for wider cultural observations, as we see in this comment by Victoria in an interview after the end of the course:

V: Do you remember the Spanish text talking about the waiter – the text of the tourist – English man who went to Spain – the one we were discussing? The first lines of the article were the description of the guy and his mother and what he did on Saturdays and his girlfriend and then once you have presented and introduced the person then you can tell the story. Its very personalised – very...they always look for an example and he and he and he and he did that and something happened to him. And its everywhere: in the news, in the radio.

CW: I hadn't thought of that until you mentioned it. Well now you mention it I think of course...

V: You think its natural, but it was new for me. It drew my attention. You need proofs in general. In British newspapers everything's got its name and surname and age and everything. Even when they go to Rwanda. And they interview a person and they always give the name and – who cares what's the name; the important thing is the opinion. They become aware of the importance of the event when they've got someone who has suffered the event and is telling it. It's because it's very important individualism here.

Critical reading: principles, purposes and practice

So, by way of summarising so far, what are the differences between critical and conventional, comprehension models of reading? I see these as clustering around differences in principles, purposes and practices. I will take each in turn here.

Principles

First, critical reading represents a challenge to the skills-based orientation of many cognitive psychological models which emphasise the building of discrete kinds of abilities based – albeit often implicitly – on some supposed hierarchy of difficulty. Moreover, its emphasis is different from the strategies view, in that critical reading focuses less on individual responses to texts and more on communally negotiated ones, by which, in classroom contexts, texts are jointly interpreted through talk around text. Also within these reader responses there is less interest in problems as located within readers, say due to supposed weaknesses of skill or strategy, than in readers' problematising of the text.

Secondly, critical reading does not see non-native speaker readers in their reading of authentic, non-pedagogic texts, as necessarily disadvantaged – on the contrary. Because they are not the primary addressees of texts written for an indigenous readership, second and foreign language learners may be more aware of the way in which texts position readers, that is, the manner in which the preferred or model reader is embedded within the text. Not being invited to collude in a text's ideological positioning, L2 readers are arguably in a stronger position both to perceive and to resist it.

Thirdly, critical reading does not privilege an author's communicative intent but is concerned with *effect*. The aim is not to converge with the author, but to disrupt or challenge the schemas called up by the text; the author is not the sole or ultimate arbitrator of a text's meaning. This is not to take, however, a totally open, relativist position, one that assumes that every interpretation is as good as another. As I argue in Chapter 1, some interpretations will be more credible than others. Fourthly, critical reading involves critiquing not just the logic, argument or sentiments expressed in texts but the ideological assumptions underpinning them. Finally and most importantly, critical readers do not just comment metacognitively, showing awareness of the cognitive strategies they make use of, but also metacritically. In metacritique we are prepared to offer challenge to our own stance to the text, aiming to gain some overall distance on our interpretations and the likely reasons for them. How do our identities and ideological leanings predispose us to read texts in certain kinds of ways?

Purposes

The purposes of critical reading as an educational project can be seen as linguistic, conceptual/critical and cultural. First, linguistic aims involve helping students to gain an understanding of the nature of ideological meanings embedded in texts as indicated by the way language is used. The aim is to draw on students' grammatical knowledge – not so much in order to aid the reading process, nor to do the kind of conventional language work by which texts are gutted for grammatical structures in rather arbitrary ways, but to facilitate reflection on the *effect* of language choice. Here foreign language students tend to be advantaged, as I noted above, over native speaker readers educated in British schools, who receive little formal grammar instruction, especially in the case of English. Foreign language students, by contrast, tend to have a well-developed knowledge of key grammatical terms which can be put to use as a tool in text analysis.

In the case of the development of conceptual/critical abilities, the aim is to develop what Wells (1991: 63) has called epistemic literacy, which means being able to move beyond the text to develop a cogent argument around it. Wells notes how even very young children will do this if provided with opportunities, for example, to discuss not just the events, but the *implications* of those events, as described in stories. They will make cognitive and critical links to their own lives, and one might call this the beginning of critical literacy in so far as children are not just understanding but questioning and challenging some of those implications. Written texts, unlike spoken interactions, offer stable points of reference for this shared debate. Moreover the talk around text becomes itself 'critical' to the extent that it is expository, reflective and does not take its own premises for granted.

Finally, when we come to consider the cultural implications of a critical reading orientation, even though the texts drawn upon in a Critical Reading class are likely to be highly culture-specific, the goal is not to teach students about 'British – or French or German – culture' (whatever we might take that to involve) but to promote insights into cultural assumptions and practices, similarities and differences across national boundaries. Indeed for the students in this study one of the most valuable aspects of the course was the opportunity to share different cultural perspectives; to see, for example, what was common ground as well as to observe and acknowledge readings taken from different cultural perspectives.

Practice

The manner in which the principles and purposes of critical reading are pedagogised in practice depends on the level and circumstances of the learners involved. The learners in my study were advanced foreign language learners, many, though by no means all, with sophisticated knowledge about language. However, with lower level learners or with children one can draw on the principles of critical literacy, by paying attention less to the detail of the hidden grammar, but to the hidden images of texts. Comber (1993), for instance, describes her work with primary aged children where she invites them to challenge the images of mothers, all white, blonde haired and middle class, which predominate in the advertisements for 'mothers' day' gifts. Arizpe *et al.* (2002) talk about the powerful interpretations of picture books offered by children, including L2 learners with little or no print literacy in English. They show how children are able to probe visual texts analytically, as revealed not by verbal responses but through drawings. In this way, Arizpe *et al.* have begun to demonstrate in very practical ways multimodal interactions between reader and text.

In considering some of the differences suggested here between conventional and critical reading, some sceptics of the Critical Reading project pose a more radical distinction by arguing that critical reading is not reading at all, that analysis of texts is not what we normally understand by reading. There is some point to this. In going against the grain of much of what counts as reading – reading for information, reading for survival, even reading for pleasure – we might want to call critical reading an unnatural act. I say this because in taking up a stance which is out of alignment with the apparent or professed intention or purpose of the text, reading critically can be said to break Grice's (1975) co-operative principle. Grice's well-known maxims of conversation, through which interlocuters co-operate to reach understanding, can be applied not just to speaking/listening but to writing/reading as a communicative act. The maxims assume that, all things being equal, listeners – and readers – assume truthfulness, relevance and succinctness on the speaker or writer's part. It is perversely unco-operative to doubt or dispute this, without good reason. In taking up an atypically suspicious stance to texts, we might want to call 'critical reading' not 'reading' in the usually understood sense at all, but rather draw on Eco's term (e.g. in 1992) and talk of *using* a text rather than reading it. Arguably, in daily life we do both. After all, critical commentary on texts of all kinds, from popular media ones to academic ones, is part of the common currency of everyday exchanges as well as intellectual debate.

In short, we might want to make a difference between reading a text analytically and 'being a reader of', for example, *The Sun* or *The Guardian* which will involve a generally convergent, co-operative stance, for the obvious reason that because we are regular readers of these texts, they reflect and reinforce our existing ideological, even aesthetic preferences (Hence the *Longman Dictionary of Culture* (1992) has entries under 'Sun Reader' and 'Guardian Reader'). Indeed one well-known journalist in a rival, popular newspaper currently refers contemptuously to *Guardian* readers as 'the Guardianistas'. This issue of reader loyalty and preference raises the question as to how far we are willing or able to *use* texts of which we are the readers. It is clearly especially important, though much more difficult, to critique what we typically accept as common sense, because in keeping with our existing world-view. Thus, one important goal of critical reading is to allow readers to change perspective – to shift, that is, from being a reader of a text to using a text for critique. In this way, critical reading – or the *use* of texts – can take its place alongside conventional reading.

Moreover, we may want to draw on a dichotomy introduced by Giroux (1983) and talk not of opposition (to texts, in our case) but of resistance. The first can be seen as an instinctive, unreflected upon response to domination, of the kind described in Willis's classic (1977) study of schooling, *Learning to Labour*, where the boys Willis describes ultimately colluded in their own oppression; the second being a considered, reflected upon, rational stance. Indeed resistance – as opposed to opposition – allows us detachment and distance from just the kind of ideological pre-judgements that some critics of CDA, such as Widdowson, have cautioned against. For it means not just that readers should be prepared to gain critical distance from texts which they would, generally speaking, align themselves with, but that oppositional barriers will be lowered in the reading of texts known to adopt a broadly different political and ideological stance from the reader's own.

Conclusion

I raised some objections to CDA and critical reading at the start of this chapter. They can be represented briefly as follows:

- Critical reading is not possible: it is not possible to argue that every single linguistic feature carries ideological weight. And if, as inevitably we must, we select when it comes to practical analysis, what motivates our selection? Finally how do we match particular linguistic features of texts to ideological effects? How is it possible to argue, for instance, that the use of a deleted agent is motivated, consciously or otherwise, by a desire to conceal causation, which in turn is linked to institutionalised discrimination against certain social groups?
- Critical reading is not only fundamentally unfeasible; attempts to engage in it are unethical. As a classroom procedure it is tyrannical. It is a way of telling students how texts should be read.
- Finally, critical reading is redundant. People are already critical readers, perfectly able to see the way in which texts position them or misrepresent states of affairs or events, certainly in those cases where the events are of interest or relevance to them. The approach is patronising.

In other words, critical reading either cannot, should not or need not be done. I shall revisit these objections at the end of this book – not necessarily to rebut them in any definitive way but to permit my reader to judge whether the description and discussion of the empirical study confirms, challenges or at least qualifies such misgivings. Provisionally, my response is offered in the conclusion to this chapter.

In answer to the first objection that critical reading is unfeasible, I would concede that its text analysis aspects involve highly selective procedures. However, while a precise and comprehensive location of ideological meaning within texts remains inevitably elusive, it is feasible and productive to note the kinds of linguistic options available to writers and some of the major effects achieved. This is so especially when linguistic choices consistently incline in one direction rather than another. CDA is able to provide some tools for offering clearer warrant to interpretations of texts – to disrupt and throw open to challenge first sight schema driven and frequently intuitive and affective responses. Critical analysis, as any other kind of language analysis, can never be exhaustive. However, it can be illuminative of the ways ideology goes to work within the texts which surround us in daily life. After all, few deny the presence of bias in public texts. If we accept the principle, then the practice of critique in classrooms, partial and approximative as it necessarily is, can be claimed to be worthwhile. Much depends on how it is interpreted in pedagogy. This brings me to the next objection.

Critical reading as a classroom project is claimed to be manipulative. I would agree that it can be, in a number of ways, several of which I will set out here. First CDA, and its pedagogic offspring CLA and critical reading, may look like a witch-hunt, in its search for villains and victims. It is for this reason that I emphasised earlier the importance of attending to the institutional and cultural circumstances of text production rather than individual authorship. It is not that the discriminatory language of individuals is of no matter. Rather that it is of greater interest educationally and culturally to look for patterns of language use at the societal level, especially where they recur across texts and across different media. Undeniably, where there is a strongly committed position on the part of a teacher, teaching is more high risk, in particular ways. However, just as no print text is ideology free, nor is the classroom 'text': teaching of all kinds is ideological, to a large degree concealing its own power base, even more so, in progressivist pedagogies than those which aspire, at least, to be more transparent.

Let us turn, finally to the third question – need critical reading be done? In particular, is it useful for second and foreign language learners? For those learners who are settled in English speaking countries, it is clearly valuable that they develop linguistic skills to critique the frequently racist and xenophobic discourse which permeates many of the texts which surround them. For the foreign language students at the centre of my particular study, the need is less clear. It must be admitted that L2 readers, especially with the educational background of the students described in this study, are frequently very good critical readers. They are certainly able to notice aspects of texts which have eluded me. However, many L2 readers welcome the opportunity to exercise their undoubted skills – opportunities not always available in the foreign language classroom. Secondly, English as an international means of communication invites critical reading. Arguably, the ideologies and cultural assumptions embedded in a wide range of English language texts are more widely disseminated in written than via spoken texts. Written English language texts of a whole range of genres from popular culture ones to academic writing increasingly carry universal authority. It has been noted for instance (cf. Kourilova 1995) that scholars wishing to be part of the international academic community in science or medicine are required to publish in British and American journals which exert their own culture-specific conventions.

In other words, the very world dominance of English invites – indeed requires – a critical response. Just as we noted in Chapter 1 that texts cannot be a neutral medium for the exercising of reading skills, English as a language cannot act as a neutral medium for the exercising of foreign language reading abilities. It carries too much baggage both from its colonial history as well as through its current global dominance. Such, at least, is the view of Phillipson, who sees both the past and continuing role of English as what he calls *linguistic imperialism* (cf. Phillipson 1992). However, refusal to engage with the language as such is unlikely to undermine its hegemony. For this reason a more feasible option might be to encourage learners to reposition themselves via the currently dominant discourses of English. This is the position which is taken by Peirce (cf. Peirce 1989) who argues the case, in the context of South Africa, not for the replacement of English as a lingua franca by an indigenous language, but for a new kind of English, which she calls 'Peoples' English, one inflected with different kinds of meanings. The ability and willingness to see how one can draw variably on the resources of a single language is part of critical literacy. Moreover, as argued above, critical literacy involves not just the reading of specific texts but makes wider reference to ways of reading and talking about texts at the start of the twenty-first century. In this sense it can be seen as part of a transnational English which does not necessarily carry with it the discourses of its colonial history.

In talking of a role for critical literacy in the context of transnational English, one inevitably needs to deal with uses of language and literacy beyond the specific and local. If foreign language students wish to play a potential part in the wider English speaking world, the kind of critical literacy we are arguing for constitutes in Gee's (1990) terms a Secondary Discourse, secondary in that it allows one to critique other primary ones, linked to our primary socialisation (cf. Berger and Luckman 1966). Gee uses the term 'Discourse' to mean ways of using language which link to various kinds of social identity, as opposed to 'discourse' which is used more conventionally to relate to specific uses of language. Bakhtin (1986) in similar ways, as noted earlier, differentiates between primary and secondary genres. Halliday (1996: 353) represents this dichotomous relationship between private and public domains as one between primary knowledge, acquired in settings of primary socialisation such as the home, and secondary knowledge which is more heterogenously constituted and specific to educational settings. In each case some kind of disjuncture is envisaged between everyday worlds and the formal educational world of schooling. Part of my argument here is that it is on this second kind of territory that second or foreign language learners need to be supported, as opposed to within primary kinds of socialisation, where mother tongue is more likely to be used. The kind of power at stake here is what Van Dijk (1996) calls the power of access, one strand of which he calls the access to 'scholarly text and talk' (Van Dijk 1996: 86). It is access to this kind of English that is frequently denied to the foreign language learner, especially within some kinds of communicative classroom, as I shall argue more fully in the next chapter.

To conclude, critical literacy, seen as a secondary Discourse involves us gaining a metalevel awareness of other Discourses, thus offering a vantage point from which to gain not just greater awareness of discriminatory forms of language but ultimately greater control over a wider range of language uses in daily life. An additional key feature of critical literacy is what I have called 'metacritical awareness' by which we become aware not just of features of texts and literacy and language behaviour but of our own responses to these.

The conceptualising of critical literacy as a secondary Discourse – in opposition to other ways of using language, including everyday forms of literacy as primary Discourses, has echoes of Bernstein's distinction between what he calls (1996: 171) 'vertical' and 'horizontal' literacies. The latter are literacy practices linked to everyday activities and may be largely learned by observation and apprenticeship. Vertical literacies, on the other hand, build knowledge in school settings and are interdependent. We need, I argue, to place the development of critical literacy firmly in an educational setting and to see it, in the manner in which Bernstein and, in similar ways, Halliday (*op. cit.*) argue, as related to but ultimately distinct from everyday literacy practices. While schooling draws on many voices, and is therefore heteroglossic, its major business is with secondary socialisation. In the next chapter, I look at the different interpretations of critical pedagogy which take account of this requirement and which might underpin more specific critical reading programmes.

3
Critical Pedagogy for Language Teaching

In the previous two chapters, I have identified some characteristics of reading as critical social practice and process. Here I want to locate my discussion within wider understandings of critical pedagogy, to pave the way for an exploration of classroom-based critical reading.

The construction of knowledge

Any educational activity must address the issue of what kind of knowledge is being transmitted, or constructed in classroom settings. A typical aim of education is likely to be, however this is achieved, to further the knowledge and understanding of topics which constitute the curriculum (Edwards and Mercer 1987: 49). This may appear to be an unexceptional point to make unless one acknowledges that much classroom interaction is less to do with building understanding than taking part in rather ritualised events where participants do not reflect – nor are invited to reflect – very deeply on the processes or content involved.

In the case of language teaching, a dilemma relates to what *kind* of content knowledge is in play. The object of enquiry may be language itself, for instance, as evidenced in written texts. This was a central focus of the class at the centre of this study. Additionally, there was an interest in the processes by which this knowledge was constructed and articulated, in particular the language which facilitated and revealed such processes.

However, a much more fundamental question centres around the feasibility of growth in knowledge and understanding. How is reliable knowledge possible? Bauman (1992 in Hoggart 1995: 1) notes that '(the concept of post-modernism) proclaimed the end of the exploration of the ultimate truth of the human world or human experience'. With the demise of the old certainties, does the pursuit of truth remain a feasible proposition in classrooms, or indeed elsewhere?

I want to argue that facts and truth do indeed matter and are necessary concerns of critical pedagogy and of critical language study in particular.

For it is the scrutiny of language which is able to reveal the difference between what happened as verifiable fact and what *would or might have* happened as mere hypothesis. Apologists for the Chilean dictator, Augusto Pinochet like to quote in his defence that he prevented a communist takeover in Chile. This is one such view, quoted in the context of the imprisonment of political opponents during that era: 'it is very doubtful whether a communist Chile, which they (those imprisoned by Allende's regime) wanted to set up, would have treated its prisoners as humanely' (Peregrine Worsthorne quoted in *The Guardian* 4 May 2002). What is at stake is a crucial difference between verifiable fact and hypothesis, revealed in English grammar by a difference between the simple past and what English Language textbooks call the 'third conditional', the unreal conditional. David Cooper writing in defence of facts, and of maintaining the difference between fact and interpretation concludes: 'However differently the murder was interpreted, one man did stick a sword into another. That was fact, not comment' (*The Guardian* 2000).

As Hargreaves (1994: 39) observes, once the pursuit of truth is denied as an objective, any endeavour becomes motivated not by intellectual principles 'entailing a search for truth or understanding, but by political and ethical principles entailing the realisation of such things as justice, fairness and equity'.

Hargreaves' point raises the question as to whether the pursuit of political and ethical principles can be seen as distinct from the search for greater intellectual understanding, to include the establishment of facts, in some cases. The view taken in this book, and discussed more fully below, is that notions of justice and equity, whether related to critique of written texts or to evaluation of classroom discourse, should be articulated within rational sets of beliefs – they must be rationally defensible and aim for intellectual clarity and coherence. While 'a whole traditional ideology of representation is in crisis', yet, claims Eagleton (1988: 395), 'this does not mean that the search for truth is abandoned'. This view is echoed by the German philosopher, Jurgen Habermas, one of whose central beliefs is in emancipatory possibilities which are sought not merely for reasons of equity but because they are intellectually justifiable.

One of the ways in which Habermas (1979) argues for universal principles regarding the pursuit of truth, without espousing a wholehearted Kantian transcendentalism is to propose a universal pragmatics, which he differentiates from what he calls 'empirical pragmatics', which attends to specific contexts of use. Drawing very much on the Speech Act literature and the work of Searle in particular (e.g. 1969), he puts the case for sets of conditions which operate in all human communication and which are orientated to the reaching of understanding. Utterances, or language in use, relate to:
(1) the external reality of what is supposed to be an existing state of affairs,
(2) the internal reality of what a speaker would like to express before a public

as his intentions, and (3) the normative reality of what is intersubjectively recognised as a legitimate interpersonal relationship. He sums this up by talking of three basic principles: truth, truthfulness and normative rightness, which relate to three types of speech action: constatives, avowals and regulatives. These validity claims, as Habermas (1979: 66) describes them, are invariably implied in speech oriented to reaching understanding and reflect the relation between the utterance and: (a) the external world, (b) the social world, and (c) an inner world. In spoken (and presumably written interaction, though Habermas is talking largely about face to face communication) 'the speaker, in a cognitively testable way, assumes with a truth claim, obligations to provide grounds (in the case of constatives), with a rightness claim, obligations to provide justification (in the case of regulative speech acts focusing on interpersonal relations) and with a truthfulness claim, obligations to prove trustworthy (in the case of expressive acts or avowals)' (Habermas 1979: 65).

In other words, different validity claims correlate with different types of speech action. With constatives, which would typify a cognitive mode of communication such as argument or discussion, the truth claim would be thematic. Inherent in the cognitive use of language, Habermas claims, is an obligation to provide grounds. 'Constative speech acts contain the offer to recur if necessary to the experiential source from which the speaker draws the certainty that his statement is true. If this immediate grounding does not dispel an ad hoc doubt, the persistingly problematic truth claim can become the subject of a theoretical discourse' (*op. cit.* 1979: 64). The overall goal is to reach intersubjective understanding. 'Speech establishes a shared relation towards truth' (Habermas, from letter to Adorno quoted in Callinicos 1999: 283). The pursuit of truth then is not seen in individualist but in dialogic terms. As Callinicos emphasises 'Habermas is as critical as Foucault of any attempt to make the self-certain individual subject the foundation of knowledge' (Callinicos 1999: 285). Underpinning any real-life communication is a formal ideal of a situation in which disagreements may be rationally resolved (Pusey 1987: 73) Habermas refers to this ideal as 'the ideal speech situation'. In such envisaged situations, not attainable in fact, there would be equal opportunities to debate. Quality of argument, through rational defence, must link with equality, that is equality of opportunity to have one's voice heard. While such situations will not exist in reality, as educators we can work towards their realisation. For this reason Habermas's work meshes with the aims of educators with an interest in classroom discourse and has been drawn on by, among others, Young (1992) and Mercer (1995b) in their analyses of classroom interaction. For similar reasons, I see this philosophical position as underpinning my own account of classroom interaction, described in Chapter 6.

To talk of truth in terms merely of the verifiability of facts will clearly not reveal much about the ideological underpinning of discourses. This is why Habermas's truthfulness principle needs to work in conjunction with the truth claim. For it is truthfulness rather than truth which is frequently either wilfully or unwittingly sacrificed in much debate and which Eagleton (1988: 387) is referring to when he claims: 'it is not surprising that classical models of truth and cognition are increasingly out of favour in a society where what matters is whether you deliver the commercial or rhetorical goods.' Frequently media reports or politicians' accounts of events might be said to be 'delivering the goods' rather than engaging in a rational debate. In such cases it is not so much that the truth in a literal sense is sacrificed but that the truthfulness claim is simply inoperable. What is at stake is not truth, as factual evidence of a kind is often adduced to support statements, but truthfulness in the sense that we are, arguably, expected to take what is said or written not as a move in rational debate but as a rhetorical ploy – as strategically motivated in short.

If this point is accepted, one can challenge the relativist claim that all discourse, including the discourse of critique, is equally motivated by interest (and therefore ideologically tainted to the same extent) by asserting that educational discourse by definition will eschew the kind of sophistry which has come conventionally to characterise the discourse typical of genres in domains such as politics. That is, the kind of theoretical discourse which, premised on truthfulness, pursues problematic truth claims, finds its proper home in educational contexts; here students – and teachers – are expected to defend positions, offer evidence and listen to counter evidence.

To argue the case, in broadly Habermasian terms, of rational justification does not mean that there is an absolutely neutral position or standpoint outside ongoing interpretation of texts or events. To claim as I have done that 'facts matter' does not mean that 'interpretations must lead in every case to a stable and unambiguously differentiated argument' (Habermas 1984: 100). It is a mistake to suppose that rational debate seeks closure. Janks (2001a: 141), for instance, describes 'educational practices which privilege rational deliberation, reflection and debate (and which) teach students to seek closure'. A Habermasian position can, in principle, support the possibility of a plurality of interpretations of any particular text. For the pragmatic universals relate not to specific and particular speech acts or speech events but provide the basis for the construction of an ideal speech situation, against which communicatively competent speakers can take their bearings. For this reason, Habermas claims that 'all speech, even of intentional deception, is oriented towards the idea of truth' (Habermas 1970 in Pusey 1987: 73). What a Habermasian position does indicate, however, unlike Foucault's for instance, is that a goal of rationally agreed interpretations of events or texts or rationally based agreement to disagree is feasible. In this way Habermas presents a case for the pursuit of truth not on the basis that there are, as Roderick puts it, 'theory – neutral facts' – timeless and absolutely neutral standpoints for inquiry – but that 'within the fallible context of human inquiry, "foundationalism" in an attenuated sense can be found within the intersubjective workings of the community of inquirers themselves' (Roderick 1986: 10).

This position on communicatively negotiated rationality is different from that of those such as Hewitt (1996), who, in attempting to understand racism in some London communities, writes of 'locally negotiated forms of reasonableness or rationality' which do not have universal applicability. However, I would argue that the local and global are mutually coreferential. Locally negotiated rationality must be located within universal principles of social justice and respect for persons. If the premises are morally or factually wrong there is simply no basis for the construction of a case, however skilfully constructed. Rational and moral absurdities should be seen for what they are: expressions of prejudice – or strategically deployed rhetoric. A recent example from the British Newspaper, the *Evening Standard*, is: 'The British, quite simply, are better than anyone else in the world' (1 August 2000). Of course one can put such claims to the test, as frequently happens in formal debate. However, a motion so certain to be defeated in rational debate would be very unlikely to be proposed in the first place. It would be naïve to believe that all assertions are so readily challengeable. People will clearly hold a range of sincerely held and rationally defensible views, which may, at first sight seem wholly incompatible with each other. However, the apparent irreconcilability of some ideological positions is no reason to abandon the search for common ground. This is especially so if we are concerned with the process of enquiry rather than closure in terms of outcomes.

Within this process of enquiry, what then, within classrooms, are allowable topics and allowable positions to take within these? That is, if we eschew a morally relativist position? Setting out the parameters of what is sayable and thinkable is clearly problematic. In some ways it is not surprising that language teachers opt for safe subjects and the approved published text book. Teachers and educational institutions are frequently more squeamish than students. At the same time neither can we entirely predict what might be decisively off limits for certain groups of students in particular circumstances, as I shall describe in Chapter 5.

Finally, in making judgements about moral absolutes, I would argue that notwithstanding the importance of openness to debate, there are constant principles which we expect everyone to adhere to in public spaces, such as classrooms: most obviously, universal views of respect for persons. Sexism and racism are wrong. That much can be agreed. Much harder of course is to reach consensus as to what *constitutes* sexism and racism, along with other forms of discrimination. For this reason constative talk in classrooms is characterised by caution rather than certainty. It is necessarily exploratory.

It must be acknowledged that as Thompson (1982: 129) notes, there are difficulties with Habermas's view that consensual agreement will be induced by the force of better argument as opposed to, for example, compassion or the commitment to a common goal, or, one might add, with reference to Hewitt's work on racism, described in Hewitt (1996), deeply entrenched prejudices. However, it is a necessary goal for education to subject all kinds of personal experience and beliefs to critical scrutiny, to challenge and rethink the taken-for-grantedness of our primary socialisation, in Berger and Luckman's (1966) terms, and its associated primary discourses (cf. Gee 1990). Moreover, strong, personal, largely intuitive beliefs and feelings are not necessarily in conflict with views arrived at on the basis of rational consensus but may be aligned with them. Held up to scrutiny they become more worth holding, more valuable. Where there is reluctance to abandon beliefs, even where rationally indefensible, subjecting them to intellectual examination at least helps one to better understand the boundaries between matters of faith and matters of reason.

An important strand in Habermas's thinking which is central to this book is the socially produced nature of knowledge. Indeed one criticism which Habermas makes of Grice (1975), with whose model of conversational implicatures, Habermas's has obvious similarities, is that it gives undue attention to individual actors and individual intentionality rather than jointly constructed meaning. As Blything (1994: 68) puts it: 'Habermas's aim is to reconstruct the general presuppositions of linguistic interaction which previous philosophers of language have only dealt with in particularistic terms.' However, I do not wish to dispense with personal agency and responsibility; rather to see both as socially located. In other words the knowing subject is social – or rather, as I would wish to argue, one cannot have any sense of the individual without seeing how the construct of the individual emerges from the social; each concept is defined by reference to the other. This is an important strand in Habermas's thinking. He uses the term 'individuation' (e.g. 1992: 152) to describe the manner in which the individual's sense of self emerges from the social, a process I see as central to the view of critical pedagogy I wish to present: 'No-one can construct an identity independent of the identifications that others make of him' (Habermas 1979: 107). This social view of the construction of the individual extends to a social view of processes of understanding and interpretation, with echoes of the notion, presented at the start of this book of 'a community of interpreters'. Moreover, the notion of 'community' persists even when, physically speaking, we are alone in our engagement with written text, as I noted at the close of Chapter 1.

More obviously in social communities like classrooms, interpretations are consensually and collaboratively agreed, even if on a tentative and provisional basis. As Young (1992: 7) puts it, 'rationality is communicatively based and action cannot be truly critical and thus rational, if it is rational for only one individual or one nation'. One of the goals of this book is to explore through the empirical part of the work the nature of such rational consensus in classroom settings.

Implications for classroom communication: universalism and relativism – commonality and difference?

In the pursuit of rational consensus on a universalist basis, how do we then acknowledge cultural difference? Where, if at all, does cultural specificity fit in? How do we balance universalism with relativism? First, we need not deny that universalism carries different culture-specific inflections: there is diversity within unity. No classroom is culturally homogeneous; there is a complex range of interacting cultural identities. And such diversity is compounded in multinational and multiethnic classrooms, where some learners will come from distinctly different traditions. One danger is then in exoticising what is perceived as difference – often being linked to students from non-European backgrounds. Hence the difficulties of well-intentioned ideas in some schools, of inviting in 'minority' mothers to do origami or display saris. In many such multicultural initiatives, only the 'other' is seen as representative of cultural diversity. I recall a conversation with the mother of a student in a class I was observing in West London. The class consisted entirely of children of African or Asian or Middle Eastern origin, and I wanted to take the opportunity as we chatted on the bus home after a school trip, to find out how Sikh religious traditions continued to be practised in contemporary London communities. After a time, Mrs Sund, previously very open and friendly, said: 'why are you asking all these questions?' She was right. I would not have expected her to quiz me on *my* religious, linguistic or cultural practices. Nor would I have questioned a white parent about her religious beliefs and everyday behaviour in the same kind of way.

Mrs Sund probably felt not resentment but puzzlement at my close questioning. She feels and is as British as myself. Indeed there was nothing about her demeanour, dress or language which set her apart from the mainstream, except a slightly darker skin tone. This is the reality of complex urban society in which younger members of groups formerly perceived as 'minority', take on, as do mainstream or dominant groups, a whole range of identities. Stuart Hall (1992) refers to these emerging identities as 'new ethnicities'. Just as I have argued against positioning the foreigner in the EFL classroom as merely and uniquely 'foreign' – and therefore in the EFL classroom typically allowed to approach texts with only this identity – so we can aim to avoid attributing a singularity of identity to students of non-mainstream backgrounds. It follows that we need not assume they will necessarily be affronted by reference to ways of life, and political or religious systems different to their own, a view which has motivated the bowdlerisation of ELT materials in some cases.

Acknowledging complexity of identity does not necessarily presuppose cultural relativism – an obligation to accept if not celebrate all cultural practices as equally legitimate. In Morgan's study of teachers and classrooms (Morgan 1997) one teacher notes that his students doubt whether they might criticise aboriginal polygamy and patriarchy as described in one children's book. Morgan adds: 'such cultural pluralism can lead to scepticism: if all beliefs are relative, then perhaps none can be preferred to any other'. My view is that critical language study is antithetical to such relativism. It is for this reason that I argue here for a conceptual and philosophical framework such as Habermas's Universal Pragmatics which acknowledges the possibility of consensus in ethical matters, including consensus across cultural divides and which includes the preparedness to put our own cherished cultural beliefs under scrutiny.

Habermas is open to the charge that the rationalist position he takes privileges Western traditions and views of development. Said notes that the Frankfurt School, of which Habermas is the leading theorist, is 'stunningly silent on racist theory and anti-imperialist resistance' (Said 1994: 336). Some feminist scholars too, such as Lather (1991), would see a rationalist stance as not only culturist but as making reference to what they see as masculine norms.

Linked to the claimed eurocentricity or philocentricity of an emphasis on reason is the debate around possibly differing views cross-culturally on what counts as rational debate and what identities are available for students to articulate in classroom settings. This is very relevant to the circumstances of second or foreign language learners. The emphasis given to critical thinking, claims Atkinson (1997), is largely a Western preoccupation and critical thinking is in itself a form of cultural imposition. Gieve's reply to Atkinson (1997) however, points out that Atkinson is assuming a cognitivist rather than a dialogic view of critical thinking (and of critical theory as linked to this). There is also a danger of a more insidious, and largely misplaced kind of cultural arrogance, which is to assume that only the West is critical. Pennycook (2001: 171), notes that rather the contrary is the case, that it has not generally been in the interests of the West to acknowledge their own world dominance, of which others are only too aware. In other words, the powerless understand power rather better than those with frequently unchallenged dominance. It is for this reason that Pennycook is able to claim with some conviction that, far from critical applied linguistics being some supposed invention of the West, as is sometimes assumed, it is a late discovery.

Rather than taking essentialist views of the 'other' as being 'uncritical', it may be more productive to consider domains where dissent or concurrence are most readily tolerated or displayed in societies and communities. Pennycook (1994b: 319), writing of his experience as a teacher in China, notes that there may be extensive discussion between teachers and students in that society, but the classroom is not generally the place where these happen. In many parts of the world classes may simply be too large, the circumstances unconducive to extended interaction. The silence of some students in the foreign language classroom is likely to be due not to any absolute disinclination to offer opinion but to different institutional norms and expectations. In many societies debate happens not in schools, but in homes, bars and at street corners.

One group frequently signalled out as 'less critical', as coming, it is claimed, from collectionist as opposed to individualist cultures, are South East Asian students. Several of the students in my Critical Reading class came from such countries, such as Indonesia, Japan and China. Leaving aside the odd assumption that individualism is to be equated with criticality (cf. Atkinson *op. cit.*), it is doubtful whether, once a number of factors are taken account of, including institutional expectations and, most obviously, the level of language proficiency, students from such countries are any less disposed to be critical than British or North American students. In my experience, while some students may be initially reluctant to offer opinions, given time and opportunity for further reflection, they may produce powerful pieces of written work. These frequently challenge some of the orthodox thinking of critical language study – to include outright attacks on it – from perspectives not readily available to the mainstream students or mainstream teachers.

One reason for enhanced critical awareness is noticeability: when it comes to interpretations of texts, including interpretations of the 'classroom text' – that is, what is going on in the classroom – the outsider reader will simply notice different things from the insider, model, usually native speaking reader, for the reason that the discourses which permeate familiar texts are part of lived experience, and therefore largely taken for granted, because reader and writer, or receiver and producer, share cultural schemas. My student Yuko (cf. Chapter 2) was able to notice, more readily than the British student, the orientalism which permeates popular culture texts, produced for a Western readership. Students and scholars from non-Western countries and traditions will also not just offer richer, less writer-aligned interpretations of texts written in English but seek out different kinds of texts for critical analysis. A Korean student of mine went to the websites of three international English language newspapers, from Britain, Japan and Korea respectively, to seek out and compare coverage of a news story which received little attention in the West, but was a major incident in South East Asia, almost triggering a diplomatic crisis in the run up to the World Cup: the claimed censoring in Japanese text books of sensitive information regarding Koreans during the war. The case itself makes the point with which I began this book: texts' matter, their distortions and omissions. Kumiko Murata, a Japanese scholar, based in Japan but who spends much time in the West, is drawing on the cross-cultural perspectives available to her in order to explore news discourse on whaling in both the British and Japanese Press. She highlights the ways in which anti- and pro-whaling discourses are formulated, by examining specific lexis and syntactic structures (Murata 2000). Murata's concern is to examine the discourses within a wide range of press reports from an intercultural perspective and to show how issues such as whaling are discussed under the influence of strong monocultural assumptions and values.

The case for common ground

To argue that certain readers may notice and interpret issues in distinctive ways is not to say that understandings will elude some people because they are not of those groups. I am thinking of the argument which goes: 'You cannot understand what it is like to be Jewish, a woman, black or gay', because you are not a member of any of those groups. At a recent day of 'dialogue' between Palestinian and Israeli peace activists at the Institute of Contemporary Arts in London, a number of participants powerfully argued the case against such identity politics, not in order to deny identity but to challenge deterministic and ultimately trivialising views of what it means politically and culturally to be an Arab, a Palestinian, a Jew or a Man. This is in the spirit of Said:

> When one uses categories like Oriental and Western as both the starting point and the end points of analysis, research, public policy...the result is usually to polarise the distinction – the Oriental becomes more oriental, the Westerner more western – and limit the human encounter between different cultures, traditions and societies. (Said 1978: 45/46)

In short, though the specific cases will clearly differ, perceptions about the need for and what constitutes social justice are universally shared. Interpretative communities consisting of people from diverse cultural origins are potentially able to demonstrate communicative rationality as these issues are debated. Admittedly, as Hoy and McCarthy (1994: 91) notes: 'the supposition of mutual intelligibility...can no longer be referred to a common cultural background with its shared schemes of interpretation and evaluation'. Nonetheless this does not necessarily disadvantage the cultural outsiders or the marginalised readers in their personal quest for meaning; also they act as a resource for others in a group of interpreters by fulfilling a schema breaking function for the rest of the class, offering a challenge to assumed shared taken-for-grantedness. Ultimately, if we accept the overriding principle of a multicultural universal discourse 'we can and must', as McCarthy says, 'rely on the background of our common humanity, as we do the interpretative work we are required and "trusted" to do in cross-cultural dialogue' (Hoy and McCarthy 1994: 92). Gieve notes, moreover, that 'as societies become detraditionalised reasons are increasingly subject to scrutiny' (Gieve 1998: 124). This means that traditional ways of life, relations between men and women, ways of doing things are necessarily open to challenge, and can no longer be taken for granted in *any* society.

What emerges from a multicultural class is the manner in which experience, while seen through different lenses, nonetheless has universal commonality because of our shared world environment both socially and biologically (cf. Andersen 1988). Or as Brumfit (1995: 30) puts it: 'Working within the range of rich and varied frameworks which people use, it is possible for individuals with goodwill to co-operate in the development of our understanding of the world.'

If we accept the importance/feasibility of the pursuit of greater understanding of global truths, then the question we should start with is: 'how can members of a community come to an agreement that something is true' (Habermas 1984 in Young 1992: 7). How can we, with all the acknowledged imperfections of societies and classrooms, 'specify the contours of the good and true life' (Held 1990: 345). These are rather grand aspirations. Nonetheless they underpin the broad project of critical pedagogy within which critical reading needs to be located. I turn to this in the next section.

Critical pedagogy

Scholars in the field of critical pedagogy such as Apple (1990), Giroux (1983) and Canagarajah (1999) talk of the wider context of schooling and society: how far the school reproduces dominant ideologies of society. Both Canagarajah (ibid.) and Giroux (ibid.) draw on reproduction and resistance theories. Reproduction theories point to the manner in which schooling serves the status quo, making the dominant ideologies appear natural and legitimate (Canagarajah: 1999: 24). This links to Gramsci's notion of hegemony by which 'powerful groups shape and incorporate the commonsense views, needs and interests of subordinate groups' (Giroux 1983: 275). Resistance theories, on the other hand, look to transformative possibilities, emphasising the way in which, for humans to be empowered, 'agency accommodates, mediates but also resists dominating social practices' (Giroux 1983: 275). In a sense, the two models offer different dimensions to a critical pedagogy; the first, providing a language of critique to deconstruct dominant schooling processes (one could add too to deconstruct dominant discourses and the texts they form part of), the second, as Canagarajah (1999) puts it, offering a language of possibility, to promote social change. In either case there tends to be an emphasis on social groups who are disempowered or disadvantaged, relative to more privileged groups or societies. Discussion circulates around who is dominated and who dominates; thus dichotomies such as men/women, black/white, north/south, east/west or centre/periphery abound. The centre/periphery one is taken up by Phillipson (1992) to describe the rich first world nations, which happen in many cases to be English speaking – that is North America, Australia and the United Kingdom as opposed to poor developing countries, often in a postcolonial relationship to centre ones. I shall draw on this terminology as a useful, if rather crude way, of distinguishing between east and west and north and south in part of my discussion later in this chapter.

One difficulty with all these dichotomised characterisations of power is that, as a number of people, following a broadly Foucauldian view of power have pointed out, such as Luke 1996, power is not so readily transmitted or handed over from powerful to less powerful groups. Nor can the presence or absence of power be so easily determined. What too of those who, as I note in Wallace 1999, may be positioned as disempowered by others, such as teachers, whilst not themselves recognising or acknowledging any such lack of power? I mention this point in light of the discourse around advocacy which typifies some versions of critical pedagogy; that teachers, for instance, should be advocates of their learners; that learners themselves become advocates of particular causes in which their own identities, for instance as black, disabled or female, are strongly implicated.

As noted in Chapter 2, 'power', as linked to ideology, is a key concept in CDA. It is equally so in pedagogic applications such as CLA and critical reading, particularly when we consider cognate terms such as 'empowerment', 'empowering' or a term similarly used – 'emancipatory'. As Lankshear (1997) and Andersen (1988) note, these terms tend to be used in very general ways with a neglect of transitivity. For it is vacuous to talk simply of being empowered, without saying what one is empowered to do or become; similarly with notions of freedom or emancipation, we need to consider freedom from *what* or freedom to do *what*. In the case specifically of language learning we may see our goal as to help make our learners more powerful users of *language*, whether of a first, second or other language. As Lankshear says 'a critical literacy approach is widely advocated as a means to making learners more powerful/empowered language users' (1997: 40).

Again though we might need to ask: powerful to what end, and in whose interest? Should critical language teachers see their role broadly as providing linguistic tools which help students combat their own oppression, or to support both awareness of and a commitment to counter the oppression of others? We may see 'powerful' language being used to different ends in different political causes. These are the undeniably powerful words of a second language user of English who has been caught up in the Israeli–Palestinian conflict. She describes each side: 'One of them has a whole dedicated army at his disposal and the other has a torn-up, wounded, humiliated nation that has nothing to lose' (Nurit Peled-Elhanan 2002). However, the person speaking is not Palestinian but Israeli, a woman whose daughter was killed by a Palestinian suicide bomber. My point in including this is to challenge identity politics or self-advocacy. It takes greater vision and courage to understand the oppression of the other.

While wishing to affirm shared experience and empathy, we find that there are difficulties also in assuming false commonalities, as happens,

I believe, in some of the citing of disadvantaged groups, for whom critical pedagogy is seen to be particularly relevant. Pennycook (1994b: 297) identifies these to include people of colour, ethnic minorities, working class students, women, gays and lesbians; Ellsworth too implies some commonality of experience across groups, from which frequently teachers are excluded. She sees it as problematic that teachers, unlike their students, are of 'white skin, middle-class, able-bodied and thin'. I believe that assumptions of comparability of experience of women, gays and fat people may trivialise substantial and multiple forms of disadvantage related to poverty and social injustice. For this reason I shall take as a working definition a view of critical pedagogy which eschews identity politics and sees its major overarching goal a commitment to social justice, to the acknowledging and combating of injustice, wherever found, and whether we personally are members of relatively powerful or powerless social groups.

But we need to ground these somewhat lofty ideals within various interpretations of critical practice on the ground. This is the aim of the next section, which looks at some of the practical orientations to critical pedagogy.

Orientations to critical pedagogy

Freirean approaches

A major figure for most critical pedagogues is one whose thinking and educational practice arose among oppressed people in the South: the Brazilian educator Paulo Freire. Sometimes seen as Marxist but more properly described as a radical humanist, his major and recurrent theme is what it means to be 'more fully human'. 'Dehumanization, which marks not only those whose humanity has been stolen, but also (though in a different way) those who have stolen it, is a distortion of the vocation of becoming more fully human' (Freire 1972a: 31). To become more fully human is, as Lankshear and Lawler in their commentary on Freire put it: 'to become ever more critically aware of one's world and in creative control of it' (Lankshear and Lawler 1989: 68). Literacy mediates powerfully in this process: 'The achievement of literacy – as understood by Freire – is a necessary aspect of functioning as a human being' (Lankshear and Lawler *op. cit.*). Moreover, there is no doubt that Freire's project has, as Lankshear and Lawler continue (Lankshear and Lawler 1989: 69), 'universalist aspirations'.

In terms of pedagogic practice, Freire is known for his challenge to what he calls the 'banking view of learning' by which bits of knowledge are deposited within learners. Freire's view of knowledge sees it as not static but 'continually created and re-created as people reflect and act on the world. Knowledge is produced by us collectively searching and trying to make sense of our world' (Shor 1987: 182). Thus Freire emphasises the collectivity of knowledge rather than individual ownership, a prevailing metaphor in progressivist discourse. The literacy programmes, described, for example, in Freire (1972b), which he and his co-workers established among peasants in Brazil in the 1960s also had a clear emancipatory objective. Built around the notion of key or generative words which encoded politically and socially significant events, objects or phenomena in the lives of the poor was an agenda for social change. Literacy was a key to empowerment, in the sense that knowing how things are named and gaining some critical distance from them as objects to be talked – and written – about gave people greater understanding of and control over the circumstances of their daily lives.

Freire's work remains a major point of reference for many critically oriented projects. Though it is drawn on and interpreted very differently from one setting to another, what is shared is a concern to offer people, through literacy, tools for the critical and creative analysis of their own circumstances, whether among newly literate adults in Nicaragua, as described by Lankshear and Lawler (*op. cit.*) or among Searle's schoolchildren in East London and Sheffield in England. Searle uses Freire's own words to describe how the children, many suffering the effects of racism or displacement, come to create poetry out of their experiences: 'they dynamize and humanize reality...by creating culture' (Searle, afterward in Lankshear 1997: 194). An example of Freirean influenced work from the United States is the work of Elsa Auerbach and Nina Wallerstein, who devised a Freirean procedure within teaching materials (Auerbach and Wallerstein 1987) by which ESL students, in a workplace setting, are invited through a series of open questions to problematise the situations presented in the form of visuals, simple narratives or comic strip presentations.

The legacy of Freire's work continues. It has been widely adapted for use in third world countries through projects such as REFLECT (Regenerated Freirean Literacy through Empowering Community). This draws on Freire's early work on 'culture circles' (cf. Freire 1972b) where an image or key word acts as a trigger or prompt to allow students to reflect on – to gain greater critical distance on – key aspects of their daily lives. I quote one example of a culture circle in practice in Uganda. In this village the culture circle produced a calendar showing the availability of food at different times of the year, and this became the code on which the following discussion and generation of key words was based. As the Reflect Manual concludes from this experience:

> The participants, most of whom were women, were finding a voice and exchanging experiences which were of fundamental importance to their daily lives – indeed to their very survival – and the literacy work was arising directly out of that context (Archer and Cottingham 1996: 37).

I noted the above difficulties with terms such as 'empowerment' and this applies to Freirean pedagogy. There may be problems in perceiving and positioning specific groups as disempowered, when those same groups may not perceive themselves as such or may simply not want to air particular issues in a public setting. This is a dilemma of which Auerbach and Wallerstein (1987) are aware and it is for this reason that their codes are designed not to mirror or reflect back students' supposed reality. The aim is not that any of the vignettes depicted – they may range from worker exploitation, or issues of pay to dismissal – should directly and specifically represent the experience of individuals in a class. The overall goal is not problem-solving but problem-posing, the identification by students of questions which are triggered by the text or visual representation. These student responses are likely to include those not envisaged by teachers or the writers of the material. The goal is to avoid the imposition of a single unequivocal interpretation of an event or situation portrayed.

The genre movement

In Australia, at the start of the 1980s, the influence of Hallidayan linguistics as a sociocultural model of language offered a new impetus to and a new dimension to critical pedagogy. It took shape in two ways – through systemic-functional linguistics discussed in Chapter 2 but, linked to this, through what came to be known as the genre movement. This originated as a counter movement to progressivism, especially as espoused by highly non-interventionist educational programmes in the United States where emphasis was given to minimally directed, experiential learning exemplified, for instance, in some process writing approaches (e.g. Graves 1983). As argued for by Martin (1989) the genre movement counsels a high degree of both teacher intervention and explicitness, particularly the need to be explicit about features of texts which exert influence within schooling and society at large; texts which are representative of what Martin and others (cf. for example Luke 1996) have called the 'genres of power'. Only when one has mastery over genres is one in a position to challenge them. Bakhtin (1986) is also emphatic about the need for full mastery of genres in order for them to be creatively manipulated. Individuality can only emerge once command of the genre is achieved. It follows, although this is not stated explicitly by Bakhtin, that the key features of secondary, powerful genres, not readily available through primary socialisation, have to be explicitly taught. Halliday too (e.g. 1996) makes it clear that one needs specific and explicit access to the genres of power before one can creatively exploit or subvert them.

One difficulty with the view that one can explicitly teach features of the genres of power, with the purpose of thereby empowering learners through schooling and in their daily lives, is that it opts for a transmission view of power rather than a relational one. As Luke (*op. cit.*) notes, and as raised earlier, it is naive to assume that power can be simply handed to learners via a set of skills or procedures. If one takes a Foucauldian view of power, whether this is a force for good or ill, power is relational and dynamic; as Andersen puts it (1988: 23) individuals do not so much have power as 'circulate between its threads'; moreover larger social structures may play a gate-keeping role in denying access to social goods of certain social groups, whatever particular kinds of abilities or knowledge they display.

Nonetheless, the genre theorists usefully pointed the way to the need for educators to make features of texts and learning processes more transparent. And this issue of transparency is key in accounts of critical pedagogy, including CLA ones, as further discussed below. It was also a principle which guided my design of the Hallidayan framework and tasks for the classroom in my Critical Reading course. As Lankshear puts it (1997: 75) 'to teach well..includes rendering the implicit explicit and the abstract concrete'. Links can be made too between some of the key principles of the genre movement and recent developments in SLA which propose greater emphasis on intervention and explicitness than did earlier ELT methods and approaches which positively favoured lack of explicitness, as suggested by some of the terms used to describe them, such as 'the Natural Approach' (cf. Krashen and Terrell 1983).

Critical Language Awareness

It was by way of Hallidayan linguistics that a critical pedagogy began to take shape in Britain through the work of Fowler *et al.* (1979) and, some years later, as a development of this earlier work, CDA, largely inspired by Fairclough. Fairclough has continued to develop and to rethink CDA as a project of late modernity (cf. Chouliaraki and Fairclough 1999). However CDA, as both social and linguistic theory does not have a pedagogy built into it and it was only in the early 1990s that a set of specific pedagogic outlines and procedures were drawn up, taking CDA as its point of departure. This was the CLA movement which built on earlier sociolinguistically inspired teaching materials to formulate a rationale for a critical awareness of language which gave greater emphasis to the ideological bases of language choice, acquisition and use (cf. Clark *et al.* 1990, 1991). This rationale was then realised in a more practical form in a series of papers which appeared in a collection called Critical Language Awareness (Fairclough (ed.) 1992a). Some of the papers in this collection offered specific proposals and procedures for the development of CLA in different educational settings. One study by Wallace (1992a) was the basis of the present study, a brief account of which was offered in my introduction.

More or less contemporaneous with the original work of Clark *et al.* was the Language in the National Curriculum (LINC) project in the United Kingdom which similarly took a CLA perspective. LINC was an in-service teacher education programme which was developed between the years 1989 and 1992, to offer a coherent language education programme for teachers which would link to the successive Kingman and Cox reports, which immediately predated the project and which were commissioned by the government. The LINC teacher training materials failed to find favour with the Conservative administration of the day and their official publication was banned. It should be said, as Clark and Ivanic (1999: ibid.) point out, that the banned materials subsequently were quite widely circulated in unpublished form and gained a certain radical currency through being seen as subversive.

There were several likely reasons for the official ban though they were never made explicit: first, there was a strong emphasis on the social circumstances of language use which, moreover, invited reflection on the circumstances of power which might privilege certain forms of language over others. Secondly, the materials embodied an approach to the teaching of grammar which was unfamiliar – and therefore unwelcome – to the politicians who condemned the material. Carter, one of the key proponents of what he himself calls the New Grammar (Carter 1990) describes this grammar, which was Hallidayan inspired, as aiming to teach students: 'not simply to look through language to the content of a message but rather to see through language and be empowered better to understand and explain the ways in which messages are mediated or shaped, very often in the interests of preserving a particular viewpoint or of reinforcing existing ideologies' (Carter 1990: 108).

The collapse of the LINC project was salutary, and points to the difficulty of the acceptance by governments of radical pedagogy. Nonetheless, CLA did not disappear, but continued to evolve in a number of ways. Both practical and theoretical aspects of CLA and its close associate Critical Literacy have taken on different emphases over the years. A macro aspect of CLA is evidenced at the language policy level where the power element which is crucial to all conceptualisations of CLA is seen in terms of the power of relative languages or language varieties. One role for CLA is to promote awareness of the unequal power relations involved in the use and maintenance of languages and language varieties within and across nations.

At the micro level of language skill, some scholar/practitioners such as Clark and Ivanic have looked at the politics of writing, challenging it as a neutral academic practice (e.g. Clark and Ivanic 1997). Others like myself have attended more to reading as both critical practice and CLA (cf. Wallace 1992a, b). Within discussion of literacy and reading certain writers, notably Street (1995), have seen critical literacy in terms of the manner in which some literacy practices are systematically privileged over others, for reasons of ideology rather than inherent value; others have maintained a specific text analytic dimension, as in the present book, building more directly on CDA. In seeing text analysis as a central micro component of critical literacy, always seen against the backdrop of contextualised macroliteracy practices, as presented in Chapter 2, CLA takes a view of pedagogy which favours explicitness and transparency. It is here that it distances itself, in important ways, from liberal, learner-centred pedagogies favoured in some progressivist educational approaches and aligns itself in spirit with the genre movement. Just as CLA, especially in the form of the LINC project in the UK, represented a response to traditional or old grammar – as well as to pedagogies which did not attend directly to language at all – so was the genre movement in Australia a reaction to progressivist pedagogy (cf. Kalantzis *et al.* 1990).

Recent conceptualisations of critical literacy and critically oriented text study have moved beyond reason, to matters of desire, pleasure and pain. Janks (2001b) notes how rationality deserted her in the aftermath of September 11th, when she was invited to scrutinise the texts of that time. A very recent visit to the United States, and the close proximity of family members to the events of those days, denied her critical distance. Later, however, she reasserts CLA as fundamentally a rationalist project. Pennycook is more unequivocally dismissive of the power of intellectual explanation, seeing the exercise of rational judgement as part of a liberal agenda of tolerance. He says: 'to develop antihomophobic or antiracist education requires much more than simply some rational, intellectual explanation of what's wrong with racism and homophobia. Rather we need an engagement with people's investment in particular discourse, that is, in questions of desire' (Pennycook 2001: 159). As will be clear, my own view is that rational, intellectual explanation is far from simple, and that rationality is continually in construction inter-subjectively.

It has to be acknowledged that critical pedagogy of whatever complexion will tend to resist mainstreaming. Critical approaches are either rejected as 'political', the case with the LINC materials, or they may be incorporated, depoliticised, domesticated and weakened into logistic 'critical thinking' approaches which tend to emphasise 'ownership for personal learning'. Finally, they may be reified into structures or frameworks which, far from empowering teachers and learners, form part of transmission pedagogy as training rather than understanding through education. This has tended to be the outcome of the genre movement. Only rarely is what we might call a strong version of critical pedagogy allowed to flourish. Societies and communities in transition may be more open to critical pedagogy. It is no accident that post-apartheid South Africa has seen a large number of initiatives, including specific classroom-based studies, several of which are documented in Chapter 5. However, in general, critical projects do not receive strong statutory support from governments in the way that mechanistic models of education regularly do. And ELT is no exception. With the ever expanding global power of English, one might expect the teaching of English as a second or foreign language to have provided fertile ground for critical language study, whether as the study of

English as a language, of English language texts or the profession of ELT. Each of these invites, one might reasonably expect, critical scrutiny. However, as we see below, this has not been the case.

Critical pedagogy and English language teaching

Janks and her colleagues and those in the LINC project show how the teaching of English as a mother tongue has drawn on Critical Pedagogy principles through both methodology and materials. Also the teaching of modern languages has in recent years taken a critical turn, particularly through dialogic cross-cultural approaches (cf. Morgan and Cain 2000) as I discussed in Chapter 2. ELT, on the other hand, has been characterised by a studied lack of criticality. The emphasis has been, until recently, on neutrality, not giving offence. The bowdlerisation of materials which Gray (2002: 159) documents under the acronym of PARSNIP (to give us politics, alcohol, religion, sex, narcotics, isms and pork, as tabu topics) was partly the result of this view. Any materials writer will bear witness to this kind of censorship. Mildly provocative texts (I recall one I wished to use about AIDS) may end up on the cutting room floor.

Challenge to the claimed and desired neutrality of ELT began with Phillipson's influential book *Linguistic Imperialism* in 1992. The debate was continued by Pennycook and more recently has been extended and revisited by Canagarajah (1999). English is necessarily – and always was – a political activity, 'rooted in the power of capital', as Holborow (1999) puts it. At the start of the twenty-first century the role of English as a second language has taken on new urgency with its ever-extending global reach. However, debates about ELT ideology still tend to take place among applied linguists or language planners and a practical critical pedagogy for ELT remains largely undeveloped, as is evidenced by the continuing dominance of what has come to be known as communicative language teaching.

Communicative language teaching (hereafter CLT) is based on the premise that the goal of language teaching is communication with native speakers in natural, everyday environments. There is a strong emphasis on speech as social action. Communicative ability is seen as linked to 'the contextualised performance and interpretation of socially appropriate illocutionary acts in discourse' (Bachman 1992: 252). Emphasis is given to experiential language which is close to the everyday experience of learners. There are several problems for a critically oriented approach with this emphasis on basic expressive and interpersonal skills: one is the priority given to talk qua talk. Pennycook (1994b) challenges the nature of what he calls *phonocentrism*, the concern with orality in ELT. This is readily observed in most ELT course books, where written texts, in the case of beginner and intermediate learners particularly, are likely to be seen as supportive of or supplementary to oral language development. The privileging of informal spoken language at first glance appears democratic. In effect the reverse is the case. It is with spoken language that debates around native speakerness and standard English tend to circulate. Written language is acknowledged not to advantage speakers of standard varieties (or at least to a lesser extent). This clearly has implications for those who are second language speakers of English. I discuss ways in which critical educators might respond to phonocentrism in the conclusion to this chapter.

A second problem with CLT is that there is a relative neglect of the *quality* of talk, of talk for learning, either as a tool for learning more about language or as a means for exploring ideas and, more specifically, of argumentative or constative speech. I have used Habermas's term: *constative speech* to refer to the language of debate, committed to the pursuit of truth and to the provision of support for views expressed. Yet, clearly one difficulty in asserting the value of constative speech is to characterise just what this kind of language looks like and, secondly, how it might be acquired. Leaving aside for the moment its manner of acquisition or learning, which I will revisit in Chapter 6, I shall present here two extracts from classroom discourse, which might show the difference between experiential and discursive or constative talk.

These two extracts are both from critical reading classes. The first consists of 17-year-old native speakers in an Australian classroom; the second is from one of the lessons in my Critical Reading course.

Extract one: the students are describing a scene from Shakespeare's *Romeo and Juliet*

Student A: It was so funny
Teacher: Okay, why did you find it funny, though?
Student B: It was so stupid.
Students: Yeah
Teacher: What was stupid about it? Why did you think it was stupid?
Student C: they were so serious and so old-fashioned
Student D: Yeah. They were so lovely-dovey
Teacher: All right, if you were Romeo and Juliet, then how would you be talking to each other?
Student E: the difference in our talk –
Student C: Nobody shows their emotions like that much any more
Teacher: So you don't think that sort of open display of emotions is something that –
Student C: Nowadays, if people, like, show that much emotion, they get all worried that the other person will think, well, hey, they need me that much, I can just treat them how I want; they'll always be there (Morgan 1997: 127)

Extract two: Estelle, a French student, is responding to one of the newspaper reports about Mandela's release (cf. Chapter 6 for a more contextualised account of this extract)

Estelle: The headline shocked me because 'Whites Out' for me it's a reference to something against blacks in fact, because..it could say 'Blacks Out' and it will, would have been a racist headline and it's very shocking because...I think that this article is racist really because of the title, because erm 'whites yes rioters shot dead as Nelson says 'Keep up struggle".. and 'whites were terrorised as young blacks er celebrated Nelson Mandela's release' All the faults are put on black people. I think you can say you can say that you can say that its racist.

The first extract contains good communicative talk: it is expressive and interpersonally appropriate. It is a model of what is often seen as desirable for L2 learners to acquire. Estelle's talk in the second extract is neither accurate in Standard English terms, nor particularly fluent but it is more elaborated than informal speech, makes explicit its grounds and provides a useful bridge into expository written language. It is talk which is exploratory, where 'partners engage critically but constructively with each other's ideas' (cf. Mercer 1995a), as opposed to the spontaneous and fluent speech which tends to be favoured in the foreign and second language classroom and which characterises Extract one. There, even though the class teacher is committed to taking a critical pedagogic approach, it is not evident that the students are stretching their language as a critical tool. The teacher has specifically invited hypothesis in 'if you were Romeo and Juliet'. Nonetheless, the students continue to offer narrative responses, close to their own experience. Estelle, on the other hand, sees the need to justify the nature of her response. She is honouring the expectation that if the goal is intellectual enquiry, participants will need to offer supports to points of view, justification for claims made and to distance themselves from the here and now. This is the kind of talk where 'reasoning is more visible' as Mercer (*op. cit.*: 37) puts it, where unlike with free and spontaneous conversation we are expected to give an account of ourselves.

Mercer (1995a) uses the term 'educated discourse' to describe the kind of talk which characterises Estelle's contribution here. Such a term presupposes that schooling, for second as well as for first language learners, involves a socialisation into language practices which are necessarily different from everyday talk, a view which echoes Bernstein's work both on elaborated codes (cf. e.g. Bernstein 1990) and on vertical discourse (Bernstein 1996) which 'takes the form of a coherent explicit, systematically principled structure' as opposed to horizontal discourse which is 'local, segmental and contextualised' (Bernstein 1996: 171). One of the requirements of discursive, elaborated speech is that it should make the grounds of opinions and judgements explicit. In doing so, it may depart in distinctive ways from conversation, which is embedded in everyday activities. It is the kind of talk which constitutes 'constative speech' in Habermas's terms. It is characterised, for instance, by elaboration and clarification and the deployment of particular kinds of linguistic and cultural resources to support points of view.

However, far from acknowledging the value of educated or elaborated talk in ELT, recent offshoots of CLT, such as task-based learning, if anything, reinforce the emphasis on contingency and on situated talk, which accompanies the performance of tasks in the classroom. Kramsch puts it thus: 'Task Based Instruction..is characterized by its local treatment of local problems through local solutions' (Kramsch 1995: 48). The stress remains on informal interaction, enjoyment and functional communicative competence. What is barely considered is the place of more elaborated forms of talk, crucial, I believe, for the development of critical literacy.

What do we do with English?

If we want to challenge CLT as the only show in town, where do we turn? 'What to do with English?' is the question Pennycook (1994b) poses. He challenges the deterministic thesis of Phillipson which sees the spread of English as a priori imperialistic, and instead favours the term *writing back* to account for the way in which non-native speakers are able to appropriate English for their own creative and critical purposes. Pennycook's examples are of creative writers of literature. Canagarajah (1999) also picks up on the theme of appropriation which he sees as an essential tool in dealing with the global dominance of English: He talks of 'the strategy of appropriating the discourses of the centre to develop a critical consciousness and voice for marginalised communities' (p. 34). Canagarajah's examples are of students – learners of English rather than the skilled users which Pennycook describes. As Canagarajah acknowledges, many of the instances of students' behaviour documented by him in classrooms in Sri Lanka show them engaging in non-reflective, rather aimless oppositional practices; not, that is, purposefully and productively resisting either English, the lesson or the teacher. One needs to ask therefore by what process periphery subjects are able, as Canagarajah puts it, to 'shift their position from objects of dominant discourses to become subjects'; to 'use the discourse critically and creatively' (Canagarajah 1999: 183).

In other words while we might agree about goals, what are the *means* by which users of English achieve the kind of critical command of the language which serves as a tool for social change and emancipation? One route for Canagarajah includes the deployment of pluralised English which he sees as 'standard grammars and established discourse being infused with diverse alternate grammars and conventions from periphery languages' (Canagarajah *op. cit.* 175). The issue raised here by Canagarajah's claim resonates very much with the genre argument: put briefly, is it possible to creatively disrupt the conventional genres of power, those needed to achieve in mainstream societies, in advance of mastery over them? Analogously with English, can students from the outset disregard the norms of language use which carry prestige or is such a healthy disregard only the *outcome* of a long process of creative appropriation? It will be clear that I favour the second position.

Canagarajah also supports a spirit of solidarity between teachers and learners, believing that teachers should 'unravel the hidden cultures of their students'. One difficulty in this kind of boundary crossing is that students may resent such incursions, inventing new ways to protect 'the underlife' – Canagarajah's own term. It has been often noted that once the mainstream appropriates the language of subcultural groups – and these flourish within classrooms – then those groups quickly relexicalise vernacular usage or private language in order to safeguard their territory.

Both Pennycook and Canagarajah share a preference for the local and particularistic over the global or universalist. Pennycook, for instance, talks of 'making the everyday and the particular part of a school curriculum' (1994b: 298). Their preference for the local over the global is in keeping with a post-modern mistrust for what they see as the totalising tendency of critical theory (Pennycook 1994b: 297). Their overriding concern is to validate forms of knowledge and traditions other than those promoted by the West through enlightenment beliefs and values. Canagarajah is particularly hostile to the enlightenment tradition, saying: 'The enlightenment led to the suppression of the knowledge systems of the periphery.' This I think is an overstatement, and indeed rather at odds with the creative appropriation view argued for elsewhere in Canagarajah (1999), where the author acknowledges the manner in which Edward Said and other scholars, originally from the periphery, have drawn on canonical texts in English. The Caribbean novelist and historian, and Marxist critic CLR James notes: 'I, a man of the Caribbean, have found that it is in the study of western literature, western philosophy and western history that I have found out the things that I have found out, even about the underdeveloped countries' (*New Statesman* 30 July, 2001). The point often made by periphery scholars such as James is not to abandon Shakespeare or Ibsen but to extend and enrich the canon, through the inclusion of texts produced by artists of the periphery. These are not just for minority groups. Chinua Achebe's *Things Fall Apart* is a text for all time and for all people.

In short, while scholars such as Canagarajah and Pennycook offer important contributions to the still sparse literature on critical pedagogy in ELT, I think there are difficulties with some of their interpretations. They relate to the preference for the local over the global, the immediate and contingent over the longer term, and for difference over commonality. I will address these points in turn, before suggesting some practical proposals for critical pedagogy in language teaching, as a conclusion to this chapter.

Orientations to critical language awareness pedagogy

Global not local

Where Canagarajah favours boundary crossing, my preference is not so much for keeping boundaries rigid as keeping the classroom distinct as a domain. This does not mean that classrooms have to maintain their traditional forms, whether typical of centre or local norms, but that their credibility as sites for learning depends on their *not* being like real life, but seen as public arenas where teachers do not appropriate the private spaces of their learners. Moreover, there is some difficulty with the arguments, as I interpret them, of pedagogues who on the one hand deplore, as I would, the trivialisation of language teaching, but nonetheless urge the incorporation of popular culture to inform learning (cf. Canagarajah 1999: 190). I would prefer to see the use of popular culture texts, which certainly are part of the repertoire of a CLA influenced critical pedagogy, more as a matter of *recontextualising* and *reconceptualising* than appropriating the everyday worlds of learners. That is, experiences, knowledge and texts which arise from primary socialisation are certainly made use of, in what Halliday (1996) calls heteroglossic ways, but explored from a critical distance.

We are talking about new ways of seeing things, what Cazden (2001) describes as 'reconceptualisations': she notes 'a great deal of education is devoted to teaching students to see phenomena in a new way, to reconceptualise circles as wheels or wheels as circles' (Cazden 2001: 112). And it is likely to be reconceptualisations of everyday phenomena – those things which are not typically talked about because taken for granted – including language phenomena, which are most illuminating.

However elusive and hard to achieve within the messy reality of classrooms, it seems crucial that we aim to maintain this 'critical distance' aspect of critical pedagogy, or 'critical framing' as The New London Group (2000) put it. Linked to a distanced, less personal stance is a different kind of language, one of hypothesis and argument. The kind of English to serve this goal, both what we teach as content and what we make use of in classroom interaction, will be a globalised not localised English, which looks outwards to other users of English worldwide, rather than inwards and locally. It is the language of social power rather than intimacy or social solidarity. It provides a basis for what Best and Kellner (1991: 212) call a 'politics of alliance', rather than a politics of difference.

Longer term not contingent

My proposal is for a critical pedagogy less concerned with personal empowerment or with immediate action, than with longer-term challenges to social inequality. One can see the role of critical pedagogy as preparation for this wider struggle, not necessarily as an immediate and direct response to events. There are critical educators who see the classroom as a 'safe place' to rehearse forms of action to take out into the public sphere. Certainly there may be cases where specific issues arise in communities which require urgent redress. However, classrooms do not have to be seen as some kind of preparation for direct action; a dress rehearsal for real life. This point relates to another, first raised by Giroux (1983) but expanded on by Canagarajah (1999), the difference between *opposition* and *resistance*. I drew on this distinction in Chapter 2 in relation to reading stance, but it can be more widely applied to Critical Pedagogy. Opposition is an immediate trigger. It may be spontaneous, not reflected upon. Much of the students' behaviour in the classes Canagarajah (1999) describes is of this ill-considered kind, as opposed to a calculated strategy, reached after dialogue with peers and on the basis of reflection. Resistance, unlike opposition, may take years in the building. It is for this reason that Giroux (1983: 285) notes, apparent acquiescence to the status quo, if accompanied with a critical questioning stance may be more politically progressive in the long run than immediate, knee-jerk opposition. I see the role of critical pedagogy and critical reading of texts as not so much oppositional to the particular as an encouragement of a critical stance which serves students in the longer rather than shorter term. Moreover, just as opposition can in fact denote submission, so can resistance accommodate agreement.

Commonality not difference

It tends to be assumed that critical pedagogy, to include the critical strands mentioned here, that is CLA and critical literacy, is only for the marginalised, those judged to be socially disadvantaged in some way. The consequence of such a view might be a form of educational apartheid, which can, much like some forms of multiculturalism or bilingual education programmes, be perceived as 'special provision' and therefore frequently stigmatised and sidelined. There is a further difficulty in assuming that only the more visibly disadvantaged are oppressed, a point made by Freire in his argument that both oppressors and oppressed suffer, are dehumanised by systemic injustice. It may be indeed that critical language study is *less* relevant for the obviously disadvantaged – they know about their own oppression – than for dominant groups, for whom it has not been in their interests to acknowledge their own dominance. It may be harder to relinquish power than, justifiably, to lay claim to it. For this reason it is both more difficult but possibly more worthwhile to do critical language study with privileged groups, as Mckinney and Van Pletzen (2001) found.

Also problematic is a pedagogy centred around difference, as opposed to disadvantage (although the two are often linked). As noted earlier in this chapter, Pennycook (1994b) talks of teaching which is committed to offering greater possibilities to specific groups, seen to be discriminated against, such as gays and black people. A difficulty with identifying specific groups as, by virtue of a particular identity, requiring specific kinds of instruction is that identities are multiple, complex and contradictory. Teaching centred around difference, diversity and particularity may be seen as irrelevant to learners' actual interests, inappropriately patronising or celebratory in the romantic, personal growth manner from which, in general, critical pedagogy is at pains to distance itself. Moreover, the celebration of difference may harden into essentialism, even stereotype, fixing boundaries rather than dismantling or unsettling them. I noted earlier in this chapter the difficulties with the attribution to students of single identities. If difference is articulated around these identities, classroom participants may opt to advance their own cause in an adversarial manner rather than in a spirit of solidarity. Ellsworth (1989) describes the students in her class as not wishing to join their voices with fellow students for fear of subordinating their specific oppressions. The emphasis is on personal liberation rather than social change in a wider sense. As Giroux says (1993: 11), 'Social betterment must be the necessary consequence of individual flourishing.' It is arguable that certain kinds of local action may not lead to social betterment in the longer term, that indeed inaction or deferred action might be the ultimately more liberating option.

One further, related point about difference (in particular difference which disadvantages) is that any consequent difference of provision from mainstream students may be resented by the people it is designed to support. McKinney (1998), for instance, who taught a critical reading class specifically developed for Coloured South Africans – seen to be a 'historically disadvantaged' group – found that they resented being 'constantly framed as 'disadvantaged' and that they understood this as 'not as good as white students'. The students in McKinney's study did not deny their disadvantage. They merely wished it to be acknowledged and addressed within the mainstream. Thus one student commented: 'I am a little unhappy about the course because it consists only of non-white students (McKinney 1998: 14). As I note in Wallace (1999) 'If we see critical pedagogy in terms of resistance from the margins, the students may feel continuingly marginalised by the very pedagogies which are committed to their emancipation' (Wallace 1999: 104).

Certainly there are no easy options. A whole range of factors, to include prior experiences of learning and the wider social and educational context will influence the kinds of judgements which are made in planning critical pedagogy. Nonetheless it seems important that educational approaches which are claimed as critical should not be concerned only with the teaching of those perceived to be disadvantaged. Ultimately the concern is with not difference but commonality, in the universalising rather than the particularising of experience. Universalism does not need to be equated with the perpetuation of a monolithic Western tradition. On the contrary, the search for common ground and, more to the point, for common causes ensures that students from different cultural traditions find ways of uniting to promote social justice and social change, rather than taking up polarised, even ghettoised positions, to promote only those issues which are close to their own experience.

Conclusions

I shall conclude the chapter with some tentative proposals, which will be revisited and expanded on in future chapters. It seems to me that a critical pedagogy needs to take account of the following key factors.

Cross-cultural dialogue

Cross-cultural dialogue can be conducted in a number of ways, either within or outside the classroom. One means is suggested by the ethnographic approaches of the kind described in Chapter 2, where students, both from mainstream, dominant cultural groups and marginalised ones may make strange their own cultural practices. In the process they negotiate a range of different cultural understandings about and knowledge of key concepts in critical language study, to include racism and sexism and the nature of discriminatory discourse more generally. They will aim to gain some distance from their readings of familiar texts, generally not much reflected upon as we go about everyday life. In a multicultural classroom a diversity of readings provides a cultural and critical resource for the whole class. Respectfully, analytically and judgementally – to answer the query which Wendy Morgan's teacher raises about aboriginal customs – students critique and evaluate, both texts arising from their own cultural milieu and that of others, always on the basis of reasoned argument and the need to take responsibility for the points of view expressed. Many cultural practices, whether they typify centre or periphery cultures invite censure. I am not prepared to celebrate football hooliganism or freemasonry as a recognisable part of the cultural world I inhabit. It is absurd therefore, on the grounds of risking offence, not to countenance the likelihood – indeed certainty – that students in critical language study will want to condemn certain practices and views linked to their own cultural identities. Ultimately the cause of critical pedagogy and CLA within this, is not best served by cultural relativism of a celebratory kind. Nor, as I have aimed to argue, is it served by a rights discourse based on identity or single issue politics. Rather, the goal of cross-cultural dialogue and exchange is empathy with the oppression of others, based on universal understandings of injustice.

Intervention and explicitness

Intervention is associated with authoritarian pedagogies. And yet to take a critical stance to dominant discourses and educational practices and to wish to promote some readings over others is bound to involve the teacher in taking a normative position. Pennycook, while generally critical of normativity (cf. Pennycook 2001), nonetheless talks of discursive 'interventions' in his own teaching. One example was his decision, as described in Pennycook (1994b) to make available to his Chinese students alternative readings (that is, alternative to widely circulated ones which cast the United States and Christianity in an overwhelmingly positive light) that drew attention to fundamentalist' right wing politics. I believe he was right. It behoves critical educators to be as clear as possible both about their agenda for change and the limits they wish to place on the acceptability of texts or interpretations. There is no doubt that this can create dilemmas for liberal educators. Mckinney (forthcoming) describes the tension she felt in her Critical Reading class between her role as the 'fair' liberal teacher, who will accept a wide range of responses, and the 'tough' or uncompromising one who takes an apparently authoritarian position in driving forward a specific agenda to promote understanding of matters of social justice. Of course all teachers need to confront this situation. However, it is likely to be more relevant to strongly committed forms of pedagogy. What we can do is to make our aims in teaching and our ideological and political leanings as explicit as possible; aim in short to make our practice visible. Importantly, we can invite challenge to our own positions as much as to the ideologies of the texts studied in class.

Tools for analysis and critique

If teachers do indeed dominate or manipulate students then students need the linguistic tools to talk back. A metalanguage can be helpful here for students to assemble a language both to challenge the teacher and, more specifically, for textual critique. Admittedly, the tools may be too cumbersome or unwieldy to do the job required of them, and this was a potential danger with the grammatical framework provided in the Critical Reading class in this study. As Canagarajah says, you can get 'bogged down in the detail of texts' (1999: 34). It is true that we need to shift focus constantly between the micro features of texts to the macro features of the contexts in which texts arise and are interpreted. However, ultimately it is attention to detail which allows us to offer plausible interpretations of texts and to provide warrant for our views, on the Habermasian principle of adducing evidence for claims. One can debate the level of specificity which is most facilitating to analysis and awareness. Nonetheless some kind of language framework provides not just a set of specific linguistic terms for textual critique but a way of conceptualising language more widely. Without such a focus, there is the danger that students may make unsupported claims about the ideological content and context of texts. In short, metalevel awareness of literacy practices and texts is more readily achieved if students have available to them a set of linguistic tools to articulate in more precise ways impressions which may be otherwise noticeable to them only at a fairly high level of generality. It is the deployment of such tools which we see as characterising debate, rather than casual conversation. Such debate is also strongly mediated by literacy, which leads to the next key point.

Literacy and literate English

The kind of discourse which is brought into play in debate is influenced by literacy, in particular by access to relatively formal continuous print text. Mercer draws on the term 'educated discourse'; others such as Clegg favour 'literate talk' which students use as they are 'trying to get a foothold in new cognitive territory' (Clegg 1992: 17). I have used the term 'literate English' to include both literacy and oracy (cf. Wallace 2002), to describe the kind of English, whether written or spoken, most like formal written English such as we encounter in public, rather than private domains. Literate English is not in itself necessarily critical, but it can more readily be deployed for critical purposes than can day-to-day survival English. Literate English may be turned to critical ends both in discussion and textual critique. We can then see critical talk and critical literacy as mutually supportive, with discussion prompting students to look more closely at text which in turn fuels further revisiting of text and discussion. And yet literacy and literate talk have been relatively neglected in ELT even though, as Pennycook (1994b) points out, written language is less classed and gendered than most forms of spoken language. It is certainly less 'native speakered', to coin an ugly term, in that, as noted earlier, it does not privilege the native speaker in the way that emphasis on the spoken medium does. Written language, or literate like language, has a necessary universality. Moreover, as I have argued at several points, emphasis on the vernacular does not provide power of access to foreign and second language students. Literate English as a secondary discourse, in Gee's terms (1990) is functionally wide-ranging, but especially powerful when used discursively rather than experientially. Hence its value in constative talk in the classroom.

Intersubjectivity

Finally it is important to conclude with a key notion in Habermasian thinking which I have taken as a major aspect of my interpretation of practical critical pedagogy; that textual critique in CLA study is conducted dialogically and that notions of the truth of interpretation or the validity of judgements are arrived at intersubjectively, consensually and collaboratively agreed, even if on a tentative and provisional basis. To quote Young (1992: 7) once more: 'rationality is communicatively based and action cannot be truly critical and thus rational, if it is rational for only one individual or one nation'. It is for this reason that educators need to ensure, as far as possible, that opportunities are available in classrooms for equity of participation as well as for the production of discourse which is committed to the pursuit of truth and truthfulness. It is for this reason that, as I show in the second half of this book, research in critical reading needs to consider not just the processes by individuals of text analysis, but should aim to capture the intersubjective interpretative processes within communities such as classrooms.

4
The Research Methodology for the Classroom Study

This short chapter links the preceding chapters which describe the conceptual underpinning of critical reading and critical pedagogy with the account of a classroom study, described in subsequent chapters. The classroom study aims to illustrate the way in which some of the principles discussed earlier come into play in a specific setting. Here I shall give a brief account of the specific procedures and tools adopted, why they were adopted and how they mesh with the larger design of the enquiry.

The classroom study

The study was centred around a fifteen-week course, meeting once a week for two hours, designed as an optional module for foreign language undergraduate students in their first year of study abroad, as well as to general language students at preproficiency level. Included in the original group of fourteen were students following a Master's degree in Language Teacher Education, who wished to observe the classroom methodology but who also were active members of the group. One of these, Monica Hermerschmidt, had a special role as a critical friend, to 'look over my shoulder' as Cazden (2001) puts it. She attended regularly throughout the course and undertook to meet me after the class on many occasions to talk through her observations of my behaviour as the teacher and to offer her perceptions of the students' responses as she worked alongside them in class. These informal discussions were tape-recorded and I used them as a basis for ongoing decision-making. This meant that I was able to take account of Monica's input as advisor and critic as the course progressed. However, the analysis is entirely my own, with the consequence that detachment is inevitably compromised.

While the classroom interaction – in particular, the talk around texts – is at the heart of the study, the course materials, student diaries, reading protocols and follow-up student interviews are also a crucial part of the overall research. What these data sets share is that they all consist of language, whether as processes or products. With the classroom interaction, I examine language data as process, that is, the interaction between teacher and students, or student and student, as a 'site where meanings are created and changed' (Taylor in Wetherell *et al.* 2001: 6). My aim is to investigate the collaborative, negotiated construction of textual interpretation; in the case of other language data, in Chapters 5 and 7, I provide a less nuanced language analysis which attends more to content or product than to process, which is more referential than constitutive. Each data set feeds into the next, in the sense that the actual course materials and methodology largely determine the nature of the classroom interactions around texts; and these two in turn influence the diary, protocol and interview data which were subsequent to or apart from the classroom interactions. In short the foci of analysis are:

1. the Critical Reading course – the design and implementation of the actual material taught;
2. the interactions in class, especially the talk around text and;
3. the input from the students, based around the class, but not actually within the classroom setting. This input consists of student diaries, 'think aloud' responses to texts and interviews with selected students.

I decided to focus on three classes from near the beginning, around the middle and at the end of the course respectively. Thus the three classes selected for more specific attention were in week four, week nine and week fourteen of the course. This offered an equal spacing of five weeks between the lessons considered in depth. Within the three lessons, I looked first at the teaching material which formed the basis of the lesson, that is, the texts selected and the tasks which supported the text analysis; secondly, I considered in each of the three lessons a characteristic episode, which was the feedback segment of the class, where individual students representing their groups were called on to offer their public response to the task. The final data set I considered consisted of the diaries, reading protocols and interview data.

Approaches to data analysis

I broadly followed the Hallidayan framework used in the text analyses in class, adjusting the questions as relevant to different modes of data. These questions are:

1. How is meaning created *interpersonally* within texts and/or constructed between readers/writers or speakers/listeners?

More specifically:
How far is the teaching material or teacher or student production dialogic in the sense that it offers spaces for a range of kinds of participation, as readers or listeners? In Habermasian terms relative openness

links with equity or equality of opportunity to participate. Linguistically speaking, dialogic features, such as the use of mood and modality, are encoded by Halliday's interpersonal function of language. A specific language question follows: *what kinds of interpersonal features are present in the data, whether in the texts surveyed in class, the classroom interaction or the students' own narratives?*

2. How does the discourse develop *ideationally*?

More specifically:

How far does the teaching material (texts and tasks) or teacher or student production in monologue or dialogue show evidence of *explicitness and elaboration of meaning* in the pursuit of truth and truthfulness? In Habermasian terms this relates to constative talk, where participants are required to offer warrants for views expressed, to justify and clarify meanings. Linguistically this relates to the *ideational* function of language; so focus is on features such as transitivity and expansion, whether for instance, circumstances are elaborated on or reasons given for events recounted or points of view offered within the print texts surveyed in class or the spoken texts we produce in classroom interaction and the additional spoken and written texts produced out of class. The specific language question then is: *what kind of ideational features are present in the data whether in the texts surveyed in class, the classroom interaction or the students' own narratives?*

In addition, we need to consider the critical dimension – within the classroom material and within the students' varying responses to the material. I shall deal with the issue of criticality in summarising comments to this chapter. First, how is the Hallidayan model differently interpreted to take account of the different data sources, namely the course material, the classroom interaction and the students' narratives? I shall elaborate on each of these in turn in the following sections.

The course material

Selection and design of texts and tasks

With both the texts and the classroom tasks which supported them, the key constructs of interpersonal and ideational meaning were in play, and linked to those of *equality and quality*. The guiding principles were that texts would be selected in the early part of the course on the basis of their predominantly interpersonal features, moving to more densely ideational texts later. Similarly there was a progression from tasks which looked at the interaction between reader and writer interpersonally speaking to those inviting attention to ideational features relating to transitivity in descriptive and report texts and elaboration or expansion of argument in expository texts.

This can be summed up in terms of shifting attention from *equality* to *quality*; at first the focus was on the balance of power/solidarity between reader and writer, and writer and subject matter, moving later to a concern with the quality of description or exposition within texts, involving attention to more hidden parts of the grammar.

A major principle in Hallidayan grammar is that texts take the form they do in order to serve particular social functions – we see a text overall as a social semiotic. This means that advertising texts will be minimally ideational and maximally interpersonal to serve their overall suasive function. Based on this principle, in the Critical Reading course, genres were selected and ordered on the basis of their distinctive social function and, linked to this, distinctive linguistic features. The course was text driven in the sense that texts were the starting point of class analysis rather than tasks or activities. There is the further point that text and task together create not just a new text, but a new *genre* as there is a pedagogic purpose in the 'text plus task' text, which is clearly missing from the text in its original non-pedagogic contextualisation.

The pedagogic purpose of a text, as distinct from its original one – if taken from an authentic source – is clearly more apparent in course book texts which are framed in pedagogic terms, accompanied by rubric, adjusted to fit a new format and so on. In the case of a CLA approach, texts may be presented within a course book frame (cf. e.g. Janks 1993) but may also be, as in my study, offered to students in their original format. This can be important in critical reading classes as textual choices related to visuals, graphics and the location within a larger text such as a newspaper or magazine are seen to be significant. Indeed this was an important criterion in planning the course – that the texts would be read in their original form, and that immediate and wider contextual framing would be specified in as much detail as possible. A second principle was to offer students access to a range of genres. One justification for this decision was that we recognise generic categories by seeing what features distinguish one genre from another. If students only ever study academic texts, for instance, they cannot readily demarcate the register differences of field, tenor and mode across different genres. For this reason generic range was seen as an important criterion in text selection for classroom use.

What interpersonal features are salient?

Tenor of discourse

The starting point of the text analysis in the course design was to look at the tenor of the discourse in the texts selected for analysis. In terms of the Hallidayan framework this meant, for instance, looking specifically at the use of personal pronouns, in genres where their presence is a salient feature, such as in advertisements or letters of different kinds. These features are what Halliday calls the 'outer layer of the grammar'; formally they are simple and recognisable. However functionally, and so ideologically, they are of some interest, a point shown so convincingly in Brown and Gillman's classic account of the pronouns of power and solidarity (cf. Brown and Gillman 1972). What counts as inclusive or exclusive *you* or *we* for instance? Clearly this can be observed in a wide range of different text genres. However, direct address to the reader is particularly characteristic of suasive texts, as are other interpersonal features, such as modality and mood, both of which are relatively accessible aspects of formal grammar for foreign language learners.

What ideational features are salient?

Field of discourse

Key, relatively visible ideational features within texts came under scrutiny about half way through the Critical Reading course. Familiar texts were revisited or new ones introduced to examine ideational features such as transitivity and agency. Questions asked related to the manner in which participants and processes were presented in descriptive and report texts, with discussion of other ideational features such as circumstantial elaboration gradually being added to the analysis. Later in the course, the concern was more specifically with linguistic features which were internal to the line of narrative or argument of the text: the manner, for instance, in which a writer expands on the account, making it more transparent and more refutable or open to challenge on the reader's part.

What textual features create genres?

Mode of discourse

The course design concluded the three part structure of *field, tenor* and *mode* by asking students to attend to the *mode* of discourse. Arguably mode of discourse is the level which should be *first* considered, rather than as the final strand, as was the case with the course design offered here. The rationale for leaving it as the final function to focus on is that unlike ideational and interpersonal meanings, textual meanings are rather the glue of a text; as Halliday puts it, they are 'what makes a text into a text' (Halliday and Hasan 1985: 23). The textual function has in this sense more of a facilitating role. And in Halliday's ontogenetic account of functions (e.g. Halliday 1977) the textual function is the last one to appear in children's 'learning how to mean'. In a Critical Reading course, it can be seen as the function which focuses on textual features such as thematisation and cohesion to offer overall social contextualisation to a text, making it generically recognisable as a popular news report rather than a broadsheet one; a poem rather than an advertisement.

The classroom interactions

My focus in the analysis of the classroom interaction was on equality of participation and quality and growth of understanding and thinking, as revealed through interactively constructed classroom talk. I wanted to chart any changes during the course in ways in which classroom interaction was structured through, for example, adjustments to turntaking and the building of conceptual knowledge. Questions tied to this goal were:

1. Given that inequality is built into teacher/learner interaction, even in a class of adults, to what extent is the teacher able or willing to relinquish power in the conduct of the interaction?
2. Secondly, how is rational consensus achieved? That is, on what basis are points of view or more extended arguments accepted or rejected? More specifically, in what ways, if any, do students draw on the linguistic metalanguage introduced through the Hallidayan framework, to support their textual analyses?
3. Finally, and crucial to critical pedagogy goals, are the students enabled to locate specific analysis and interpretation of texts within wider sociocultural contexts in order to show awareness of ideological constraints and possibilities, as evident within texts and more generally within social life?

With these questions in mind, key interpersonal and ideational features of the classroom interactions were selected for analysis. Examination of interpersonal features of the episodes, relating to concern with *equality*, involves scrutiny of patterns of turntaking, mood and modality, specifically the function of types of questions while focus on *quality* involves consideration of ideational features such as conjunctive relations which serve to elaborate, extend or enhance argument.

What interpersonal features are salient?

Tenor of discourse

Interpersonal features were selected so as to offer judgements about the extent of equality in interaction. How is the discussion genre maintained, allowing for the fact that a classroom setting will differ from those where discussants are readily acknowledged, at least in principle, to have equality of rights to speak? To what degree is it possible – or desirable – for the teacher to relinquish the conventional control over rights to speak and topic selection, so that there is greater than usual approximation to the kind of debate among equals to which constative speech aspires? We need to keep in mind that while there are legitimate forms of power in the teacher's gift, there are equally unsustainable and unproductive ones, in the light of the aim of moving towards some Habermasian ideal of unconstrained contributions.

More specifically, what mechanisms are used for distributing turns to offer equitable access to the floor? The effectiveness of interaction can be judged not merely, in quantitative ways, from equal opportunities to speak, but from the extent to which the classroom discourse, as managed by the teacher, maximises opportunities for students to present points of view and elaborate arguments, drawing on rich linguistic and cultural resources and the collaboration and support of other members of the classroom community. This is consistent with the aim of seeing classroom learning and knowledge as building from contributions offered by all the students and the teacher.

Footing. One way of looking at the overall tenor of interactions is provided by Goffman's notion of 'footing'. Goffman uses the term 'footing' to mean (1981: 28) an 'alignment we take up to ourselves and the others present as expressed in the way we manage the production or reception of an utterance'. In Goffman's (1981) terms, teacher and students do not embark on any form of classroom interaction on an equal 'footing'. However, within the inevitable constraints imposed at an institutional and wider sociocultural level, the teacher has options in the manner in which she interprets her role. In Chapter 2, I introduced the notion of footing as related to the reader's alignment to a written text, drawing on Widdowson's (1992) adaptation of Goffman's roles of the reader as *animator, author* or *principal*. But, as Kramsch (1993: 38) notes, the notion of footing usefully allows us also to think of the roles we take on in the classroom – whether as teachers or learners – as shifting and flexible within the inevitable, wider constraints. In Goffman's terms teachers are necessarily 'principals' much, if not most of the time, in the sense that the authority of what they say is a function of their institutionally ascribed status as teachers. However, they might shift roles to become either animators or authors, that is, they might animate the classroom material, such as by reading from a course book (less relevant in the case of this study) or they may speak with an other than professional identity – and become 'authors' of their utterances – as, for example, in what Kramsch (1993: 40) calls 'side-plays', where teachers and students may shift outside their classroom roles, to speak, for instance, as parents, members of the local community or football fans. Of course as teachers adjust their footing, so do students. And while teachers, as more powerful participants, usually take the lead in the change of mutual footing, this is not always so. Students too will occasionally prompt a change in classroom tenor by spontaneously shifting out of role as learners and into other roles which offer them opportunities to express a wider range of identities and experiences.

Questions. Questioning procedures accompany and signal changes in footing. As often observed, teacher-questions frequently function as a way of controlling and allocating turns where the teacher, as principal, is managing the interaction rather than participating in it. Even where questions are substantive, the teacher may be 'steering students to the envisaged answer', as Reynolds (1990: 130) puts it. Drawing on Young (1992: 100), I identified three kinds of questioning in my classroom interactions: managerial, substantive and exploratory.

Managerial questions are to a large degree, as the term suggests, not questions at all but function as directives and will be responded to by some kind of student action, to include taking the floor. Substantive questions require responses to specific questions about content, in this class largely centred around textual features. They may take the form of what Young (*op. cit.*: 102) calls Guess What Teacher Thinks (GWTT) questions, where the teacher is pursuing a very specific agenda. However we might add a subsidiary question, related to GWTT, but which can be seen to be even more subtly (or indeed not so subtly) manipulative. I call these *Guess what teacher wants you to think* questions. These are an occupational hazard of CLA in that teachers are likely to have investments in particular political positions, to a greater degree than in other pedagogies. It is this kind of question which can be embraced by the useful categorisation offered by Blum-Kulka and Peled-Elhanan (2000: 76) who talk of 'ideological' questions. They note how the syntax of questions, for instance in signalling what is new and given, positions students to offer one kind of answer rather than another. The clear assumption with such questions is that there is no other interpretation or point of view. Blum-Kulka and Peled-Elhanen are describing the strongly ideologically loaded classrooms of Ulpan classes which offer religious education for refugees into Israel. There is a tacitly agreed and specific agenda in these classes. Nonetheless they share some features with other ideologically committed forms of teaching, such as CLA.

Finally there is one kind of question which is not really a question at all: exploratory questions. Unlike ideological questions which I see as closing down further debate, exploratory questions keep it open. A defining characteristic of exploratory questions is that they will not invite answers and may indeed be responded to with further questions. It is not just that neither participant knows the answers, but that answers are not readily knowable. Exploratory questions are necessarily reciprocal – jointly authored, that is, they show participants acting as authors of their own thoughts and ideas, but also adjusting and qualifying those in the course of the interaction. They can be said to be indicative of greater equity in interaction. They include the kind of questions which problematise – that is, pose problems rather than attempt to solve them – and acknowledge uncertainty, dilemmas and contradictions. An example from the data shows Yuko exploring several possibilities of interpretation:

This "support" (she refers to a word used in the newspaper article headline)...is it supporting her being racist or is it supporting her being a childmind – good childminder? We don't know that yet.

Modality. Accompanying a stance or footing of uncertainty, of the kind which Yuko demonstrates in the extract above, will be varying degrees of modality. Modality covers both modalisation and modulation in Halliday's (1994) terms, one reflecting a speaker or writer's attitude or stance to what he/she is saying, the second the stance to an interlocutor. A key part of the tenor of the speech event will relate to how the participants align themselves not just with each other, but with a particular point of view. Although modality is sometimes seen to suggest powerless speech or writing, I want to suggest the reverse in the case of constative speech. As Clegg (1992: 16) says, 'talk for learning manifests an underlying stance of uncertainty or tentativeness'. Modality as a typical feature within such talk is therefore as likely to signal reflectiveness, the search for truth as it is to indicate lack of confidence. It is as important not to overstate one's claims as it is to assert opinions and judgements unequivocally; modalisation is a necessary support for the presentation of tentative or provisional claims. For this reason I examined the use of modality in the classroom interactions.

Challenges. Features to note in establishing the degree of equality in debate are expressions of agreement or disagreement with other group members and how conflicts or differences of interpretation are resolved. And of particular relevance to an assessment of the critical tenor of the interactions will be the occurrence and nature of certain kinds of *challenge*, whether to texts, student to student and student to teacher. Habermas's theory of communicative action tends to emphasis consent rather than dissent. It is claimed (e.g. Best and Kellner 1991: 253) that Habermas 'exaggerates the desirability of consensus and downplays the importance of dissensus'. However, within what we might call a consensual environment, challenge to dominant views is clearly a key principle of critical pedagogy, on condition it is offered in a spirit of resistance rather than opposition; that it represents sincerely held views rather than being strategically motivated. Constative speech, while designed to reach shared understandings, does not converge on orthodox interpretations of texts or situations. As with other speech acts, however, it is not easy to identify what constitutes a challenge. It is very unlikely to be signalled performatively, with 'I challenge' or even with 'I disagree'. It may be prefaced with 'why' or 'what if' questions, but finally the presence of challenge can only be assessed by close reference to the immediate and wider context of communication, as some examples in the classroom data reveal.

To sum up on equality of interaction, it is worth emphasising, as Peled-Elhanan and Blum-Kulka (1998) do, that the mere incidence of exchanges of turns and questions does not in itself signal a dialogic classroom. If the exchanges are routine and the questions designed merely to test knowledge then the classroom ethos remains monologic; conversely teacher monologue, if it offers reflective spaces for learners, potential points for challenge or enquiry, can be dialogic. Moreover it is of little value to have interpersonally equitable classroom interaction if the substance is inconsequential. Indeed this was my objection to some versions of communicative language teaching, as noted in Chapter 3. For this reason we need to attend to the *quality* of the discourse, which can be covered, in Hallidayan terms, by field. I turn to this next.

What ideational features are salient?

Field of discourse

Opinions. How willing are the participants, especially the students, to give opinions at all, to make value judgements? Although, in the language classroom, opportunities may be offered to practice the function of 'giving opinion', this is of little value in the development of constative talk, if the matters offered up for judgement are essentially trivial. It is for this reason that the PARSNIP model, described in Chapter 3, may create difficulties for the development of opinionated discourse. It became clear in my study that the opportunity to offer a point of view was seen as a major role of the Critical Reading class from the student' perspective (cf. Chapter 7). However, one is bound to ask how often learners in classrooms are genuinely invited to offer an opinion. If we accept the value of opinion giving, then students need a language to encode this, beyond the formulaic chunks regularly provided for practice in the language course book. Opinion might be simply marked by statements such as 'I think' or 'in my opinion' or may be modalised in a range of ways, adverbially or through the use of modal verbs. Although modality, both modalisation and modulation are included under Speech Exchange and so linked to 'tenor' in Hallidayan grammar (Halliday 1994), it is clear that modalisation serves an ideational function too in modifying the propositional content of statements, in particular in qualifying opinions or judgements of the state of affairs. However differently articulated, an awareness of personal judgements and values, and how these may differ from those of others, is key to participating in argument.

Warrants. A feature of constative, exploratory talk is that people do not simply express feelings or opinions but offer supports or warrants for them. As one kind of evidence of the quality of classroom discussion, I examined the classroom data for the incidence of certain kinds of conjunctive relations within and across clauses, which encode such warrants or supports. Motivating this selection of feature is the view, argued above, that adequate argument involves the presentation of reasons for beliefs or points of view. In particular, circumstantial expansion (cf. Halliday 1994: 225) allows an argument to be made explicit and therefore more readily either accepted or disputed. Halliday (*op. cit.*) offers an account of expansion which includes three main types of conjunctive relations: extension, elaboration and enhancement. Tools for looking at quality of argument, in particular through instances of expansion, drawn from Halliday, will be specified in Chapter 6.

Resources. Crucial to the quality of the overall interaction is the degree to which students, especially in a multicultural class such as the one described here, are able to draw on cultural and linguistic resources which may be uniquely available to them as members of linguistic or minority ethnic groups. As noted in Chapter 3, the goal is not to essentialise or exoticise this experience, but to allow it to be articulated as a highly pertinent cultural resource which illuminates debate about issues of social justice and discrimination. Students' narratives – of cultural rather than personal or intimate experience – can resonate with the comparable experiences of other class members, constituting 'memorable moments' in Mercer's (1995b) terms.

Resources are also provided by the lessons themselves; students refer intertextually and interdiscoursally, as Victoria does in Chapter 7: Episode three, where she comments: 'this is like the Noddy text'. This kind of observation might be accompanied by metalanguage explicitly introduced during the course, by terms such as 'genre' and 'model reader' and 'intertextuality' – concepts introduced to develop contextual awareness of the cultural milieu in which texts arise.

In addition, a key requirement of this particular course was the need to adduce various kinds of linguistic evidence to support interpretations of texts. Thus, a further question relates to the degree of specificity with which students are able to draw on linguistic terminology which relates to lexiogrammatical features of texts. Moreover, is the linguistic analysis offered for its own sake in tokenistic or display fashion or is it put to use in furthering rich and insightful interpretation?

The student produced data: diaries, protocols and interviews

One problem with looking just at interactional processes within classrooms is that time and space for reflection is not available for students and teachers to re-evaluate in-depth and gain further distance on readings of texts or situations. Differently articulated views may emerge through other media such as, in this case, student diaries, protocols and interviews. In this sense, discussion extends beyond the classroom. Broadly speaking, interpersonal and ideational meanings are still in play, and, at the same time, issues of equality and quality. Equality is evidenced in the manner in which the student locates him or herself within the discourses of these additional texts. How far do students feel empowered by earlier debates in class with peers and teacher to air opinion, to develop personal lines of enquiry? For this reason, in the case of diaries and protocols, I centre on the manner in which the students locate themselves in their own discourse by for instance, indicating varying degrees of commitment to the views they express. Quality is evidenced, I want to argue, as with constative speech in general, in the degree to which warrants for points of view are provided through modality or expansion of their argument. This therefore is a further focus in the analysis of diary and protocol data. In the case of the interviews my major interest is in how the students see their own ways of reading in light of the experience of the Critical Reading course. Questions I ask of this data are designed to capture students' views of changed ways of reading, the role of the classroom itself in facilitating these and what level and kind of critical awareness they have gained for the longer term.

In general I aimed to offer a less structured analysis of the data which I have called 'student produced'. My overall aim here is to try and capture what were the major themes which emerged in student narratives across all three genres: diaries, protocols or 'think alouds' and the interviews. In doing so, I have kept in mind the four questions raised at the start of my study:

1. What ways of reading texts can be described as critical?
2. How far is it possible or desirable to address social and political issues in the language classroom through text analysis?
3. What kinds of language analysis procedures promote critical reading?
4. What sense do students make of CDA approaches in the classroom context?

Answers to these questions emerge with varying degrees of clarity from the different data sources. Clearly it is the last question which is the overriding question to be addressed and to which the other three are subsidiary. Overall then, the purpose of this final data set is to gain some answers to these questions from the students' own point of view. What is their interpretation of critical reading, in the light of their experience of the particular course? Specifically has the course, in their view, changed their ways of reading in any significant way?

Conclusion

The critical dimension

We are still left with the dilemma of how far such a reading course can be called 'critical'. Can we talk about *degree* of criticality or growth of critical-ity? While it is not possible to measure criticality in the sense I intend it, that does not mean that judgement of its absence or presence cannot be sought. Finally, the critical perspective embraces all modes of discourse considered here: it is embedded within the textual critique but also the classroom talk around texts and the commentary, both spoken and written, which arises from reflection on both texts and the classroom. There is a constant shift of focus, out to the wider parameters of the broader social and political contexts in which texts arise, narrowing into the examination of the linguistic features of specific texts. Part of this shifting focus involves gaining a critical perspective on our own ways of reading. So questions to ask are whether students envisage kinds of social identity and interpretations other than their own? Do they make reference to texts and parts of texts and to other texts introduced in the course of the class in critical, not merely unproblematic ways? Moreover, to what extent are the contributions cumulatively, not just individually, critical?

More specifically, is there any evidence that students and teacher are able not just to critique the texts but to gain greater awareness of the possible interestedness of their _own_ observations, thus moving beyond metacognitive to what I have called metacritical awareness? We might expect to find this level of awareness emerging not during the lessons as such, but during occasions at some distance from the class, where there is opportunity for learners to reflect on the nature of their own evolving awareness.

While the development of CLA more widely and critical reading more specifically is a longer-term project, nonetheless I want to claim a strongly mediating role for the classroom; that it is within the classroom community that students begin to find a personal voice which emerges out of the social, as intersubjectively realised. The nature of this classroom community is taken up in Chapter 5.

5
Critical Reading in the Classroom

This chapter will describe a specific context of use for practical critical discourse analysis (CDA), beginning with the notion of classroom as critical community. It will continue with an account of some classroom-based studies which fall under the broad umbrella term of 'critical language awareness'. Against the background of these, I set out my own Critical Reading class, describing the texts and tasks chosen; finally I provide some vignettes of classroom procedures. The chapter views the classroom and the course very much from my own perspective as the teacher, and it is my voice which is dominant here, especially in the early lessons of the course. Gradually, however, the students' own voices begin to emerge.

The classroom as a critical community

Much of the discussion of critical pedagogy and related work such as critical literacy has been at an abstract level. There has been, as Usher and Edwards in Pennycook (2001: 82) note, a 'curious silence on concrete pedagogical matters'. Indeed Pennycook (2001) himself, while he offers a comprehensive account of critical applied linguistics, including a chapter on the Politics of Pedagogy, says little about actual classroom procedures. Canagarajah (1999) looks critically at his own classroom practice in teaching EFL. However, only in a further source (2002) does he offer practical proposals for the application of critical principles to his teaching of writing.

A further problem with most critically oriented study is its singly authored nature. If we turn to the textual critique favoured by critical discourse analysts, the interpretations produced by critique are not generally opened up to communities of interpreters. CDA has tended to be done by the lone armchair critic, giving rise as O'Regan points out, to comments by opponents of CDA that critical analysts promote textual exegesis by proxy on behalf of the supposed 'uncritical reader' (O'Regan in preparation). One advantage of drawing on specific teaching experiences and learner data is that we can concretise some abstract ideas about pedagogy and language; secondly, we have access to a class of students who offer us a ready-made interpretative community, who bring different knowledge and cultural resources to bear on textual critique.

This immediately raises the question of what we mean by 'community'. I have drawn on the idea of 'interpretative community', based originally on Fish (1980), to describe reading as a social practice, that we read not as individuals but as members of a more or less readily identifiable social group (cf. Wallace 1992a). Londoners will be aware of the literacy preferences of regular travellers on the Tube. It seems, from my observations, that there are distinct communities: the Central Line readership is different from the Northern Line or Piccadilly Line one. In *The Importance of Being Earnest* by Oscar Wilde, when the hero Jack Worthing announces that he was mislaid on the Brighton line as a baby, Lady Bracknell's famous reply is: 'the line is immaterial'. In our case, the line is material. Central line travellers are strongly *Guardian* reading; Piccadilly line readers, at least at certain times of day, favour *The Sun*. And, as often observed, women, rather more than men, on all lines are readers of novels.

Talk of the 'classroom community' is now common, as a way of validating and promoting solidarity and mutual support in classrooms. However, as Cazden (2001) notes, the notion of community is in danger of becoming clichéd and fairly empty, unless we specify in some detail what characterises the creation of community. Even more problematic is what we mean by a *critical* classroom community. The investigation of classroom interaction in Chapter 6, aims to embark on this discussion, while not presuming to provide definitive answers. Provisionally we might say here that membership of such a critical community involves both teacher and students being alert to how power relations are embedded not just within the texts we critique in class, but are continually reproduced in and through classroom interactions. We might agree to observe how far power is applied collaboratively and productively or used strategically for specific and individual, even destructive, purposes. Also, ideationally speaking, members of a critical classroom community articulate awareness about matters of social justice in the contemporary world. In a class centred around text analysis, this means pointing to the unequal treatment of participants within texts, the manner in which the reader is positioned and the relative openness of the discourses in a text, all textual features, which as argued in Chapter 2, are amenable to investigation through systemic-functional grammar – the tool for analysis selected in the Critical Reading course. This is linked to the broad goals of critical pedagogy noted in Chapter 3: the desire for social change and commitment to social justice. It is important to add that empathy is a key factor here too; in the view of critical pedagogy I have opted for here, which privileges distance over involvement or desire, one has to understand the principle of social justice, as *apart from* one's own involvement. One of the students on the course, Yuko, sums up my point

here, in the interview I had with her at the end of the course (this is reproduced more fully in Chapter 7).

CW: Do you think it was interesting having people from different backgrounds?
Y: For example, I think it was the French girl – I can't remember her name –
but she was studying British...
CW: British National Party.
Y: ...National Party yes BNP BNP. It wasn't about her country because she
was from France I think but she was so against it.......and then for
example for me, Japanese, I do understand Nazism and things like that
but it wasn't so, how d'you say, *close* to me at all – until she showed her
consideration and she take it so seriously...
CW: her concern
Y: ...it's not even about her country I thought..I thought if I was asked
my opinion I thought I can't say anything because I never thought of it.
I never experienced it...
CW: that kind of racism
Y: ...yes but I can understand what they're saying yes, but I didn't have my
particular opinion.
CW: Did you feel at the end of the course you were more aware about some
of these issues?
Y: Yes yes I thought now...but before I didn't I just didn't care at all. I felt
a bit ashamed of it because you should be aware of these kind of things.

As I read Yuko's words, I take her to be saying that what she gained from the
classroom community was not an understanding of her own oppression.
What was new for her was the value of seeing the notion of oppression
and injustice more widely, as it affected others than herself.

The Critical Reading course

This was how the course was presented to students:

Beginning in October 1993

A Special Course in

CRITICAL READING

A one semester class from 3.00 pm to 5.00 pm
Open to students who have successfully completed Cambridge
First Certificate or University equivalent

Do you want to improve your critical reading skills in English?
Do you feel that you would like a fuller understanding of the written texts which you encounter in your day-to-day life in Britain?
 This class aims to help you:

* read between the lines, that is, understand the hidden messages of written texts;
* understand some of the cultural meanings in written texts;
* see how texts persuade us to behave or think in particular ways;
* appreciate the ways in which texts are written for different audiences;
* see how texts may be read in different ways by different people.

We will look at a whole range of different kinds of texts, collected by all of us in the course of daily life, including:

* advertisements
* newspaper texts
* leaflets and forms
* textbooks
* magazines.

It is important to see this particular course in a social and historical context. The course took place in one of the new universities in Britain which was developing a particular interest in media studies and encouraged the development of innovative options. It was also the successor to a number of similar courses, all of which shared two basic principles: an interest in everyday community texts as legitimate objects of study and the development of some specific linguistic tools as a means of analysis. The first of this series of courses offered at Thames Valley University (then known as the Polytechnic of West London), albeit to a slightly different student group, is described in Wallace (1992a). The Critical Reading course took the shape it did, both in structure and content, because of its base in London and the particular aims and interests of the students who opted to attend. For this reason it is instructive to look at the ways in which critical pedagogy has been interpreted in other contexts before taking a close look at my own course. I turn to some of these studies in the next section.

Classroom studies in critical pedagogy

The classroom studies set out below illustrate varying interpretations of critical practice – favouring in different ways, Freirean problem posing approaches or more text analytic ones. What they share is the fact that they are all classroom-based investigations. Secondly, the teacher scholars who provide these examples are prepared to problematise as much as promote their own practice. The studies are themselves *codes* in the Freirean sense. In different ways, they encode some of the tensions and dilemmas around critical practice in classrooms as interpretative communities.

Ellsworth (1989), teaching undergraduates at Minnesota University, set up her course in media and anti-racist pedagogies against the background of the nationwide eruption in 1987–88 of racist violence in communities and on campuses across the USA. The course was therefore planned as a political response to a particular situation: racism on campus. Where the class ultimately failed, in Ellsworth's view, was that students were unable to reach some sense of resolution or shared purpose in combating racism and other forms of discrimination. Ellsworth attributes this failure to the limitations of the rationalist position which she associates with theoretical critical pedagogy. However, one wonders if her frustration and disappointment might be due rather to her interpretation of empowerment, which takes a rights orientation within identity politics. She says (1989: 309), 'the concept of critical pedagogy assumes a commitment on the part of the professor/teacher toward ending the student's oppression'. No teacher can, in my view, make such a commitment – nor should they expect to. The difficulty with such an interpretation of critical pedagogy is that ultimately, although the concern is certainly with access and opportunity, the struggles are pursued in an individualist spirit, in terms of personal empowerment. Even the title of Ellsworth's paper: *Why doesn't this feel empowering*? suggests an individualistic ethos, and one which favours the affective over the rational.

Hilary Janks was one of the first to take a specifically CLA perspective to critical pedagogy in South Africa, beginning her work, as she notes in Janks (2001a) at the height of the struggle against apartheid. Janks and her colleagues (1993) produced material which takes an explicit CLA position in a series of books which, as the general introduction to the series states: 'deal with the relationship between language and power... the materials attempt to raise awareness of the way language can be used and is used to maintain and to challenge existing forms of power' (Janks 1993: iii).

These books represent the first attempt to take a coherent CLA approach across a series of distinct but related non-fiction texts and topics, and involve specific analysis of texts. In addition, Janks (1993, 2001a) offers a critique of the use of the pilot version of these materials, called *Language and Position*, in a multiracial school – an independent school which had 'opened its doors to students of all races before it was legally allowed to do so' (Janks 2001a: 140). In this school the workbook generated conflict of a kind which did not appear to be amenable to transformation into greater mutual understanding. In answer to questions posed about the position of men and women in child-care arrangements, the white girls and the female teacher adopted a strong feminist position. The black boys defended the idea that patriarchy was part of Black culture, and the black girls were largely silenced in the debate through perceived tensions between their identities as both women and black.

The Janks' study highlights the difficulty of doing critical work in some contexts. The black girls set out as trebly disadvantaged, as girls and as black and as working class, within the specific school setting, institutionally and in the wider society. It was their identities which were on the line, not those of the already dominant participants, the boys and the white girls and, of course, the teacher herself.

In a very different way the identities of the students of McKinney (2002) were also on the line. These students were, arguably, at the opposite end of the social spectrum to the black girls silenced in the Janks' study, being first year undergraduates on an English studies course at a relatively privileged and predominantly 'white', Afrikaans university in South Africa. McKinney examined her own classroom data by teaching two courses on South African literature to a group who were mainly Afrikaans first language students (including two coloured students). Her aim was to take a critical literacy focus on issues of social inequality in South Africa; specifically to develop students' ability to read texts critically, whether these are literary texts or other genres such as films, news reports or advertisements. Many of the students expressed resentment at the course and at the manner in which they felt positioned by the texts they explored, which examined the apartheid experience. McKinney notes that there was a tension between the desire to escape the past, feelings of guilt and a wish to move forward to the creation of a new, non-racist South Africa. Far from feeling empowered by critical language study, some students felt stranded in a sense of powerlessness, and trapped, as McKinney puts it, 'in critique and frustrated at not being able to move beyond this position'. In reflecting on pedagogy which might pursue critical study of this kind more fruitfully, McKinney proposes a move beyond critique to what she calls a process of design, which involves students producing their own texts. As she concludes: 'Perhaps giving students the opportunity to produce their own alternative fictional texts which represent South Africa *now* (my emphasis) is one possibility' (McKinney 2002: 12). McKinney has drawn on Gunther Kress's construct of design here. He says: 'While critique looks at the present through the means of past production, design shapes the future through deliberate deployment of representational resources in the designer's interest' (Kress 2000a: 160). McKinney notes that those students who were fully engaged in a writing task which arose out of textual critique began to show deeper engagement with issues of social justice. In other words, they were, we might say, deploying creative resources to counter their sense of helplessness. Janks in her recent work (e.g. 2000) also talks about 'design' as central to her synthesis of four interdependent orientations to critical literacy: domination, diversity, access and design. It is design which allows for reconstruction and transformation. I shall return to the implications of the inter-relationship between critique and design in the concluding chapter to this book.

Few studies offer close examination of verbatim classroom interaction within a critical pedagogy framework. Morgan (1997) is an exception. As she says: 'critical pedagogy theorists have rarely turned their attention to the nature of the talk that goes on in classrooms – unless it be in the more general terms... concerning the politics of teacher–student interaction and the desirability of open, equal dialogue' (1997: 110). Wendy Morgan's work is of particular interest to my study because she looked closely at both the content and structure of talk, and the way students make their own kind of sense of critical language study. Morgan took a less risky option than did Janks and Ellsworth: unlike Ellsworth, she was not investigating her own practice; unlike Janks, the teaching context was a less volatile one – the students' own identities as mainstream white Australians were less threatened. Systematic oppression of aboriginal groups in Australia continues. However – and this in itself says much of the persistence of inequality over generations of political struggle – this conflict is less raw for these young people than the apartheid experience of McKinney's students. Also they were studying not specially prepared critical material, or contemporary literature, but a classic text *Romeo and Juliet*. The teacher Lindsay, whom we observed in the extract in Chapter 3, offered a systematic introduction to critical literacy (Morgan 1997: 115). He started from four principles: that texts and their meanings are produced within the cultural contexts that condition them; that texts therefore offer a partial (both in the sense of 'incomplete' and 'interested') version of 'reality'; that they are nonetheless capable of multiple readings, since readers draw on diverse ideologies in their own contexts; and that the work of texts (their production and use) is political. The task was to explore gender roles in *Romeo and Juliet*. Drawing on aspects of Hallidayan linguistics, Lindsay initiated work on the ways women are described by themselves and others: as acting, acted upon, simply existing in some state or as ordered to do something. Both the content of the textual analysis and the teacher/student and student/student dialogue, that is, both ideational and interpersonal language functions, diverge from orthodox classroom practice, as this brief extract suggests.

Student A: Sir, does 'enrich the hand' come under anything, or is that just a load of babble?

Teacher: Well, the lady is enriching the hand of yonder knight

Student A: Yeah, so you reckon it's an action – enriches?
Teacher: Yes, it's a funny sort of action, though, isn't it?
Student A: Yes, because its not something you can actually physically do.

This dialogue, which does not at first sight look particularly critical, nonetheless shows teacher-mediated textual analysis of a kind which is drawing students' attention to the way that discourses about women – in this case about Juliet – pattern in texts. Interpersonally, though the student seems keen to know the teacher's own view (so you reckon...?), the teacher is resisting the pressure to provide correct answers, not so much in the relativist spirit that there are not preferred responses but because he is anxious to maintain a dialogic approach to the analysis which favours knowledge construction rather than knowledge transmission.

Mellor and Patterson (2001), writing about texts and readings with 8–10-year-olds, acknowledge and argue through one particular dilemma in critical literacy and in critical pedagogy more widely: the privileging of one reading over another. The assumption has been that once conscious of the deceptions of the received or model reading of the text, students would be free to produce alternative, critical readings, abandoning earlier, first glance ones. However, this was not the case in the class investigated here. Children were likely to stay with their initial readings. Mellor and Patterson, reflecting on this unexpected outcome, are forced to acknowledge that they are not just encouraging analysis of texts and the production of alternative readings, but that they are actively working towards *adjustment* of readers. In short, critical text analysis of this kind is likely to be inter-ventive. Mellor and Patterson conclude: 'We have come to feel that we have to acknowledge the normativity of our practice in arguing for the pro-duction of particular readings over others.' They proceed to an example: 'It seems to us that the teaching of multiple readings of *Mein Kampf* might be dismissed in favour of teaching a specific reading of it as racist' (Mellor and Patterson 2001: 132). This acknowledgement, one I would concur with, concedes the importance for teachers of using their power legitimately to promote certain readings over others, as much as to resist others' use of power. It also affirms the incompatibility of critical pedagogy, at least a CLA inspired one, with a relativist stance whereby any reading is as acceptable as any other, or that texts are ideologically permeated in com-parable kinds of ways.

The studies above reveal the tensions and compromises which emerge when critical theory, as variously interpreted, is put to work in classrooms. Will greater conflict be the outcome, rather than, – not necessarily an align-ment of positions but at least, an agreement to disagree? This was the outcome of the classes described by Ellsworth and Janks. Will students direct hostility – more oppositionally than with critical resistance – against the class and teacher rather than at racist texts or social injustice, as was the case with some of McKinney's students? Or will they resolutely stand by their initial readings of texts or situations, opposing any encouragement to gain some critical distance from them, as was the case with the Janks' classroom and the children in the classroom observed by Mellor and Patterson. Morgan too notes the compromises and uncertainties which characterise classroom analysis of texts in her study of Australian classrooms. Ultimately the value of such studies, however, is to balance the grand narratives of theoretical critical pedagogy with on-the-ground real instances of classroom interaction.

While there are few studies of practical CLA for first language speakers, there are even fewer for foreign language learners. Some of the studies designed to enhance cross-cultural awareness, such as those by Morgan and Cain (2000), take a critical slant in challenging stereotypes through encouraging students to collect and exchange a range of textual material which then forms the basis of dialogue between student groups in different countries, mainly European ones. Similarly Quist (2000), drawing on Bakhtin, takes what she calls a 'dialogic' perspective to text-based work in the teaching of Dutch to adult university students, encouraging her students to problematise the cultural values within a range of popular texts. Her aim is, by making use of the concept of 'Kulturtext' (Meijer 1996), to show how the discourses which permeate popular texts continually reconstruct, sometimes in quite subtle ways, cultural values and attitudes, as well as notions about national character and identity.

Background to the Critical Reading course

As I revisit my analysis of the Critical Reading course, these other studies offer me a clearer perspective and some distance on my own course. In many ways my students were similar to McKinney's, of a comparable age and education. Why then were they not – apparently at least – threatened? Simply I believe because there was less at stake. The students came to the course, which they had opted for, neither with the guilt of an oppressor class nor the passionate and specific agendas of an oppressed group. Though neither mainstream nor exclusively white, they would not claim oppression in any specific way. While the diversity of Ellsworth's class resulted in fragmentation of interests and eventual conflict, my students, with fewer axes to grind, seemed able and willing to suspend personal and immediate grievances, to participate in the sharing of experiences and perceptions of their class mates. Indeed it was these differences of perception and experience which motivated much classroom discussion. This is not to say that there was not some resentment within the class about group behaviour, as emerges during one of the end-of-course interviews, discussed in Chapter 7. Nor have my experiences with approaches to critical language teaching been problem free. I started a very recent course called *Ways of Reading*, with a text about the US and British bombardment of Afghanistan. Military action had just been declared the previous evening and I felt I could hardly ignore this in a course dedicated to the reading of contemporary texts, including news texts. The text I chose to centre on, from an influential British broadsheet newspaper *The Daily Telegraph* expressed views on Arab nations, which I believed needed to be critically addressed. However, for seven of the eight Arab students in my class, from Bahrain, this was too raw. They did not return for the subsequent lessons of the course.

I reproduce part of the text here, leaving my readers to do their own critical analysis:

IN THIS WAR OF CIVILISATIONS THE WEST WILL PREVAIL

This war belongs within the much larger spectrum of a far older conflict between settled, creative productive Westerners and predatory destructive Orientals. It is no good pretending that the peoples of the desert and the empty spaces exist on the same level of civilisation as those who farm and manufacture. They do not. (From John Keegan *The Daily Telegraph* Monday 8 October, 2001.)

The Critical Reading course

Aims of the course

Wider principles of CDA which underpinned the study need to be seen together with practical goals. I have argued that it is these practical pedagogic goals which distinguish CLA, and critical reading within this, from its CDA antecedents. These wider principles were those which were stated at the outset of this book and are grounded within:

Views of society:

- CLA addresses social and political issues
- CLA is committed to the pursuit of social justice.

Views of pedagogy:

- CLA is interventive
- CLA is dialogic in process or means towards outcome.

Views of text:

- no texts are ideologically neutral;
- texts arise out of social relationships, in particular relationships based on power;
- texts relate to each other intertextually; they have a history as do the discourses embedded within them.

Views of reading:

- reading is a social process;
- interpretations are negotiated within communities;
- interpretations may or may not be aligned with the model or expected reading.

The Critical Reading course should also be seen intertextually. In planning this class I took my bearings not just from earlier courses I had taught, but more particularly from one which directly preceded this, which acted as a pilot. I wanted to incorporate the feedback from this earlier course into the main one. This feedback had proposed five major recommendations:

- Students should make a commitment to bring material into class and to take an interest in current affairs. Without an interest in news and contemporary social life, intertextual knowledge was simply not available for learners.
- The teacher needed to present the students with a clear agenda as to expected ways of working on the course.
- Because of some of the difficulties with culturally loaded texts, that is, where there is a high degree of culture-specific reference – largely inevitable with community texts – it might be best to begin with familiar genres and relatively accessible language.
- Within each lesson there should be an extended 'pre-reading' phase in advance of the text analysis. This would be done jointly by the whole class, as a schema-building exercise, where existing knowledge, opinions and cultural resources could be shared, before embarking on more focused tasks around text in small groups.
- There might be an initial open-ended 'response to texts' assignment, as a way of discovering what kind and level of critical engagement with texts students drew on at the beginning of the course.

This advice, which came mainly from the key participant observer of the pilot group, Ros Tobin, resonated with some of the major underlying principles of CLA. For instance, the first point acknowledges the key factor of the social and political content of CLA, along with the need to read texts intertextually, to read text against text. Equally the need for transparency and explicitness is key to my view of critical pedagogy, as argued in Chapter 3. Others are more tactical and specific in nature, relating to practical pedagogy. However, they largely meshed with my own observations, and I took them on board in planning the main course, the outline of which is included here.

The course programme

Week one	Introduction. Ways of noticing texts and readers in different environments in our daily lives
Week two	Talking about texts: Introduction to genre. Classifying written texts under topic and readership
Week three	Talking about readers (1) How can we tell which texts are written for which readers? Focus on advertisements
Week four	Talking about readers (2) Why are texts written and presented in particular ways? Focus on advertisements for cars and perfume in Men's and Women's magazines
Week five	Introduction of the Hallidayan Framework for text analysis. Talking about topic (1) Why are people, places and things described in particular ways? Focus on magazine and newspaper articles
Week six	Talking about topic (2) Why are events reported in particular ways? Focus on newspapers
Week seven	A closer look at advertisements and other texts which aim to persuade us to behave in certain ways
Week eight	A closer look at magazine articles, in particular the different ways in which language is used to represent participants in texts
Week nine	A closer look at newspapers, in particular the ways in which the same events are reported differently
Week ten	Poems, songs, folk tales and romantic fiction. Do we want to read these texts critically?
Week eleven	News reports. Front page stories. What makes the news? How are participants, processes and cause and effect represented? How is point of view represented?
Week twelve	Comment on the news: the role of editorials. Features of expository comment
Week thirteen	News articles and features. Differences and similarities between a range of newspaper genres.
Week fourteen	Open for group to select own genres and topics to analyse
Week fifteen	End of course evaluation and in-class assignment

Course objectives

Firstly, the Critical Reading course drew on the two strands of critical literacy awareness described in Chapter 2, that is the macro-awareness of literacy practices in social settings and the awareness of effects in specific concrete texts. In other words, the aim was to embed a close study of texts in a wider understanding of who reads what, where and why in different environments; also, although there was greater emphasis on the context of reception, in keeping with this as a *reading* course, I also wanted to take account of different circumstances of the production of texts. The hope was that one outcome of the course would be that students would be able to use the fine-grained study of specific texts in intertextual ways to gain deeper understanding of the language and literacy practices surrounding them in everyday life. Pedagogically the two strands of awareness are realised in three phases in Lankshear's (1994) procedure. This procedural cycle, offers a heuristic, as I argue in Chapter 2, by which to capture the progression of a Critical Reading course from early awareness raising activities, to focused work on specific texts and finally a revisiting of both texts and practices in daily life and in academic contexts which is accompanied by more finely tuned critical awareness abilities. That is, students more readily shift into the kind of critical gear I describe as characterising critical literacy in Chapter 2. This final phase is likely to be at the end of the course – or indeed some time later – as students experience new ways of noticing aspects of texts and reading which had earlier been less salient to them.

A related goal, because this was after all a class for foreign language students, was to promote a richer awareness of the uses of English (and by implication of other languages) and an ability to articulate observations and support cases for certain points of view with conviction, confidence and clarity.

A final goal was to collect evaluative feedback of various kinds: both evidence of learning from the course and learners' critical responses to the course and the quality of the classroom interaction. Indeed these can be taken together in that one learning outcome of such a course might be expected to be a greater preparedness to critique the class itself – not in conventional ways but to critique critically. In short, the class itself should be open to critical scrutiny with channels made available for observations to be noted, through student journals for instance.

Choosing texts

As noted at the start of this book, I made a decision to centre critical reading around what I call, following Luke *et al.* (2001), 'community' texts, those which circulate in everyday life. It might be argued that populist texts – as opposed to academically serious ones – have no place in the classroom. However, one is at liberty to resist the reader positioning offered in such texts, that is refuse to treat the trivial playfully. This is consistent with the critical reading principle of 'reading against the grain'. Hoggart (1995: 176) argues 'to assume that popular culture can be explored with crude tools because it is assumed to be crude, uncomplex, easy to read is a serious mistake'.

A further justification for the inclusion of community texts is that these texts are influential in the wider cultural climate. This in itself is of interest to foreign students and was the motivation behind Quist's use of Kulturtexts, noted earlier. Admittedly the 'knowingness' of texts, particularly media texts, signalled by a fake kind of inclusiveness can be irritating for mainstream readers and perplexing for the outsider. One reason for avoiding the playful and the ephemeral, especially for foreign language students, is the parochial nature of such texts. There may be too great a density of culture-specific information, an excess of highly esoteric references. However, difficulties of accessibility can be partly resolved through building in the role of intertextuality on the principle that any particular text (including texts of the academy) needs to be read in the light of other texts, and indeed only then begins to take on wider sociocultural meaning. Without an understanding of some of the cultural points of reference embedded and continually reinforced across both community and academic texts, students may miss many intertextual clues in their wider reading in the foreign language.

Pedagogically, the intertextual principle can be exploited in a number of different ways, around the principle of text sets, or intertexts which can be clustered or grouped in different ways, to show different kinds of cross-textual links. One might, for instance, show how the same genre, even the same story, can select different discourses. This is the basis of some of the material produced for 'Changing Stories' (Mellor *et al.* 1984) which shows, for instance, how five different versions of 'Little Red Riding Hood' create different overall ideological effects through the making of systematically different kinds of linguistic choices. Students are better able to appreciate the effect of the 'divergent' texts by reference to the unmarked traditional version. The same principle can operate in the case of other genres such as news reports, where one can discuss what might motivate the different linguistic options made in the writing of the same news item across different publications. The individual readings of each 'version' of the story take on extra resonance by reference to each other. This is the principle on which the 'Mandela' set of texts described below was selected and exploited in the classroom. Alternatively, one can take sets of texts from the same or comparable sources, which appear not on the same day but serially, to be read against each other over several weeks or months. With this in mind, we examined a series of texts from the women's magazine *Marie Claire* which revealed a clearly identifiable discourse about the lives of women in distant places. To be eligible for the particular 'Society' slot which was a regular feature of the magazine, to have the appropriate level of exoticism, the communities described had to live in remote parts of the world – remote, that is, from northern Europe and North America. The Singapore text which I introduced in Chapter 2, came from this 'Society' slot. Once one had acquired familiarity with this particular genre the occurrence of certain discourse, regularly brought into play to serve the purposes of identifying 'the other' in Said's (1978) terms, became highly predictable.

While students might legitimately complain of a waste of intellectual energy expended on the essentially worthless, that it is harder but more rewarding to look critically at the texts of the Academy than at an article in *Marie Claire*, it is possible to argue the case for community texts not to replace canonical literary or academic texts but to be read in conjunction with them. In the same way the new, especially electronic literacies, do not replace but are used alongside – are indeed complementary with – print-based ones. On recent critical reading courses, such as the *Ways of Reading* course referred to earlier, students regularly brought in texts from the Internet. These were analysed alongside conventional print texts. All of these textual resources are, one can argue, part of a broad critical literacy education for the twenty-first century.

The selection and progression of material for the Critical Reading course

Texts were drawn from a wide range of community sources: letters through the mail, advertisements, posters taken down from billboards, political manifestos, travel brochures and newspaper material of various kinds. Both the students and myself brought texts into the classroom to add to the pool. However, it was then my role to decide on the use of these texts, and to put them into text sets, to enhance intertextuality.

Particularly with a group of students from diverse cultural backgrounds, it is interesting to compare the existence of genres and how generic conventions are realised in different social contexts and what social purposes are served by established or newly evolving genres. For this reason, I took the concept of genre as my organising principle in choosing the way in which particular texts fitted into a coherent course structure.

However, one is still left with choices as how to order the genres to offer some rational kind of progression: the choice here was made to begin with interpersonal texts as more accessible in a number of ways to foreign language students, moving on to descriptive and report texts and concluding with expository texts. Within these broadly defined text types which are universally identifiable are located culture-specific realisations of these, in the shape of genres, such as advertisements, political manifestos, leaflets, and newspaper editorials.

In making practical choices relating to syllabus content, cultural and ideological factors are implicated as well as linguistic difficulty. For instance, even when material is generically familiar to students, it might, in terms of content, be culturally inaccessible. I took the decision to begin with advertising, because, while culturally obscure in many ways, it is noticeable and attractive for students. Moreover, the linguistic content may be minimal. So in beginning with the analysis of predominantly visual texts, students are introduced progressively to greater density of written text, with a lessening dependence on visual image.

One can certainly dispute the claim of easier access to the visual. Clayton (1995), for instance, points out how CDA proponents have neglected to offer adequate analyses of the visual images which, especially in popular texts, accompany conventional print. Analyses of the visual will, potentially, be as complex and sophisticated – and as critical – as print-dependent ones. This is one principle of the multiliteracies project described in Chapter 1 (Cope and Kalantzis 2000). However, the professional preparation of most foreign language teachers still predisposes them to orthodox linguistic analysis rather than to visual analysis. This poses a further problem in wishing to use texts which are, as Kress (2000b: 184) puts it, 'constituted by a number of modes of representation'.

As well as criteria related to linguistic and cultural content and to variability of mode is the issue of ideological content. This is a central and defining concern of a course in CLA. The position argued in this book is that ideology is a feature of texts rather than merely a matter of interpretation. Moreover ideology is not equally salient. Lack of salience, of course, does not mean relative absence of significance – quite the reverse, as noted in Chapter 2. In terms of text selection, then, does one opt to begin with texts whose ideology is worn 'on its sleeve' so to speak, moving on to those whose ideological loading is more covert? My choice of texts in terms of their relative ideological weight was influenced by the progression which Halliday describes (1990) by which certain features of texts are more noticeable than others. Thus certain genres and specific exemplars of genres will fairly consistently show a greater incidence of personal pronouns or strongly connotated vocabulary than genres, such as, for instance, expository texts of various kinds whose significant ideological effects will be more readily observed at clause level.

Designing tasks

Just as the texts were selected and ordered so as to pose progressively greater demands on students, so were the accompanying tasks. As well as the major principle that the tasks should progress in the kinds of demands they made on the learners, another key principle was that the task should mediate between the text and the Hallidayan framework, which was presented as a resource for the class, rather than a task design as such. Features of systemic-functional grammar were introduced only gradually so that the full framework, reproduced on page 39, was only presented in session five.

Thereafter it became a point of reference for the students in completing the specific tasks around texts.

There seem to be two potentially opposing principles in task design when a task supports text analysis. First, the task should match the text (cf. Wallace 1992b: 90) and therefore be tailored to aid access to the specific text. Secondly, however, tasks should have some generalisability and consistency for students so that they can see some coherence of approach across the course as a whole, and in order to ease the pressure of preparation time on teachers. This apparent dilemma can be overcome if one sees tasks as matching not specific texts but genres. Thus the same task format might be used to support analysis of advertisements of similar kinds, assuming, of course, that there is a shared purpose to the text analysis. There is a further dilemma in that the task is part of the text used pedagogically (cf. Chapter 4), and in a critical reading approach should invite resistance along with the accompanying text. One can hardly propose resistance to the activities in published ELT text books while our own designs remain loftily immune from critique. Although this was an issue I failed to address adequately in my own task designs, materials writers such as Littlejohn (1998) offer a rationale by which students themselves redesign, in creative and critical ways, the task material they are presented with.

I include in Figures 5.1–5.4 four task types which represent ways of analysing texts at progressively greater levels of specificity and as related to different genres. The first example, in keeping with the fact that *genre* was the organising principle of the Critical Reading course, is a genre awareness task.

An early classroom activity, which was related to the initial consciousness raising phase of the course, centred around the construct of genre as central to the course. This is an activity which aims to draw students' attention to the sociocultural nature of genres. Working with a wide range of types of text brought into the class by all of us, the students in groups attempted a generic classification, using the framework in Figure 5.1:

Try to classify the texts on each table. Suggested categories might be: requests from charities or causes; public information leaflets; professional reading material; reading for entertainment or leisure

(a) Who produces them: e.g. public bodies, commercial enterprises, local authorities?
(b) For whom are they produced, i.e. who are the consumers or the expected readers of the material?
(c) Why has the text been produced?
(d) Is this type of text of interest or relevance to you?
(e) Choose one text from each category which particularly appeals to you, either because of its style or content and discuss with other members of the group.

Figure 5.1 Genre awareness task.

An incidental outcome of this kind of activity is that students can select specific texts for future detailed analysis during the course. They can, that is, be added to 'the pool' of shared resources. This was the case with a text which Yang, a Chinese student in the group, came upon in the magazine *Marie Claire*. In the feedback from the task, Yang, who had been one of the intellectuals who went to the countryside during the Chinese cultural revolution, responded to the text, which was about the working lives of women in a remote part of China, very much as a code in the Freirean sense, commenting: *This reminded me of my own experience of my own work in the countryside in the 1970s.*

The kind of task we used in a later phase of the class when we were looking at readership, is represented in Figure 5.2. At this stage of the course the students were able to work with some preliminary contextual and textual terms, such as *model reader* and conventional grammatical terms, already familiar to them, such as *verbs* and *nouns*. This task was applied to the advertisement for a car: *Power and Control* (Figure 5.2.1. on page 110).

This reader is	because	the text uses this language			
		Nouns	Adjectives	Verbs	Other
e.g. male working class European		.....	.....	.....	.....
After your comments on the text, note: 1. Do you think that *you* are the 'model reader' of this text? Why? Why not? 2. Is this a culturally familiar text to you? Why? Why not?					

Figure 5.2 Focus on readerships as indicated by linguistic features.

About half way through the course we moved attention to the news report genre, and consequently I provided a different task type to capture the level of analysis which the students were doing at this stage of the course. Figure 5.3 represents the stage at which the class was beginning to refer more closely to the Hallidayan framework and explore ideational meanings within report texts, in particular *participants* and *processes*. The example used in Figure 5.3 relates to the *Violent Homecoming* text, which formed the basis of lesson 9 discussed below, but it is generalisable to other report texts or expository texts. It is what we might call, following Wallace (1992b) a *parallel discourse task*, similar to the one about Singapore, described in Chapter 2, where students are asked to notice how competing

110

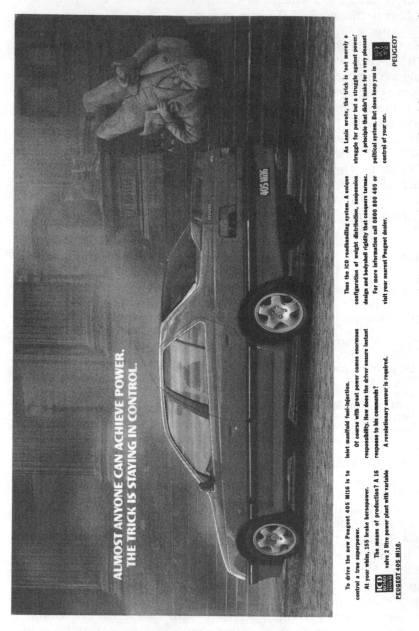

Figure 5.2.1 An advertisement for a Peugeot car alongside a falling statue of Lenin. Reproduced by permission of Euro RSCG.

Read the text *The Violent Homecoming*

1. Identify the major participants within the text?
2. Can you observe any patterns in the ways the participants are described?
3. Do they readily group in any clear way?
4. What noun phrases or verb phrases are associated with each set of participants?

Below is a typical response to this activity, in the form of a parallel discourse task:

Mandela supporters	*Mandela opponents*
Violence and death	White extremists
Mobs ran wild and looted shops	There was bloodshed
Sickening scene of savagery	(An ecstatic black ANC follower) was shot in the
Knifed a man repeatedly	head and killed by an unidentified white man

---

Figure 5.3 Parallel discourse task.

participants are set up in opposition throughout a text. The nature of these oppositions will vary: in the text, *Singapore*, they could be conceptualised as 'Singapore the State versus Singaporeans as powerless citizens'. I have interpreted the set of oppositions which arise from *The Violent Homecoming* as 'Mandela supporters versus Mandela opponents'. This is on the basis of successive readings of this text by students, who have tended to see this divide among the text's participants. Moreover, as a coincidence, Michael Stubbs chose this text for a critical analysis in his inaugural professorial address at the Institute of Education (Stubbs 1990). I have drawn on the additional insights he offers in subsequent use of this text with students. I have also analysed this text along with intertexts, in the form of other news reports. Below, I reproduce first the major parts of the key text – *The Violent Homecoming*, together with three additional 'support' intertexts in the form of the opening paragraphs of news reports which appeared on the same day in February 1990. Each must be imagined in the original format to which the students on the Critical Reading course had access. For instance, the main text was accompanied in the original by the now famous image of Nelson and Winnie Mandela giving a clenched fist salute.

Text extract one: Key text

THE VIOLENT HOMECOMING

Violence and death disfigured the release of Nelson Mandela yesterday. Mobs of his followers ran wild and looted shops in Capetown, where police fired on the crowds.

There was also bloodshed by white extremists in Johannesburg and Port Elizabeth.

Mandela, speaking to a joyful audience in Capetown, warned that the armed struggle by his African National Congress organisation would continue.

He also said his release and other concessions by the government did not mean that international sanctions against the apartheid regime must be relaxed – as Mrs Thatcher has proposed.

SALUTES

With clenched fist salutes, Mandela now a potent symbol of freedom for millions of South African blacks, walked amongst ecstatic well wishers at the prison gates before travelling on to Capetown.

But on the streets of the cities, tension was already boiling over.

At least two people died and more than 200 were wounded in Capetown. In one sickening scene of savagery, Mandela supporters knifed a man repeatedly until he was mortally wounded and then beat and kicked him to death.

In Johannesburg, an ecstatic black ANC follower was shot in the head and killed by an unidentified white man who escaped.

Four people were killed and 17 injured in Port Elizabeth when a car ploughed into a group of people celebrating Mandela's release.

Jubilant blacks also clashed with police in the tribal homeland of Ciskei. Three people were shot dead, with 20 wounded.

In Natal, where ANC supporters have been feuding with a more conservative black group, police said 12 blacks were killed in factional fighting. One black was reported dead and five injured at Inanda, a black township outside Durban, when police fired at a celebration.

The situation in Capetown was highly volatile throughout the day as thousands massed in Grand Parade in front of City Hall, where Mandela was due to make his freedom speech. (From *The Daily Mail* February 1990)

Text extract two

MILLIONS CELEBRATE AS THEIR HERO WALKS FREE

OUT OF PRISON

WE CONTINUE THE ARMED STRUGGLE, VOWS MANDELA

Nelson Mandela walked to freedom yesterday...straight into the fury of South Africa's shotgun wielding police (from *The Daily Mirror* 12 February 1990)

Text extract three

> Mr Nelson Mandela walked out of prison a free man yesterday, and within hours told an ecstatic crowd of supporters in Cape Town that the armed struggle against apartheid would continue (from *The Guardian* 12 February 1990)

Text extract four

> ## WHITES-OUT
>
> RIOTERS SHOT DEAD AS NELSON SAYS: KEEP UP STRUGGLE
>
> Black fury erupted in South Africa yesterday as freed leader Nelson Mandela vowed that the guerilla war against apartheid must go on (from the Sun 12 February 1990)

An activity of this kind highlights for students a clear and consistent inequality of treatment between the participants linked to Mandela and those linked to both white people and the police, both latter groups being set in opposition to the discourses about Mandela in the key text.

In the final lessons of the course, students were working regularly with the full Hallidayan framework, that is, analysing texts at the levels of tenor, field and mode. Typically students would work in pairs, focusing in some detail on one function before sharing their findings with the whole class. Figure 5.4 presents the task which supports analysis of the *Childminder* text, and which the students in pairs were asked to complete. The text for analysis follows the task. Here I have extracted the beginning, part of the middle and the final paragraph. In the original it is accompanied by a photograph of the smiling figure of Mrs Newton, proudly displaying the golliwog and a teddy bear.

Complete the columns below, making reference to the key text and the Halliday framework for text analysis

1. Interpersonal Meanings	2. Ideational Meanings	3. Textual Meanings
Note any use of:	Note who the major participants are and what verbs collocate with what nouns	Note what kind of text this is
• Personal pronouns or ways the reader/writer or main participants are referred to		• How is information presented?
		• What comes first?
• mood and modality		
• language items such as nouns which reflect writer attitude		

Figure 5.4 Making use of the overall Halliday framework of analysis: *Childminder*.

SUPPORT FLOODS IN FOR CHILDMINDER WHO REFUSES TO GET RID OF 'RACIST TOY'

COUNCIL SEEKS COMPROMISE OVER GOLLIWOG

Support is growing for the childminder who faces another confrontation with social services this week over her refusal to give up a golliwog.

Letters have been pouring into Deena Newton's home in Thamesmead, southeast London, from parents and childminders all over the country who back her stand against Greenwich council

The Labour-controlled local authority has refused to issue a registration certificate to Mrs Newton because one of its inspectors, Lorrie Lane, a Rastafarian, is offended by the 'racist toy'. Mrs Newton has compounded the sin, in the eyes of the inspector, by reading Noddy stories to the two children she cares for....

Mrs Newton said...'As for Noddy, they might think he is racist but I am not throwing out the books. I will keep reading them to the children. They have got the attitude problem, not me'...Mrs Martin (a Council Inspector) left Mrs Newton and her husband Paul, a booklet by the Working Group Against Racism in Children's Resources, which says the 'golliwog' has no place in society...

Mrs Newton, who has three grown children and has cared for Chinese, Colombian, Indian and African children, is prepared to work without money to care for the two children. "If they refuse to register me I will not have any choice. Both myself and their parents want me to stay with the youngsters until they are school age. When I look at my golly I think Greenwich, where I have lived for 18 years, has gone quite mad" (from *The Times* January 1994).

Below I shall embed these texts and tasks within some sample lessons procedures:

The lessons

The very early lessons of the course aimed to promote awareness raising of literacy practices and texts, in the ethnographic cross-cultural spirit of the work of Morgan and Cain (2000) and Barro *et al.* (1993) noted in Chapter 2; the middle phase moved into the study of specific textual features, while the final sessions aimed to relate texts to their wider context of use, by drawing more freely on the full scope of the Hallidayan framework. This progression reflects the Lankshear model which starts with a broad look at literacy practices, focuses in on text and then widens out to revisit and relate the readings of specific texts to readings of cultural practices within social settings.

This last phase is embodied not just in the critical work done towards the end of the course, but in the understandings of critical literacy which may remain with students after the end of the particular Critical Reading course.

Once we came to the text-focused phase of the course, the lessons were guided by what I call orientating questions which were originally adapted from Kress (1985), and expanded in Wallace (1992b). They were continually revisited and fleshed out during the course but in their original form were:

Why has the text been written?
To whom is the text addressed?
What is the topic?
How is the topic written about?
What other ways of writing about the topic are there?

Although we moved back and forth among these questions, there was a progression in emphasis in that readership was an early focus in the course, while the issue of discourse options at all levels of field, tenor and mode was largely left to discussion at the end of the course when we had covered more of the detail of the Hallidayan framework. Only then could we begin to answer the more complex final question of 'what other ways of writing about the topic are there?'

As the whole course progressed from looking at literacy practices in quite general ways to close textual analysis, so did the content and tenor of individual lessons evolve over the lifetime of this fifteen-week course. For instance, some of the curriculum knowledge relevant to this class was conveyed transmissively. This kind of transmission teaching was weighted towards both the beginning of the course and the beginning of each lesson where there was often a period of extended teacher talk where key concepts were introduced. Here I shall give an account of three of the lessons, near the beginning, in the middle and at the end of the course, looking in particular at the way in which texts were used and talked about at different stages of the course. The first lesson focuses on the reader, the second on participants and processes, while the final one, at the end of the course, considers, more holistically a set of texts within their contexts of use.

Week four: *Power and Control* – who is the reader?

One of the key concepts which the course aimed explicitly to introduce was that of readership, in particular the notion of *model readership*, and this was the focus of lesson four. Consequently our major question was *Who is the text addressed to?*, which involved identifying the readership of an advertisement for a car. I call this text *Power and Control* and it was the key text for this particular lesson. Preceding the pair work, where students made use of the task in Figure 5.2, was a lengthy stretch of expository teacher talk, part of which I reproduce here, to give a flavour of this kind of pedagogic discourse, heavily metalingual in function. I first introduced the Hallidayan categories as follows:

Note on transcription: a series of three dots:...signals missing information.

When we're looking at texts, we need, these are the things we need to think about generally, OK, in the text, and I've, I've presented here three bits of terminology. For those of you – I know some of you are interested in linguistics, this is taken from Halliday,...and it's a simplified version of his work and that's what we are going to be looking at in detail. And the first thing we need to consider is the field of discourse

This exposition continued for several minutes and included within it the focus for the day's class:

When we're looking at the writer and the reader and how the writer makes contact with the reader, which, as I say, this is what we're going to look at closely today; this is indicated in the text by names, proper names and pronouns in particular. An obvious but quite important thing to look at is personal pronouns – I, you, we, they – how are those very simple words used in the text, and what do they signify?...So you see, this course is not just looking at texts, its also being a little bit analytical about language.

As noted above, the course assumed the need for a working set of terms to talk about both context and text, and this is what had motivated my input here. This kind of transmission teaching is also used to signal what is to come later in the course, which motivates the following section of discourse:

Now these questions down here (on the Overhead Projector) are the ones we're going to move on to: how is the topic written about and what other ways are there of writing about the topic? These two questions are central for critical reading, because what we'll be doing is considering always, how could the text have been written in a different way...we'll be moving on to these questions because these relate to the detail of the language within the text.

Finally I set the scene for the analysis of the car advertisement by preparing the ground for some of the cultural allusions. The Statue of Lenin in the advertisement, makes the point about the ephemeral nature of most advertising. Fifteen years after the end of the Cold War, the cultural reference is likely to mystify the contemporary reader. Even for this group of students, in 1993 closer to those events, I felt that it required contextualising:

And there was, there were a whole lot of advertisements after the end of the so-called Cold War, that looked positively, that erm referred positively to the links between East and West…so what you find then in advertising is the reference to cultural events, to contemporary cultural events and this brings us to the car ad, and the statue of Lenin.

I then moved to the actual instructions for the task:

I want you to look at the nouns, adjectives and the verbs which signal to you a particular kind of reader.…I want you to look at some of the vocabulary in the the car text to work out for instance is the reader,…we use the term 'the model reader'…is the reader of the text educated – or not? Is it possible to say what social class this person is, through the language used? What political views?…in other words we're looking at tenor at the moment.

Commentary

What is striking in the transcript of the lesson is that the early expository part of the lesson consisted almost entirely of input from myself as teacher. It is also strongly directive, as in 'I want you to' twice repeated. There were very few instances of student initiations, mainly to ask for clarification. Only one student, Isabelle, offered a spontaneous challenge to one point I made about advertisements. My comment was that, although advertising was ubiquitous, it was not embedded within genres such as political manifestos, to which Isabelle says:

Why shouldn't they do it? If they are trying to sell and this attracts a readership, so why shouldn't they do it?

Isabelle's intervention here was the longest turn which any student took during the whole of my exposition. One needs to be cautious perhaps in judging such monologue negatively. As noted earlier, classroom dialogue can be monologic in effect, if student contributions merely support the teacher's. Equally teacher monologue can be dialogic, as evidenced, for instance, by students' non-verbal responses and the creation of open text, which aims to prevent the closing down of communicative opportunities, even if those options are not exercised. The patterning of interaction changed considerably from one lesson to the next in the Critical Reading course, and from one class episode to another. Even then, as, noted in Chapter 4, merely to quantify turntaking tells us little about the *quality* of collaboratively produced talk, which I try to capture in more detail in Chapter 6. What one might provisionally conclude is that it is important to consider any single lesson within the context of others, following the principle of intertextuality. That is, any classroom event needs to be considered in the context of what precedes and follows. Indeed it is for this reason that we need to conceptualise a classroom community as evolving over time.

Week nine: *The Violent Homecoming* – **how is the topic written about?**

This class began with our revisiting of three of our four orientating questions: (1) *What is the topic?* (2) *Why has the text been written?* (3) *To whom is the text addressed?* These then were our starting questions, progressing towards the major question for this particular lesson which was: *How is the topic written about?* This question was calculated to move us into analysing the discourse choices within the texts surveyed. The text type under consideration was newspapers and we began the lesson by looking at the headlines of the day's newspapers which we had all brought into class, as previously agreed. After some minutes examining these, we discussed them, by using our three key questions. Not surprisingly, some of these headlines provoked more insightful and interesting discussion than others. For instance, one headline *France facing terror wave by Islamic Groups* promoted an exchange, part of which I quote here:

Estelle: I noticed that usually in Britain we don't speak, er, a lot about France. France is not an interesting subject – France, Italy, Spain – Germany sometimes. But er Brit-Great Britain and the United States...
CW: That's interesting. Some of you, the rest of you, are nodding. Have you noticed this as well? Would you say?
General: Yes
Carlos: Nothing abut Europe
CW: Nothing about Europe
General: Nothing. No

As if to confirm the parochial nature of British newspapers, the main item of news in most of the day's newspapers was *Sunday shopping*, about to be introduced in Britain. The newspapers included headlines such as: *MPs vote for shopping on Sundays, Go Ahead for Sunday Shopping, Bye Bye Sunday*. I drew on these headlines to raise our key questions of what the topic was about, why it had been written and for whom the topic would have interest or relevance. This in turn lead to the discussion of a set of newspapers which I had collected over the previous weekend. I turned to them at this point as they allowed me to move to the next phase of closer textual analysis and to introduce the key question for the lesson: 'how is the topic written about', with reference to *participants* and *processes*. In particular, I wished to show how the protagonist of a news report can be variously positioned as agent or patient, as causer of events or as acted upon, as victim. The texts all related to the news that Princess Diana had decided to have a private life subsequent to her divorce from Prince Charles. These were my words: *How does this locate Diana as the subject?...If we take Diana...is she doing all those things voluntarily? Is she an active agent or is she a helpless victim?* We agreed that she was positioned as victim, and one student, Carlos, added: 'She is the goody'.

The notion of agency and victimhood and, in particular goodies and baddies, allowed me to introduce the texts for the day on *Mandela's release*, with the words: 'these sets of texts represent a momentous event for many of us around the world'. Brief discussion confirmed that this was indeed the major news event for that day in February 1990, for all the countries represented in our group. I reminded them of the language of newspaper headlines by reference to previous work on text headlines such as *Violence Erupts* and *Mob Stone Police*, with the words: 'I gave you these texts (to show how) the same event – more political events (than the claimed retirement of Princess Diana) can be represented through the language in different ways. For example when an intransitive verb is used, it doesn't say who caused the violence.'

We then turned to the texts which were the major focus of the day's lesson. They consisted of four versions of the 'Mandela release' news story; the main one, *The Violent Homecoming*, is reproduced above. The other three, from three British newspapers: *The Daily Mirror*, *The Guardian* and *The Sun* were to serve as intertexts. The aim was to ask students to judge the degree to which the text producers had differed or coincided in the lexicogrammatical selections they had made in presenting the event, and to evaluate the effects. This task was introduced after the presentation of the Hallidayan framework and was designed to encourage a closer examination of some of the key features of continuous texts. While earlier lessons had looked at interpersonally orientated texts such as advertisements, letters and written versions of political speeches, which specifically address a reader – often through some form of second person pronoun – the newspaper texts introduced in this lesson represented a shift to reporting language. They offered the opportunity to introduce some features of ideational language, with a focus on the representation of participants and processes, in particular the way in which the major participant of all the texts surveyed – Nelson Mandela – was variously portrayed. We began our discussion on these texts by looking at the choices of wording in the banner headlines, in particular the word 'homecoming' in *The Violent Homecoming*, noting the striking juxtaposition of apparently anomalous lexical items. Pierre's account of what might motivate this kind of contrast anticipated the task I was about to set. He noted: 'In the text we've got a strong opposition between the whites and the blacks.' My teacherly response was to say to this: 'You've gone ahead of me Pierre. You've already observed one of the things I want you to look at!'

I then proceeded to set up a task which was a warm-up to that represented in Figure 5.3, as follows:

'I'd like to ask you to look at the opening three paragraphs of these four texts and consider how Mandela is talked about. The way – you know the nouns used to talk about him; the verbs that are associated with him. So what we're doing, we're looking at the ideational language. Mandela is the major participant, that's pretty clear. How is he talked about? and the (other) question is what other groups or what other participants are mentioned in those first three paragraphs? So,...look at them on your own and then turn to your neighbour and see if you notice the same things or if there is some disagreement.'

Commentary

There are more instances of challenges to the teacher than the single instance noted in *Power and Control*. These challenges remain, in this initial teacher-fronted part of the lesson, exchanges between a single student and the teacher. On the subject of Sunday shopping, Carlos challenges my implication of triviality, incidentally claiming the last word in our exchange:

CW: Why has this been chosen as the front page news? I mean, why this rather than all the other things that might be happening in Europe and not just in Europe – but in Africa, round the world...why do you think?
C: Because that's very important for the economy
CW: You think it...
C: for the economy
CW: is important?
C: Yeah. Definitely it is

The syntax of my question serves to close down rather than open up interpretations. 'All the other things' presents these 'other things', not in fact selected as significant, as more important than the 'Sunday shopping' topic actually selected. We could call this an 'ideological question' in that I clearly invite an affirmative response through the wording of my question. For this reason Carlos's challenge is all the bolder. Later there is a further exchange where Carlos similarly pursues a point, implicitly challenging my presentation of the main Mandela text, and incidentally alluding to the importance of intertextuality.

C: Was was this the first report about his release or there was something else before this, er article because...
CW: no I...
C: it makes a big difference
CW: it does
C: Maybe before, they said Mandela has been released. The next day, they say *The Violent Homecoming* – makes a big difference.

I quote Carlos's contribution here, because not only is it substantively astute, but it signalled one of the first occasions when a student began to claim some equality of membership in the class community, till then strikingly dominated by myself.

Week fourteen: *Childminder* – **What other ways of writing about the topic are there?**

This was the penultimate week of the course, the final one being reserved for the end of course assignment. My aim was to return to the context/text relationship on which the course had been broadly based, that is, to reaffirm the need to see any concrete text as arising in specific situational and wider cultural contexts. With this in mind, I introduced the four texts we were to work with on this occasion, all intertextually related: the key 'childminder' text, first brought into class by Monica and read at home by the students, along with three support texts. These 'intertexts' were an update on the childminder case, from a recent newspaper report: *Noddy and Golly are cleared as council backs off*, an extract from one of the original Enid Blyton Noddy books *Noddy Goes to School*, where a golliwog is featured as one of the characters, and a dictionary definition of 'golliwog'.

After setting up the broad genre category of news story, and the set of texts we were to work on, I elicited from the students some of the categories we had used during the course to describe the way in which texts are grounded in social and cultural contexts, and which, by the same token, make particular demands on the readership in terms of background knowledge. In other words, what kinds of non-linguistic knowledge did readers need in order to offer adequate interpretations of the texts under scrutiny here? I noted that text and context worked in parallel, saying: '...it works both ways. What happens is that you use the context to understand the text... but as you read the text that helps you again in understanding more about the context....so there's an inter-relationship, all the time, between the actual text and the context'. I then asked for contextual categories from the class – a question which generated this set: general knowledge, culture-specific knowledge, knowledge of recent events or local knowledge, knowledge of genre, knowledge of writer. The first specific task of the lesson was then to look at the text (the key *Childminder* text) again and think about the kinds of contextual knowledge needed to understand the text. In other words, what had created difficulty for the students when they were doing their first 'response' readings at home, in preparation for the lesson? what kinds of contextual factors helped or frustrated them?

The students then worked in small groups and the following conversation gives some flavour perhaps of the way two Spanish students and one Chinese student negotiated their understanding of what the term 'childminder' means in a British cultural setting:

Valle: Is there a difference between childminder and babysitter?
Yang: uhu
Victoria: Do you have childminders?
Yang: We have farm girls, from countryside, from the countryside and but really, take care of one child

Victoria: One child?
Yang: and lives with someone's family and that's like er this child[mind
Victoria [minder
Yang: who can just look after three babies or three children
Victoria: We don't have those things in Spain
Valle: What's the difference between childminder and baby sitter?....
Yang: the difference is not so....in China, baby sitter lives with the fam,
    family, and paid by the family without any certificate, registrations.

While the meaning of 'childminder' was fairly readily resolved in such discussion, the issue of racism and what constituted racist behaviour was, understandably – and necessarily – problematic. The following extract shows the students' exploratory talk about golliwogs, during further pair work which discussed cultural and contextual difficulties. In particular, Yang and Victoria are trying to understand the racist connotations of the black doll, at this point by reference to the main *Childminder* text.

Victoria: Are they racist, er dolls or not?
Yang: ..what...
Victoria: I don't know, I don't know, from the text I cannot get it. I think
    that they, they say that it's a racist erm doll, but I cannot see any racism
    in playing with er black doll or white....I cannot see – its <u>good</u> if you
    play with it, it means that you're accepting'

The students then had an opportunity to look at the Noddy story which I had brought in. I reproduce an extract of this here. The book is called *Noddy Goes to School*.

"You go away," he said to the little golliwog. "And don't come bothering me. I'm going to wash my car". The little golliwog didn't go away. He just stayed, and watched Noddy get out the hose and begin to wash his car. "When are you going to clean its teeth and brush its hair?" asked the cheeky golliwog, presently. "I'll wash your face and clean your teeth first!" said Noddy fiercely, and he turned the hose on to the small golliwog. The water splashed into his face and made him yell. Mrs Tubby Bear came over from next door and laughed. "That just serves the cheeky fellow right" she said. "He's a scamp. He keeps coming and knocking at my door and then running away. Its clever of you to wash his face for him so suddenly!" Noddy felt pleased. He watched the little golliwog running down the street, water dripping from his naughty black face.

After looking through the book, from which this piece is extracted, Victoria was less equivocal about the racist implications of 'golliwog' as articulated within this particular story:

I think this story is racist, the way they say...the white child is happy of, er, doing harm to the black one, I don't know. I wouldn't like if it was a, a white erm, child either...do you underst – its its the attitude of the white child, what, I don't like and besides the the weak person here is the black child, so that makes it racist. I don't know

Similarly Yang commented to the whole group:

When I read the story (that is, the original *Childminder* text) I really didn't think about the racist er racism, because I think we can use all kinds of colours er to make toys, but when – with this connection between this er Noddy and er golliwog, I think that really is not so right, to let small children get very clear pictures in their brain about black boy er black small child and a white faced child

We see Victoria and Yang linking past readings with present ones, still not making any definitive judgements about whether golliwogs are racist toys, but exploring how the discourses around skin colour within children's - stories might construct racist stereotypes. Their initial hesitancy to use the term 'racist' makes the point that interpretations evolve and change in the course of further readings, reflection or discussion with their class mates.

After the group work in which students had explored some of the cultural meanings within texts, as a whole class we continued to explore, refine and rethink these key concepts (supported by access to the intertexts). A prolonged discussion of racism and naming, particularly around the offensiveness of 'wog', in the context of 'golliwog' then led to this contribution by Yuko:

CW: Yes, if you say 'nigger'..that would be a very shocking word. Negro less so. Because of the way these words. Because all words have a history you see, and that history is changing of course...There are disagreements. There was a Conservative politician on television the other day saying it didn't matter what you call people, but I think if you say that to most black people..I mean sometimes Japanese and Chinese people are called rude, rude names aren't they.

Yuko: Oh yeah. I was called erm face to face..the English officer called me 'Jap'

CW: Really

Y: Yeah. I was very offended but because I was just in front of, you know, going through immigration, so I didn't say anything..

CW: So how did it come up then, what did he actually say?

Y: Um, I don't know. He was standing behind other immigration officer, she was dealing with me and then he just erm, he looked very bossy, and he just took all the paperwork and he said, erm, something like, and then said: 'Oh this Jap' and this was very offending to me.

Commentary

Yuko's comment on her experience is partly invited by my question, addressed to the group as a whole, which included Yang, the Chinese woman, rather than directly to her. Even so, it is a fairly rare moment of disclosure in the course as a whole. It is possibly no accident that it occurred towards the end of the course and within a relatively smaller group. It was also introduced in the context of a lengthy discussion on racism which had brought us to this issue of name calling. It was personal but also timely, and not gratuitous in the way personal sharing approaches can be, as I suggested in Chapter 3. It should be emphasised too that Yuko did not volunteer this kind of personal detail earlier in the course.

Conclusion

I reproduced the extracts from this final lesson partly to show that interpretations of texts and judgements about unequal treatment in text, here articulated around racism, are not readily and immediately arrived at. A criticism of CDA has been that ideological meanings are merely lifted from texts, or more insidiously, with strong mediation by committed CDA pedagogues, implanted in learners. It is certainly possible to identify instances in my classroom data of unjustifiable closure of interpretation, especially through ideological questions. However, viewed over the longer term of a course in critical language study, the processes of making sense of texts are tentative, and exploratory, with earlier judgements being revisited or discarded at different stages of lessons and the course as a whole. Also, even though we have some evidence from the students' words above of adjustment to their initial interpretations, these remained provisional. They had still to undertake the more in-depth analysis of the texts, supported by the task on page 113. Moreover, while progress towards greater truthfulness and truth is a goal, the ultimate aim is not for closure. The talk changes in tenor to become constative, more carefully elaborated, rather than conversational, but is still not dedicated to the articulation of definitive conclusions about the nature or content of the texts under scrutiny. In Chapter 6, I look at the classroom processes which support some of these more fine-tuned interpretations.

6
Talk Around Texts: The Analysis of the Classroom Interaction

In Chapter 5, I offered a preliminary account of the classroom procedures in the Critical Reading course. Here I take a more fine-tuned look at the classroom text, in particular the manner in which the social and the pedagogic intertwine, as students and teacher share their responses to texts.

The episodes featured in this chapter are from the same lessons as introduced in Chapter 5. Following the opening episodes discussed in Chapter 5, the students moved into pairs or groups to conduct closer textual analysis by working with the framework and the task. Subsequent to this close analysis of the texts, where students made notes on the task sheet, came the class feedback session which is presented here. We see the students, led by a spokesperson for each group, sharing their analyses within the wider classroom community. The expectation is that this feedback episode will feature more discursive and extended talk to reflect the fact that students have had the opportunity to gain insights from each other within their groups, as well as the planning time to prepare more considered responses to the texts under scrutiny. Broadly I am focusing on the functions of selected communicative sequences within these three classroom episodes, which I shall refer to, following the key texts we discussed, respectively as *Power and Control*, *The Violent Homecoming* and *Childminder*, all reproduced in Chapter 5.

Just as I used field, tenor and mode to interpret the context of the texts studied in the Critical Reading lessons, I shall draw on these same parameters to interpret the context of the classroom text. Of course it is, in practice, hard to tease out the ideational, interpersonal and textual functions. In use they are necessarily woven together. Nonetheless I have drawn here on tenor and field – to a lesser degree, mode – as a heuristic in the analysis, a way to illuminate some key features of equality and quality in the classroom, or, in terms used by Sarangi (1998) in his analysis of classroom discourse, the manner in which what he calls 'task talk' and 'procedural talk' work together.

Tenor, field and mode revisited

Tenor

The key question is, how far is it possible within the constraints of a classroom setting, institutionally ascribed as an unequal encounter, to move some way towards reciprocity in teacher–student exchanges in order to acknowledge the principle of equality of contributor rights in discussion genres? Goffman's overriding notion of footing can be linked to tenor. Footing is signalled by a whole range of behaviours, apart from verbal language, such as gesture, stance and eye contact, none of which, in the absence of video, I am able to capture in my analyses. Accompanying these shifts in typical classroom behaviour may be the changing use of modality and mood, in particular the use of questions. It is less interesting to note the mere occurrences of questions than the function they serve in the overall speech event. For instance, the teacher as animator may use questions to steer students towards the anticipated answer, animating not just the syllabus or the textbook, which may prescribe particular answers, but, more widely, reproducing the ideology of classrooms and of language teaching. Even when substantive, that is, directed at the elicitation of real answers (rather than rhetorical or managerial) the questions may be ideologically charged, as I note in Chapter 4; these are questions of the kind 'guess what teacher wants you to think', slightly differently inflected, as noted earlier, to Guess What Teacher Thinks questions. Finally the teacher as author may be interacting in her own voice, still in role as teacher but adopting a questioning style which is exploratory and interactive and which does not guide students to some pre-envisaged response.

Of course, it is not just the teacher who can shift or initiate new footings. Students too can, through their own adjustments of footing, by certain use of questions or challenges for instance, initiate or contribute to a wider change of tenor within the classroom community, always on condition that the teacher, as overall controller, either acknowledges such openings for realignment or permits any mitigation of power relations. As I argue later, it is only when all participants are acting as authors, that some approximative equality of tenor can be achieved and we might offer some defence of the classroom as a critical community.

Field

The key question is: how is reasoning and reflectiveness made visible in the classroom exchanges through the manner in which teacher and students expand on the points of view expressed and the claims made? In strategic talk the goal is to persuade, through a range of classical rhetorical devices; in casual conversation we might simply state that X is the case, assert a belief or comment experientially, as in the extract from Morgan, quoted earlier in Chapter 5 where the class teacher asks why his year 10 secondary school students laughed during the screening of romantic scenes in *Romeo and Juliet*. The students' answers stayed close to their own experience. What I aimed to do in my class was to push students beyond the experiential, in order to examine the way in which argument is developed across rather than within individual student and teacher contributions. One feature which will accompany constative or discursive talk is the use of modality (one might wonder, for instance, what my own use of *will* is adding discursively to the previous sentence). Modalisation is important ideationally, as well as interpersonally, in the sense that it contributes not just to the manner of speech but more substantively to the quality of propositional meaning, in its signalling of the commitment of the speaker to the truth and truthfulness of what is said.

As a further kind of evidence of the quality of the discussion, I shall examine conjunctive relations within and across clauses. Motivating this selection of feature is the view, argued above, that adequate argument involves the presentation of reasons for beliefs or points of view, as well as the preparedness to elaborate on and qualify statements offered. In particular, circumstantial expansion (cf. Halliday 1994: 225) allows an argument to be made explicit and therefore more readily either accepted or disputed. Halliday (*op. cit.*) offers an account of expansion which includes three main types of conjunctive relations: extension, elaboration and enhancement.

Expansion: extension, elaboration and enhancement

Extension

In extension, one clause extends the meaning of another by adding something new to it (Halliday 1994: *op. cit.*). This is the most common type of expansion to be found in the classroom data presented here and is exemplified by statements which introduce a further point or which are adversative. Students may extend their own or others' contributions. An example is in Episode one, where Carmen offers two successive extensions to the argument around the readership of the text, the first solicited by the teacher, the second spontaneous:

Carmen: Its for men especially

   (Several lines later she adds)

Carmen: And the language is quite difficult as well I mean

Elaboration

In elaboration, one clause clarifies or rewords what has preceded it. The secondary clause does not introduce a new element into the picture but restates, clarifies or refines (Halliday 1994: 225). Teacher reformulations are good examples of moves which may aim to sum up, put more clearly what a student has been saying. An example from Episode one is:

CW: so, we've got an educated reader, someone with political and economic power and male

But students may also elaborate each other's contributions, as Carlos does:

Well, we have the same as them – I mean, you know, intellectual, maybe male, we agree with that (Episode one)

Enhancement

Cases of enhancement are evident where one clause qualifies another by reference to time, place, cause or condition (Halliday 1994: 232). Examples would be the use of clauses prefaced by 'so', 'otherwise' or 'similarly'. Most relevant in discursive talk are clauses which provide conditions, concessions or which offer reasons for beliefs or states of affairs. An example, taken from Episode two is by Pierre:

Pierre: In most articles…Mandela was referred to as the leader because he's the one who talks as if he was the brain..

These circumstantial relations may not be made explicit through grammatical marking in discursive talk. However, even in the absence of the specific linguistic signal it is possible to observe and comment on the presence of expansion and the role it plays in argument.

One precondition for the investigation of talk which is expanded in this way, is that the talk needs to be sustained. Silverman (2001: 21), writing about therapy discourse, notes that the therapist might consciously or otherwise organise talk for maximum or minimum uptake by the client. Much the same applies to teachers. How is the talk, largely under their control, organised for maximum uptake by students? There would seem to be both institutional and wider cultural norms. Alexander (2000: 400), in his extensive cross-cultural study of school classrooms, observed the fullness of some of the answers provided by the Russian pupils in his study, in contrast to very limited responses by students observed in other countries. Certainly in much of the literature on second language classrooms a striking fact of classroom discourse is how short the turns at talk are. In Van Lier's extensive classroom data, provided in his 1988 book, I could find no instances of student turns beyond two lines. Clearly, single clause or brief utterances offer limited opportunities for expansion, although there may be expansions across turns. However, cross-turn expansion of student utterances is also rare, as most student turns revert to the teacher.

Expansion is more frequent and arguably more varied in particular types of extended discourse, more so say in exploratory, constative talk than in narrative. Constative talk will also make reference to other points of view more readily, consistent with its need to be accountable. To rehearse Mercer's point once more about exploratory talk: 'knowledge is made more publicly accountable and reasoning is more visible in the talk' (1995a: 37). It is this visibility of reasoning which I am largely concerned with under 'field of discourse'. Of course reasoning will be present in the absence of its verbalisation and as Adjer and Hoyle (1998) in Cazden (2001: 177) note, it is difficult to tease out the difference between actual developmental progress, whether linguistic or cognitive, and opportunities for its display. Elaboration of syntax in itself does not indicate complexity of thought – it may be empty verbiage. Nonetheless, greater explicitness through verbal expansion, at least allows students to rehearse more complex kinds of talk, at the same time offering fellow classroom participants specific warrants which can be either accepted or challenged.

Also under the broad category of field of discourse is content and knowledge building. What evidence is there that the students are drawing both on the linguistic resources provided by the framework for analysis as well as their existing cultural resources, and developing new ones to gain greater awareness of the manner in which language, both as a phenomenon in the real world and as used within specific texts, reinforces or challenges prevailing ideologies? In other words, what particular tools do students use to articulate awareness at both a macro level, related to awareness of the context of production and reception of texts, as well as at the micro level, related to the ability to offer specific warrant for interpretations?

Mode

I shall not comment specifically on mode within the classroom analysis, on the grounds that the structuring of classroom discourse is largely given. Mode is here more constraining, because lessons are institutionalised to a greater degree than speech genres such as casual conversation, with assigned roles to teacher and learners as participants. However, adjustments of tenor and field, even within fairly circumscribed events such as lessons, may ultimately reshape mode, challenging dominant orders of discourse which continue to privilege certain ways of doing things in classrooms. Bakhtin talks of the plasticity of genres, the possibility to 'reaccentuate' even familiar and structured genres (1986: 79). Under what kind of circumstances might orthodox patterning of classroom interaction be reaccentuated? What space is there for learners as well as teachers to reshape the lesson genre in more or less fundamental ways?

A note of caution

One needs to be careful in making claims that the infringement of normal rules of discourse, in this case classroom interaction, necessarily signals some kind of qualitative advance in classroom-based critical language awareness. Lapses in usual turntaking procedure might signal not enhanced reciprocity or dialogicity but that the teacher has simply lost control of the proceedings! Nonetheless, atypical occurrences, marked shifts in footing, can be revealing in that they signal the potential for change in positive ways – change in the way both interpersonal and ideational meanings unfold in classroom discourse. A key question therefore is one which, as argued earlier, is central to critical analysis and critical pedagogy: how could things be different? The challenge is to taken-for-grantedness; about both *what* we say and *how* we say it; what spaces can be opened up to facilitate critical enquiry around texts in the classroom?

In short it can be of interest to note occasions which go against the grain of typical classroom discourse, which, for instance, infringe the general rule that student turns will be specifically solicited by the teacher and that some kind of Initiation, Response, Feedback structure will prevail. As Young (1992: 76) puts it: 'The optional components (of genres)...may be crucial in analysing the critical potential of them.'

A further note of caution relates to the danger of getting lost in the micro analysis. Just as with the texts studied in class, so with the analysis of lessons themselves, in looking at the detail, it is easy to miss the wider picture. How do the course participants relate discourses within the texts we survey to wider discourses in society (one of the criteria given earlier of a CLA perspective)? In my summaries to each episode, I try to open out the discussion to bring in some of these broader implications.

Selection of segments

I have selected key exchanges, called *segments*, from within the three feedback episodes, on the grounds that they demonstrate both typical classroom interaction, but also occasional departures from established patterns, thrown into relief when set against conventional discourse. Seeming infringements may be realised either in unusual patterns of turntaking or atypical footing or a greater degree of expansion on the students' part.

Notes on the extracts

1. The turns are numbered for ease of reference. The literature on turntaking notes the difficulty of establishing what constitutes a turn, as opposed to a supportive interjection. Here I have not counted as turns those occasions where a speaker 'talks across' another contribution – especially where it forms a minimal response – and does not specifically acknowledge it.

2. With no video recording I was unable to capture wider semiotic features. However, I have occasionally noted one or two which are of special significance, such as laughter.

3. I have simplified transcription conventions for purposes of readability and clarity. This means that while the transcription aims for a faithful record of what was said, minor hesitations and overlaps are omitted. Because classroom interaction frequently involves turns which are assigned by the teacher, with relatively little spontaneous interruption, I have noted occasions which go counter to this, that is, where students intervene rapidly either in interacting with each other or the teacher. These rapidly succeeding turns are indicated by a series of three dots at turn end. Prolonged pauses, on the other hand, are signalled by (...) to indicate the number of seconds of silence. In the segments under closer scrutiny I have indicated the following features:

- Overlaps: [
- pauses over one second: (.), the number of dots indicating the number of seconds
- rapidly succeeding speech:... at turn end
- Emphasis: –

4. The episodes are each about 15–20 minutes in length and were selected from weeks four, nine and fourteen respectively of the fifteen-week course. In these episodes the students are reporting back from their group or pair work analyses. The talk is therefore relatively planned, and they are referring to notes they have made and the completed tasks, which featured in Chapter 5. The episodes were recorded with students speaking into the microphone.

Week four *Power and Control* – readerships

Students in this episode are: Hanna from Germany; Carmen, from Spain; Carlos, from Spain; Victoria, from Spain; and Yuko, from Japan. (We join the episode at the point when Hanna has been arguing that the text *Power and Control* constructs a reader who is educated, has some political knowledge, and is probably fairly well off.)

1 *CW*: Anything else you want to add? That's good so far.
2 *Carmen*: Well, its for men especially, because its like men are in politics, they know more about the war, what's going on, I mean its......
3 *H*: They're sup<u>pos</u>ed to know more.
4 *C*: Yeah, well, they're supposed (general laughter)
5 *CW*: Yes. You always.. yes...

6   C: and the language is quite difficult as well I mean...
7   CW: and men can understand more difficult language, you think?
8   C: (laughs) No, I don't think so but they may think so
9   CW: Yes, this came up I think in [that..in]
10 [C: especially compared with this one]
11 CW: Yes, when you look at the other one (another advertisement) –
    that makes the contrast doesn't it? I think some of you had the chance
    to look at this one, which is, you can see, clearly for women – the
    heart shape and so on. So, we've got an educated reader, someone with
    political and economic power and male. Let's move on and see if we
    can. . . . Thank you very much. That's good.

Comment

Tenor

I open and close this segment as principal, in charge of turns at talk and taking on the classic teacher role, as I reformulate, at the end of the segment,
Hanna's contribution preparatory to handing the floor to the next group.
Questions are managerial rather than substantive. They tend to function as
polite directives as 'Anything else you want to add?' or are broadly phatic as
in the tag question 'that makes the contrast, doesn't it?' – where I offer no
opportunity for students to respond. Evaluations do not refer substantively
to the quality of the student's argument, so much as impose closure on
an exchange, as in 'Thank you very much' and 'That's good'. It is Hanna
who triggers a shift of footing. Her unsolicited turn in 'they're supposed
to know more', with the second syllable of 'supposed' heavily emphasised,
produces the kind of sequence which Kramsch (1993) calls a 'sideplay' in
classroom interaction. The turns which follow her intervention do not
move the interaction forward, but in the way they echo what has just been
said, they build the social text of the classroom, offering some mitigation
of teacher power. In a series of rapidly exchanged turns, Hanna, Carmen
and myself offer mutual solidarity (we know what men are like!). A similar
overlapped sequence, shortly afterwards, in turns 9 to 11, further shows
how overlappings can be interpreted as offering solidarity as much as
indicating interruption. The tenor of the discourse becomes more egalitarian
as I adjust footing to take on more of an authorship role, relaxing if not
quite abandoning my role of principal in the classroom discourse as a whole.
Finally, however, I take control of the floor and move on to the next
exchange with Carlos.

Field

Through joint scaffolding in the rapid series of exchanges, there is the beginning of a collaborative construction of argument: first Carmen adds to

Hanna's contribution, enhancing it with her reasons for assuming a male readership. The point is then elaborated, that is, qualified spontaneously, without teacher intervention by Hanna's: 'they're supposed to know more'. Then in the following turn Carmen extends by first echoing Hanna's comment and then offering new information regarding the difficult language. Half humorously I interpret this as an enhancement – I pretend to assume a cause/effect relationship which is unintended by Carmen, who gets the joke and laughs. The only long turn is taken by myself and used to make a categorical statement, which is briefly illustrated but not expanded: 'some of you had the chance to look at this one (talking of a second advertisement for a car) which is, you can see, clearly for women. The heart shape.' I then reformulate the discussion, a classic managerial move on my part, and offer the floor to the next group:

12 CW: Carlos?
13 *Carlos*: Well, we have the same thing as them – I mean, you know, intellectual and all that, political, maybe male – we agree with that. And just to say two more things: it employs technical speech, a little bit of technical speech to give security to the potential buyer I think er – when it says all this about 'inlet manifold fuel injection' – I don't know if the common reader knows about that – what do you think?
14 CW: manifold fuel [injection..?]
15 *Carlos*: [When you think about] 'manifold fuel injection' you have to be into the matter to know about that, so it gives importance, I mean it gives security to the potential reader. What else do we have here? Excuse me (looking at the prepared notes) I believe that the whole advertisement doesn't make sense at all (general laughter) and I think they do that on purpose. I think they do that on purpose because that way...
16 *Victoria*: [It does. It makes sense]
17 *Carmen*: [It makes sense]
18 *Carlos*: [It makes sense? The whole thing?]
19 *V*: It makes sense. Yes very clear
20 CW: Christine is it?
21 *V*: No, Victoria
22 CW: Victoria, I meant Victoria
23 *Carlos*: I wish everybody could explain to me (laughs)
24 CW: OK Victoria thinks it does make [sense.
25 *V*: [Yes it does
26 CW: So would you like to say what the sense is?
27 *V*: It does, because the car is a super car. It's a powerful car, so it's like a big enterprise, like a country. Lenin, applying his principle, was not able to manage the political system in his country and he fell, but you, applying this system, and being responsible, and with control, you can control this super car.

Comment

Tenor

This segment is bounded by two relatively extended turns which sandwich a series of brief exchanges. Interpersonally two features stand out. First, Victoria claims the floor supported by Carmen with a direct challenge to Carlos, in the form of an adversative extension contradicting his claim. Second, rather than welcoming this spontaneous extension of Carlos's turn as an opportunity for the students to build their own classroom discussion, I maintain bogus control. My question, 'So would you like to say what the sense is?' is a managerial question which serves no purpose, as Victoria is clearly about to offer her interpretation of the text in any event. This question follows a redundant – even obstructive – intervention on my part: 'OK Victoria thinks it does make sense', an unconscious desire to broker the exchange between Carlos and Victoria. I am intervening with a display of power, 'snatching a turn' from a student as Reynolds (1990: 125) puts it. At the same time, though my failure to respond to Carlos's direct address to me – 'what do you think' – at first looks like non-compliance, closer listening to the tape reveals that Carlos's question is phatic, as he offers no space for me or other participants to reply.

Field

In his extended turn, Carlos acknowledges membership of the class community with the use of 'we' to signal the shared interpretation which has been arrived at in his group, for whom he is the spokesman. At the same time he also makes reference to prior contributions in the class: 'we have the same as them'; 'we agree with that', briefly reformulating the text of the previous pair of students. He then extends the text of Hanna and Carmen, at the same time as elaborating his own text, by giving reasons for the chosen wording in *Power and Control*: 'to give security to the potential buyer'; 'so it gives importance...to the potential reader'. A few lines later Carlos addresses the whole group, making reference to the classroom as an interpretative community: 'I wish everybody could explain to me'. This shift of footing subverts the norm by which the teacher holds rights to the distribution of turns.

Victoria's long turn which closes this segment is similarly discursive. She enhances her claim that the advertisement makes sense with the use of a clause of reason: 'because the car is a super car'. She then elaborates with: 'it's a powerful car'. She extends this clause with a clause of manner: 'it's like a big enterprise, like a country'. The following clause contains further enhancement with a clause of result, although this is not explicitly marked: Lenin was not able to manage the system and (consequently) he fell. There then follows an adversative clause introduced with 'but', to mean 'on the other hand'. In addition there is an embedded clause of condition though not explicitly marked; 'but you, applying this system, and being responsible, and with control, you can control this super car.' We understand this to mean: 'on condition that you apply this system and are responsible then (unlike Lenin) you will exercise proper control'.

(In the final segment selected from this episode, I bring in the contributions of a third group, which includes Yuko.)

28 *CW*: You were saying..?
29 *Yuko*: Pardon?
30 *CW*: You were saying...she's shy (laughing) that you picked out some of the vocabulary that gave you the impression of a male reader.
31 *Y*: Oh yes yes. I thought especially the phrase, it says: A 16 valve 2 litre power plant with variable inlet manifold fuel – injection.
32 *CW*: Yes, yes, you see its not just 'manifold fuel injection'. It's that whole phrase [isn't it?
33 *Y*: [Yes, it's a whole phrase]
34 *CW*: It's a whole noun clause, isn't it: 'a 16 – you can hardly say it – a 16 valve 2 litre power plant with variable inlet manifold fuel injection'. That's all one noun phrase.
35 *Y*: That's right [yes
36 *CW*: [But why does that suggest masculinity to you?
37 *Y*: Because its about car and if you're talking about car maniac its normally a male. For example, my brother is crazy about cars (laughs) – I mean automatically, it's indicate to me it's about men.

Comment

Tenor

This segment represents a more typical classroom sequence than the previous ones in its demonstration of the teacher's exercise of her right to allocate turns. While the other students show relatively marked assertiveness, taking the floor spontaneously on several occasions, Yuko risks a different kind of infringement of classroom discourse through her initial reluctance to speak at all. In fact classroom turntaking rules require a response; Yuko has no option of silence and has to at least say 'pardon' as she resists being selected to talk. Nor can she say that she has no view whatsoever on the matter which is an option in non-classroom genres. At this point in the class Yuko is a less confident participant than Carlos and Victoria. Nonetheless while this justifies some cajoling, a more open invitation to contribute of the kind I offered to Carlos would have allowed Yuko to formulate, not just her own position but that of the group of which she was part. As it is I position her with my prompt: 'You were saying that you picked out..vocabulary that gave you the impression of the male reader.' I allow her only a reactive turn. In listening to the tape what is also striking is the speed with which I interrupt, in turn 34 and intervene, especially as Yuko's echoing response: [Yes, it's a whole phrase] indicates that, given more space, she might have elaborated on her own contribution.

Field

Yuko's response offers an enhancement, with a clause of reason to support her judgement of the maleness of the advertisement. However, she does so with reference to her personal experience rather than any supporting evidence from the text or the context of situation in which the text arose. My intervention, ostensibly an elaboration to reformulate Yuko's contribution, simply repeats her own observation adding little new of substance apart from the confusing claim that the phrase beginning 'A 16 valve' – Yuko herself has already used the term 'phrase' – is both a Noun Phrase and a Noun Clause! At least my final question 'why does that suggest masculinity to you?' is substantive, one of the very few in this episode. As such it produces an expanded response from Yuko.

The wider picture: from text to context

Critical language awareness is characterised by close attention to text but also the need to move beyond commentary on specific texts in order to draw wider social and ideological inferences from the existence, content and design of text. Specifically I have argued that in critical language study there is a text/discourse dimension, which focuses on specific textual features; that this relates necessarily to the context of production and reception which is, in turn, linked to the wider social/political landscape from which the text takes its ideological bearings. How far are these wider as well as more specific purposes of CLA in evidence here?

At the micro level of attention to specific textual effects the students' comments remain at a fairly general level, with little use of metalanguage, as in, for instance: *the language is quite difficult; it (the text) employs technical speech; the phrase...gives the impression of a male reader.* When we turn to the context of production and reception, largely constrained by the nature of the task which required them to consider *readership*, the students focus on the context of reception, rather than the context of production. Teacher and students discuss the model reader almost entirely in terms of gender, particularly by reference to the use of technical language. The theme: 'reader as male' is extended across the text: first introduced in turn 2 by Carmen, it re-emerges, later in this sequence:

CW: Who is 'you' by the way? When you say: 'you can control?'
Victoria: The man (hesitates) the economic power, you know
CW: The male reader?
V: I don't know why 'male', because I didn't find anything but you get that
   feeling

Carmen: yeah you get that feeling…
V: that it's a man. I was looking for something here that would tell me that it was a man, the reader, but I couldn't find anything, but you have that feeling.

There is some evidence that the students are developing a concept of reader which includes not just the actual, real-life reader but the intended or model reader. Thus we have, forming some kind of lexical cohesion across the text from different contributors: 'the reader, readership, the reader, the potential buyer (as a reader of an advertisement), the common reader, the potential reader'.

At the more macro level, we might have expected students to widen out their commentary to embrace the extended political metaphor in the advertisement. However, the students make only very generalised reference to political discourse, through allusions to 'political system,' 'political power' and the mention of Lenin himself. Victoria interprets the metaphor of Lenin embedded in both visual and text. However, she does not extend her interpretation to what might have motivated the choice of political discourse to carry the more expected sales discourse; in particular the students make no mention of an ironic/humorous stance to communism taken by the text producers through references to 'revolutionary', 'superpower' and 'the means of production'. We see how the advertising text, quite typically, as Fairclough (1989) has noted, colonises discourses from other spheres of public life. The students do not note the resonance it is assumed this text will carry for the contemporary Western reader, appearing as it did at the time of the collapse of communist regimes across Eastern Europe. Indeed they seem to have only a vague notion of Lenin's role in twentieth-century history, 'the war' being mentioned unspecifically by several students. As we look again at this text, a few years into a new century, one is bound to wonder whether anyone would now draw on Marxist discourse, at least in the public domain. This reaffirms the point, raised in Chapter 5, about the ephemerality of genres such as advertisements.

In short, we see that the students are beginning to use some metalinguistic tools to make judgements about the readership of a specific text. However, they are not, as evidenced here at least, moving much beyond the particular text; that is widening out their readings to offer implications for social life about the prevalence of certain genres and the discourses embedded within them which daily confront us.

Week nine: *The Violent Homecoming* – participants and processes

Students in the episode are: Pierre (French, arrived since lesson 4), Estelle (French), Carmen (Spanish), Carlos (Spanish), Victoria (Spanish), Monica (German), Christine (German).

(The students are referring to four texts about Nelson Mandela's release. The opening paragraphs of three of these, along with the text of *The Violent Homecoming* are reproduced on pages 111–13.)

1 *CW*: (Switching on the tape recorder. General laughter) I feel a little bit like a a showman, or a showwoman with this. *OK, Sssh* Quiet then. I heard some very....Can we start then with this end – Pierre, do you want to say something?

2 *Pierre*: In most articles, especially this (he indicates the main text: *The Violent Homecoming*) Mandela was referred to as the leader because he's the one who talks um..um..as if he was the brain and then there are the followers – the arm – and the only difference was in the first paragraph where we noticed that he wasn't the subject of the sentence...

3 *CW*: this one here? yeah...

4 *Pierre*: as if was taken over by the events, as if he didn't control the the flow of violence.

5 *CW*: Well yes...

(Carmen signals directly to Pierre that she wishes to come in at this point, by claiming the microphone from him.)

6 *Carmen*: I don't think so.

7 *CW*: You don't agree?

8 *C*: No

9 *CW*: You want to say something more about that?

10 *C*: I think yes they talk of him as a leader but he's the leader of a criminal gang – is like he is the baddy, no, and the black people are the baddy, er I don't know. So he is going out of the prison so he more or less implies that eh he knows what is going to happen when he's released but he doesn't care or something like that.

11 *CW*: Thank you that's interesting you were taking slightly – well different views but you, that..em...

12 *Pierre*: especially the first one.

13 *CW*: Yes that in a sense is he the sort of victim of events or is he..? – I think both are true...

14 *General*: yes, yes...

15 *CW*: in a funny sort of way eh oddly be..because texts can mean two things at the same time. Let's remember that, there isn't you know because this is where language is so complex. So I know what Pierre was saying – if I can come in – where it says for instance it talks about 'the release of Nelson Mandela' whereas what do the other texts say, did you notice? How do they describe..yes?

16 *Victoria*: In the rest of the texts he's the subject – he walks to freedom or walks out of prison or – he's the subject and there's one interesting point that Estelle noticed: in the first text (*The Violent Homecoming*) the rest of

the participants are accompanied by the possessive 'his followers', 'his African National Congress Organisation'.. 'his release'. So its somehow blaming all the violence on Mandela, all the violent erm participants are related to Mandela explicitly.

17 CW: This is why I think both what Pierre was saying is true and what – you know both those impressions were made, because it's true 'his followers' – All the way through the violence is associated with Mandela but at the same time he's not. he he's made powerless er by because the opening subject is 'Violence and death disfigured the release of Nelson Mandela'. Good. Did anyone want to comment still any more on the way Mandela is the subject of these opening paragraphs.

Comment

Tenor

A striking feature of this extract is Carmen's direct challenge to Pierre, 'I don't think so' accompanied by a non-verbal signal that she would like the microphone to be handed to her. However, again I mediate in this exchange, 'you don't agree?' (turn 7), showing a reluctance to allow students to take the floor from each other. Many of my turns consist of managerial questions which select students for a turn, for example: 'you want to say something more about that?' (turn 9), which are largely redundant in view of the apparent willingness of the students to pursue autonomous debate. I appropriate or steal turns directed to others. The result of this behaviour overall is to restore the classic Initiation, Response, Feedback (IRF) pattern, whenever it is at risk of disruption, and to keep turn allocation in the teacher's gift. However, as an attempt at compensation, I redress a subsequent intervention, with a mitigating 'if I can come in.' which can be seen as some acknowledgement of parity of speaker rights. One kind of question which, as argued in Chapter 6, has a more fundamental potential to shift overall tenor, appears here. My question in turn 13, 'Is he the sort of.. victim of events or is he?'.. while hesitant and ill-formed, because authored 'on the spot', is exploratory, formulated within continuing, negotiated debate. This kind of discourse is of its nature reflective and hesitant, and relatively rare in classroom interaction. However, the feedback or evaluative move remains standard, as I claim superior status by offering thanks for contributions (cf. e.g. turn 11).

Field

Pierre in turn 2 begins by enhancing his claim, through simile, that Mandela is seen as the leader ('he talks as if he was the brain') and then elaborating metaphorically on the notion of 'brain', seeing Mandela's followers as 'the arm'. He then provides a further extension of his argument by offering an exception to his overall case, with reference to the first

paragraph of *The Violent Homecoming*. This point is in turn elaborated
through exemplification, more particularly figurative expressions, as in: as
if 'taken over by events' and 'as if...he didn't control'. Carmen's spontaneous challenge to Pierre: 'I don't agree' is based on her reading of the
conflicting discourses within the texts, especially *The Violent Homecoming*
one, which constructs Mandela as both hero/villain, agent and victim
of events. However rather than allow her to develop this idea more fully,
I reclaim the floor and curtail the development of this discussion. I reformulate for Carmen rather than allow her to elaborate. I also speak on
Pierre's behalf in: 'so I know what Pierre was saying', rather than allowing
him to complete his point, or allowing both Pierre and Carmen to
construct their own argument. Such attempts at closure are typical of classroom discourse. However, there is one new departure here: at several points
I offer authentic, authored reflective responses to the ongoing discussion.
One example is in my attempts to reconcile the position of Carmen and
Pierre: 'Is he the sort of victim of events or is he – I think both are true.'
And, following on from that: 'because texts can mean two things at the
same time. Let's remember that'. Arguably this shift in both field and tenor
of discourse facilitates Victoria's unsolicited entry into the discussion at
this point. What is striking about her contribution is both the use of
metalanguage (still not often volunteered by the students) as in 'participants' and 'possessive', but also her acknowledgement of her partner as a
resource: 'There's one interesting point that Estelle noticed'. Victoria does
not just show accountability to the learning community but proceeds to
enhance Estelle's observation, with a clause of result: ' so its blaming all the
violence on Mandela'. I then elaborate on Victoria's point about the use of
'his', bringing in the twin discourses of violence and powerlessness. Overall
there is a sense of co-construction of argument. These are unplanned and
therefore more authored contributions, particularly from myself, noticeably more hesitant than earlier ones, the turntaking less smooth but which
signal a stronger engagement with the substantive arguments presented.

(I introduce the next segment with: 'We haven't had Carlos and Franco.
You're not usually shy. Do you want to add anything?')

18 *Carlos*: OK. About which one, this one – or this one – or which one?
     (referring to the four texts)
19 *CW*: Well let's take <u>any</u> of them because they're different aren't they?
20 *Carlos*: OK well it's quite interesting the beginning (cf. *Daily
     Mirror* text on page 112): 'Nelson Mandela walked to freedom
     yesterday straight into the fury of South Africa's shotgun wielding
     police' er the police here are the baddies I think and Nelson
     Mandela is the goody in a way. You see 'police opened fire on a
     section of the welcoming crowd in Cape Town' so its you know

giving the active role to the police instead of to the black crowds and erm then after this in this one, this is a very good one, this is a very good report about what's going on- it gives relevance to the fact that he has be...

21 CW: I think Carlos means this one (the Mandela text extracted from *The Guardian*, cf. page 113)

22 *Carlos*: Yes this small one here, I think this is quite a good one because it gives emphasis first to the release of Mr Mandela – and it says 'Mr Mandela' which is a good treatment I think. And now this last one is unbelievable (from the *Sun* newspaper, p. 113). It says 'Whites Out'. It's quite violent, shocking. It says: 'Black fury erupted in South Africa yesterday as freed leader Nelson Mandela vowed'. etc. etc. and 'Black gang clashes' and all that. This is quite violent, shocking. And that's it.

23 CW: OK. Thanks very much.

Comment

Tenor

At this point the tenor shifts back to smoother turntaking. Carlos waits to be invited to take the floor, offers his interpretation, which does not make reference to his group's discussion, being presented in the first person, and closes it formally and rather baldly with 'that's it'. The tone is less discursive and maintains classic non-reciprocal rules of exchange. He offers a contribution, and I thank him for it because he has performed the classroom task. This is rather different from the more substantive and authored responses I offer to Pierre, Carmen and Victoria in the first segment of this episode.

Field

Carlos offers a fluent and expanded response. He elaborates the claim that the police have the 'active role', are 'the baddies'. However, although he exemplifies and enhances to the extent that he offers a reason why the *Guardian* treatment of topic is good because it thematises Mandela, he fails to elaborate on his reason for saying *why* 'Mr Mandela' is 'a good treatment'. Carlos tends to reiterate at the affective level through use of strong adjectives such as 'unbelievable', 'shocking' and 'violent', but does not support his claims with fuller enhancement nor clarify with elaboration.

24 CW: Does anyone want to look at how the groups, the participants are grouped together in the other texts? We've already said a little bit about this. Anyone want to say anything more for instance about 'Whites Out' (cf. *Sun* text, p. 113) Estelle?

25   *Estelle*: The headline shocked me because 'Whites Out' for me it's a
     reference to something against blacks in fact, because..it could say
     'Blacks Out' and it will, it would have been a racist headline and it's
     very shocking because...I think that this article is racist really because
     of the title, because erm 'whites erm – rioters shot dead as Nelson says
     "Keep up struggle"..and 'whites were terrorised as young blacks er cele-
     brated Nelson Mandela's release'. All the faults are put on black people.
     I think you can say you can say that you can say that its racist.

26   *CW*: Do people agree with Estelle on this point...

27   *General*: yes, yes...

28   *CW*: about that fourth text in particular from *The Sun* – no surprise –
     that the participants are polarised in terms of blacks versus whites?
     And in fact those of you well you've looked at this text most of you.
     What did you notice? Let's take the blacks and whites as two sets of
     participants. It's quite interesting to look: blacks versus whites, police
     versus crowd, you know, to look at groups in opposition. What did you
     notice about *The Guardian* text? About the blacks versus whites?

29   *Carlos*: This is from *The Guardian*?

30   *CW*: This is from *The Guardian*, yes.

31   *Student*: It's neutral

32   *CW*: It gives the impression of neutrality but there's a reason, a very
     clear reason why that is, in terms of the participants in the text, who's
     talked about simply. Have another look at that in terms of the blacks
     versus whites. It's quite interesting I think. (....................about
     20 seconds pause) Anybody want to comment? It's pretty...

33   *Estelle*: the crowd the crowd is called 'supporters' which is positive.

34   *CW*: Yes, very good. The crowd are supporters, which is positive, of course,
     not mobs. But what do you notice about the blacks and whites also (..)

35   *Student*: There's no opposition (.)

36   *CW*: Christine?

37   *Christine*: Hold on a sec

38   *CW*: Hold on a sec. All right. I won't rush you. (..)

39   *Ch*: He's more, in a way he's more em I would say compared to the others
     one there's more objective. He just says actually what's happening and
     he's not like telling you that, like the last one, that as soon as you just
     have a look at it you know that, which side it is. The other ones is more
     more more relaxed in a way.

40   *Monica*: I think he talks about 'apartheid' and the others don't., I mean
     I'm not too sure, but I think.

41   *CW*: Well what I was thinking of – I don't want you to guess what's in
     my head – it's simpler than that really. The fact is I think in *The Guardian*
     text that blacks and whites are not mentioned at all. Maybe that was
     too obvious to you. It's quite important that the crowd are not identi-
     fied as black.

Comment

Tenor

What is striking about this segment in terms of tenor is the sequence of turns beginning: 'What did you notice about the *Guardian* text – about the blacks versus whites?' This signals the start of a string of GWTT questions and I am aware of – and uncomfortable about – the motivation of these questions, shown by my commentary on my own practice in turn 41: 'I don't want you to guess what's in my head!'. The students' responses are tentative, there are long pauses and uncharacteristically unconfident bids from participants such as Monica: 'I think he talks about apartheid, and the others don't but I'm not too sure'. Christine in turn 39, produces a far less coherent response than usual, in the rather desperate effort to 'find out what teacher thinks'. At least she offers some resistance with the words: 'hold on a sec'. Overall, the turntaking pattern consists of rather futile bids from the students, which are noticeably brief and relatively unexpanded, as they struggle to come up with the expected answer. This sequence reveals how GWTT questions may close down constative talk, not surprisingly in view of the fact that they have an inbuilt power dimension, one which would seem to be peculiar to classroom discourse; it is hard to imagine another kind of speech event which would feature one participant inviting others to imagine what he/she is thinking of, apart, that is, from certain parlour games!

Field

The longest and most interesting turn, ideationally speaking is Estelle's (turn 25). This links indirectly to Carlos's in reiterating the notion of shock about the *Sun* news report on Mandela. However, while Carlos tends to affirm: 'Its quite violent, shocking', Estelle expands on her initial response and moves the quality of the discourse on in a critical sense by hypothesising what the effect of a different wording would have been, honouring the paradigmatic principle of CDA by which we imagine the effect of different substitutions: she justifies her judgement that the headline is racist by inviting us to imagine the effect of a direct replacement of the actual words in the text – 'whites' – with the word 'blacks'. She first enhances with a clause of reason: 'because "Whites Out"...and elaborates on this point before further enhancing with the hypothesis: if it had said "Blacks Out" that would have been clearly racist. She then further elaborates her position in a summing up of her overall argument, concluding with an implied enhanced clause of consequence, to the effect: therefore you can say the article is racist or "considering that..." you can say that its racist.' In other words although some ultimate opinion on the presence of racism is offered quite decisively, we see the reflective process through which this judgement is reached. The reasoning is visible in the talk, in Mercer's terms.

The wider picture: from text to context

At the micro level, students offer more references to specific text linguistic features than in the first episode, particularly around the key notion of the lesson: *participants*. Thus we have:

he (Mandela) wasn't the subject of the sentence (turn 2)
he's the subject (followed by exemplification) (turn 16)
the rest of the participants are accompanied by the possessive (turn 16)
the violent participants are related to Mandela explicitly (turn 16)

Most of these comments come from Victoria, who was far more willing than other students to offer specific textual warrant for her comments. More typically, for instance, Carlos notes the effect of linguistic choices without, however, elaborating on the manner in which grammatical choices have combined to create that effect, for example in turn 20: 'police opened fire on a section of the .. crowd' is 'giving the active role to the police' and in turn 22: 'it says Mr Mandela which is a good treatment I think'.

In terms of knowledge of immediate context, the students have been informed that these were all front page news reports of the same event on the same day. The critical reading tasks based around the Mandela texts had required the students to note the different discourse options selected by different newspapers. This involved drawing on some background institutional knowledge about the varying political allegiances of the British press. Much of this knowledge had been introduced via analysis of news texts in earlier lessons. The students were able to recognise a broadly left stance in one of the newspaper articles. However, rather than allowing the students to articulate and develop this knowledge explicitly for themselves, I gave the students very restricted options for comment, with ideologically loaded questions such as 'is it from a left wing or a right wing paper do you think?' (not included in the transcript here).

It is Estelle who, in turn 25, introduces the theme of racism into the classroom discourse by way of offering a supported and elaborated judgement on one particular text. In doing so she moves beyond micro-interpretation to social implication. However, I fail to build on her contribution, deflecting this line of enquiry in which the students show interest, as suggested by their interjection during my turn 27, of 'yes, yes' and pursuing a related but more specific point about equality of representation in a different text.

Week fourteen: the *Childminder* – ideational, interpersonal and textual meaning

The students in this episode are: Yuko, Victoria, Franco, Monica.

(We join the episode at the point where Yuko and Victoria, who have focused on ideational meaning, are about to offer their interpretation of the text.)

1 CW: So Yuko are you going to be
2 Yuko: Oh yes
3 CW: report back on your discussion?
4 Y: Yes we found lots of participants here er the main participant is the council.
5 CW: mmm, well, I think the council, I suppose yes the council…
6 Y: and childminder yeah, and childminder Mrs Newton and also in relation to 'support' the parents and other childminders are very important as well we thought.
7 CW: Yes do you want to say a bit more about why why the parents come into the picture – not the children so much but the why – yes because the other noun, the noun that leads the whole article is 'support' isn't it? Do you want to say something more about it, whose support and what kind of [support?
8 Y: [Yes erm what we found confusing is a bit like erm support for what? – we are talking about. Is it..well because this Mrs Newton's attitude…its not so clear, – clearly said here, we don't know if she's a real racist or just doing her job as a childminder. We don't know that. We have to know that first and 'This support' meanings become a different meaning as well – is it supporting her being racist or is it supporting her being a childmind, good childminder? We don't know yet (laughs)
9 CW: That's very interesting yes. what evidence is there in the text for those, positions do you think. or why – let's put it differently why is it ambiguous?
10 Victoria: She never says she's not a racist. She never says that. I think she's so convinced of the way she's been brought up and everybody's been reading these stories for a long time er well maybe we're all racist and we don't realise. It's a part of our conscience – consciousness.
11 CW: What is racist? this is the thing…
12 V: and maybe the council is trying to reject this and trying to..trying to erm separate the concepts and tell you that this is racist, I don't know.
13 CW: Who's trying to say that? Sorry?
14 V: The Council – the Inspector, but its also funny that the Inspector is Lorrie Lane – they give us the name and they also straight away they say that he is a Rastafarian.
15 CW: 'Lorrie Lane, a Rastafarian', [that's right
16 Yuko: [Yes
17 V: Yes. Its maybe they are saying that he is, erm, he considers the toy a racist toy because he's a Rastafarian not because he's an Inspector. It's like he's not objective.
18 CW: Mmm
19 V: Maybe
20 CW: That's an interesting point. That the first desig, desig, well it does say 'because one of its inspectors Lorrie Lane a Rastafarian' but then you might say is that relevant? Do we need to know whether he's a Rastafarian?

21   *V*: Yes, that's why – why do they say it?
22   *CW*: Sure and it's always an interesting thing when you're looking at participants, what information is selected er and what is relevant?
23   *V*: It's like when we were talking about 'the naughty black face'
24   *CW*: Yes
25   *V*: The same
26   *CW*: yes, that's right you can make that connection. Why mention something? Because one of the…we don't state the obvious.

Comment

Tenor

Yuko responds unhesitatingly, even though she waits to be addressed. The 'we' shifts in her discourse from the *we* of the pair who looked at ideational meaning (i.e. Yuko and Victoria), as in 'what we found confusing', to the *we* as part of a wider community of (critical) readers: 'We don't know' (repeated three times). Her initial quite firm declaratives as in 'we found lots of participants' give way to a series of interrogatives and negative statements: 'support for what?'; 'Mrs Newtons's attitude – its not so clear – clearly said'. The questions are not clarificatory questions directed at me. They are exploratory. Yuko takes up a different footing to that typically adopted by students. Her apparent hesitancy need not be interpreted as lack of confidence, as evidenced in the strong modality of: 'we have to know that first'. This asserts the need for caution in reaching an interpretation. My response 'that's very interesting' is authored. That is, I am responding substantively, not in role as principal, as when merely acknowledging and validating a turn. I do indeed find it interesting, and have not anticipated Yuko's response. Her observation of the textual ambiguity in the title is not one I had noticed. In short, I have largely abandoned any reformulating or evaluative role. So in turn 7, although I push Yuko to extend her answer, I do not evaluate it in terms of some pre-specified notion of adequacy.

In the subsequent series of turns, between myself and Victoria who self-selects to take the floor, there is a further shift in teacher role towards what Young (1992) calls 'fellow enquirer'. The tenor is characterised by uncertainty, evidenced, as with Yuko's contributions, by the assertion of not knowing as much as knowing and questions which are exploratory; that is, they are neither intended nor received as requests for answers to specific questions, as in 'what is racist?'. Not only do I as the teacher not have the answers, the questions are not readily answerable Questions are responded to not with answers but with expressions of uncertainty or with further questions, as in 'Do we need to know whether he's a Rastafarian?', 'Yes that's why – why do they say it? Sure'. This exchange is less status-marked than most classroom interaction in that it is hard to identify teacher or learner roles. This is apparent too in Victoria's comment: 'Its like when we were talking about the naughty black face.' Here the 'we', unlike in Yuko's earlier usage, refers to the classroom community, that is, our earlier shared discussion of *Noddy Goes to School*, p. 122. This manner of referring to texts and discourse, as in 'remember when we looked at the other ad' (Episode one) is usually in the gift of the teacher. Finally there is also a relative absence of the evaluative or feedback move. The three short turns of mine (nos 11, 13, 15) can be seen as supportive or clarificatory rather than an attempt at reassertion of control, in view of the fact that Victoria's continuations are not responses to my interventions, but rather spontaneous expansions on her own train of thought.

Field

Yuko initially uses material and unmodified relational verbs to signal strong agency and a degree of confidence in her assertions: 'we found lots of participants; the main participant is the council; and other childminders are very important as well we thought'. Then in turn 8, she extends on my prompting her initial turn by posing a problem around the interpretation of the text. However, a surface hesitancy masks a confident toleration of uncertainty, as we see by Yuko's extended and elaborated enhancement beginning: 'Because this Mrs Newton's attitude and ending... We don't know yet'. Her point is not that she personally does not understand but that the text headline is open to several interpretations. She thereby acknowledges the principle of textual ambiguity. My response is evaluative in a substantive way of Yuko's point and my question, 'why is it ambiguous?', functions not as an invitation for someone to take the floor with a specific answer to the question, but as an exploratory open question: 'Lets think about why....' Victoria acknowledges this function by not attempting to answer my question in any direct way but by elaborating on Yuko's discourse about racism. The sequence which then follows proceeds, as noted above, by a reciprocal extension of points or echoing of questions, which are posed not in the expectation of an unequivocal response but in order to problematise the text:

27 CW: I forgot to ask Monica an important question – why she chose this (text) in the first place – It's *The Times*. *The Times* is a fairly...
28 Y: Con[servative
29 V: [Conservative
30 CW: Conservative paper – not as much as the other *The Standard* (from which a second article about the Childminder case was taken) but nevertheless there is a tendency to have an idea of what we call 'loony left' councils – you know what 'loony' means – mad – you know these extreme left wing councils who are always making a fuss about racism – you know. (The overhead projector collapses.)

31   CW: what happened!
32   V: It's a loony...machine!
33   CW: It's broken (laughter). Anyway, we can't use that. Well are there any other observations you want to make about the verbs perhaps that are used?
34   V: They're all mental processes – more, the majority of them
35   Y: It's 'off[ended' or 'refused'
36   V: [Offended
37   V: and for instance, they don't stress that the parents and the child-minders wrote the letters. They say 'letters have been pouring in'. They start a sentence like that. They don't stress who is..It's later on that you get the er – it's impersonalised. I don't know how to say it in English.
38   CW: Yes it is its they want to emphasise it seems to me the...
39   V: support...
40   CW: the support. That's that's the main subject. Perhaps you found that in looking at the textual features. Let's move on to talk about the text, textual features because it all comes together really; textual features are how the language is put together really what is..Do you want to say something Franco?
41   *Franco*: Well, we have been focused on how the information is presented. So we have direct speech and indirect speech. The first one – direct – we have the council spokesman, Mrs Newton, the council spokeswoman, and then Mrs Newton again. In the indirect speech we have Mr Lane, the Inspector then – well we are not very sure if this part.
42   CW: Which part is that?
43   F: about the booklet which says 'the golliwog has no place in society' we are not sure if this is indirect speech. (.)
44   CW: Which column is that? (reads) 'Mrs Newton – no Mrs Martin left Mrs Newton a booklet by the Working Group against Racism in Children's Resources which says the "golliwog" has no place in society' – that's an interesting example because – no that's indirect speech erm "the golliwog" has no place' – golliwog in inverted commas

(explanation continues for several minutes)

Any other comments you want to make? (.)
45   F: Well apart from this, we have been commenting on the whole text, because we thought that the writer is for Mrs Newton. It's not for the council. The council is in a weak position here.
46   CW: How's that indicated do you think by the language? If it is, is there something in the text that suggests that?
47   F: Yes, let me see Yes, let me see...............
48   M: ......What the council says as well – nothing much, they want the compromise now. But Mrs Newton is very strong, she knows what she is doing.
49   CW: That's right [yes.

50 *Yuko*: [I think the last bit as well – it's within a quotation but it says: "has gone quite mad". (general laughter) It doesn't say – *The Times* won't say that kind of thing but <u>she</u> says

51 *CW*: Yes, that's nice, that's nice. Well put.

52 *Y*: It's [within quotations

53 *CW*: [She's allowed to say that, so *The Times* – exactly – you know, might seem like it's a more serious newspaper, and that's the importance of where you place, what prominence you place....like you know, it ends with....Mrs What's her name has the last word. Mrs Newton has the last word.

Comment

Tenor

Overall there are more unsolicited turns from the students than in earlier episodes. Monica, Yuko and Victoria all volunteer turns, with Franco the only one who contributes only when selected by myself. Noticeable is the echoing of responses, with slightly overlapping turns, as in

Y: Con[servative
V: [Conservative and
Y: It's 'off[ended' or 'refused'
V: [Offended

One shift of tenor both in terms of taking the floor with a change of topic and in terms of the substantive quality of the contribution occurs at the end of this segment, where Yuko volunteers a turn, even though she was not in the group which was considering textual features. In turn 50 she overlaps my minimal response *That's right yes* with the words: 'I think the last bit as well'. Nonetheless, rather than allowing Yuko to pursue her point I retake the floor, interrupting her attempt to elaborate in turn 52 and myself claiming the final word and closure of this segment of the lesson. Like Mrs Newton I have to have the last word!

Field

There is little expansion of my own point of view here. However, there is greater encouragement of expansion of students' positions, through the use of substantive questions, as in 'you mean the writer?'. Franco here does not voluntarily extend arguments beyond his prepared turns. This is partly because he is dependent on Monica with whom he has been working, and he defers to her in this feedback episode. However, the other students in this group are beginning to spontaneously expand their own and others' talk. Again one notes how Victoria in particular extends on points I make, not waiting for specific invitation. This happens in a sequence which begins:

CW: '..any other observations you want to make about the verbs, perhaps that are used' and ends with
CW: ...they want to emphasise, it seems to me, the
V: the support
CW: the support (turns 33–40)

Finally, Yuko's intervention in turn 50 is not just interpersonally significant as an unsolicited intervention but ideationally and substantively introduces a fresh topic linked to the textual function. As with her earlier observation on the ambiguous meaning of *support*, hers is an insightful and pertinent contribution, in this case related to the manner in which the use of quotation allows the text producers (*The Times* newspaper) to distance themselves and ultimately disclaim responsibility for a point of view.

The wider picture: from text to context

Metalinguistic terms are used more frequently in this episode than in earlier ones though still sparsely. In this task students, in pairs, were asked to comment specifically on ideational, interpersonal and textual features respectively. Yuko, in the 'ideational' pair with Victoria, introduces the key notion of 'participant' and then goes on to exemplify the major participants in the text. However, this metalinguistic term is not kept consistently in play through the discussion of ideational features. Victoria in turn 34 introduces the term 'mental processes', though only in response to a prompt, as follows:

CW: any other observations you wish to make about the verbs perhaps that are used?
V: they're all mental processes – more, the majority of them
Y: 'offended' 'refused' (turns 33–35)

Orthodox grammatical terms, not specifically dependent on the Hallidayan framework are more readily used, as in:

Franco: So we have direct speech and indirect speech. The first one – direct – we have the council spokesman, Mrs Newton, the council spokeswoman, and then *Mrs Newton* again. In the indirect speech we have Mr Lane, the Inspector.

More frequent than the use of metalinguistic commentary is reference to the effects of wording in the absence of specific labelling. This is evident where a section of text is problematised as in:
Yuko: Support for what? – its not so clearly said here (turn 8)

Victoria: They give us the name and they also straightaway they say that he is a Rastafarian (turn 14)
Victoria: They say 'letters have been pouring in. They start a sentence like that. They don't stress who is..It's later on that you get the er – it's impersonalised. I don't know how to say it in English (turn 37)

We see that Yuko and Victoria allude to the underlying or hidden grammar, as in 'support for what?'; 'they don't stress who is' (i.e. who is writing the letters) but largely dispense with the metalinguistic apparatus.

At points where references widen out from the effects of textual wording to the making of links between those wordings and the context of production and reception, the most frequent references relate to the political allegiances of the newspapers under discussion. It is noticeable that I position the students with rather narrow ideological questions. An example, from elsewhere in this episode is: 'Anybody want to say any more about the "Labour controlled Council" – is that just innocent information perhaps?' My question clearly favours a negative response: of course not! Yuko's comment in turn 50: '*The Times* won't say that kind of thing but she says so' is a more sophisticated observation, in that it relates to a deeper layer of grammar. My own comment relates just to lexical wording – the choice of 'Labour controlled' to qualify 'council' – a feature which is generally more visible in the grammar than the effects achieved by punctuation to which Yuko makes reference.

Finally some of the students begin to address the wider socio-political context in ways, I have argued, which are key to a macro view of CLA. On this occasion this wider discussion is conducted around race, especially in the exchanges between Victoria, Yuko and myself. The matter of racism is introduced into the discourse by Yuko: 'We don't know if she's a real racist or just doing her job as a childminder.' In topicalising race, Yuko is privileging the interpretative community over writer intentionality. It is unlikely that the producers of the *Childminder* article would wish to claim race as salient in their text, in response to the key question: What is the topic of this text? Certainly the lexical item 'racist' features more frequently in the oral classroom discussion than in the written text, where it collocates not with Mrs Newton, as in the classroom text, but with 'Noddy' or 'toy' (and then equivocally and ironically, as the use of inverted commas around 'racist toy' appears to suggest). In the early part of this episode, race is a major theme across the first 6 or 7 turns of the interaction, kept in play largely by Victoria who elaborates on it in a number of ways. Thus we have:

Y: 'we don't know if she's a real racist' – 'supporting her being a racist'
V: 'she never says she's not a racist' – 'maybe we're all racist'
CW: 'What is racism.'

We see how the theme of race is elaborated across turns, through particular uses of mood and modality: the uncertainty indicated by the use of interrogatives, for example, 'what is racism' and the strong use of modal expressions to qualify statements, particularly Victoria's repeated use of 'maybe' suggests an exploratory search for meaning rather than the need to reach definitive interpretations. The effect is to problematise the concept of racism.

In opting to make this the dominant discourse within the text, the students may have been influenced by the many discussions we had on race throughout the course. As a discourse it circulated in various guises, for instance as orientalism, exoticism, xenophobia or prejudice against people of colour, in many of the texts we surveyed.

Summarising comments

Let us revisit the key questions for the classroom analysis set out in Chapter 4:

1. Given that inequality is built into teacher/learner interaction, even in a class of adults, to what extent is the teacher able or willing to relinquish power in the conduct of the interaction? How can the classroom speech event become more dialogic?
2. Secondly, how is rational consensus achieved? That is, on what basis are points of view or more extended arguments accepted or rejected? More specifically, in what ways, if any, do students draw on the linguistic metalanguage introduced through the Hallidayan framework, to support their textual analyses?
3. Finally, and crucial to critical pedagogy goals, are the students enabled to locate specific analysis and interpretation of texts within wider sociocultural contexts, in order to show awareness of ideological constraints and possibilities, as evident within texts and more generally within social life?

Overall the purpose of raising these questions is to challenge the lesson genre, to reaccentuate it, in Bakhtin's terms (1986: 79), in particular to rethink our expectations of what happens in language lessons. How far is it possible to challenge the transmission view of knowledge about language, which is, I have argued, typical of communicative as much as traditional classrooms? How far can we envisage lessons where foreign language learners, rather than being positioned as inexpert, as novices, debate and construct views about language, especially language ideology?

Observations on features of equality: the tenor of discourse

By and large within the classroom data analysed here, rather than entering into the debate, as a co-participant with the students, I use my turns managerially, acting very much as principal in Goffman's term, in order to locate the present discussion within my wider brief for the course. This is especially so in Episode four, *Control and Power*. My turns do not 'invite a responsive attitude' as Bakhtin (1986: 76) describes it, as we see in: 'This is what we're going to try and do...' 'This is why I gave you this'. The longer turns are used to make categorical statements, which are not supported by argument. Certainly, one might expect tighter framing of classroom interaction early on in the lifetime of a class, with the teacher adopting a footing more in keeping with her role of principal or animator than of author and this is borne out by the teacher turns in Episode one where the teacher talk is almost entirely managerial. The interaction is tightly controlled, even though there are occasions when students are signalling a readiness for direct engagement with each other and a readiness to take the floor.

By the second episode, when the students settle into this discourse community and understand its rules, there is some evidence of a loosening of framing by the teacher. Nonetheless, the students are denied opportunities to respond on their own behalf to challenges or queries from each other. Pierre's intervention in Episode two, turn 12: 'especially this one' signals a willingness to keep the floor, a wish denied him by my insistence on attempting some kind of formulation of Carmen's and his own positions. In particular, there seems little to justify the persistent GWTT questions evident in the series, 'What did you notice' and 'Have another look', especially with students who are showing an ability to engage in discussion in more independent ways.

By the final episode, possibly because of the reduced size of the class on this occasion, there is some evidence that the tenor of the classroom setting has shifted. This is evidenced in a greater number of exploratory questions, more spontaneous turntaking by students, and mutually supportive talk both between the students and between teacher/student. This is apparent in the sequence of turns between myself and Victoria which, while still dominated by me, are echoic in effect: for example,

It's like when we were talking about the 'naughty black face'
yes
the same
yes. that's right.

However, it is important to add that this kind of smooth exchange of turns tends to occur only between the teacher and one particular student. It may be that in granting the floor to one student who is eager to take and hold it, other students' floor rights are being infringed. Sarangi (1998) discusses how teachers position learners through their talk so that, perceived less able students are engaged with largely through procedural, more managerial talk, more substantive talk ('task talk' in the terms used by Sarangi) being reserved for the perceived 'able' students, of whom Victoria would certainly be one, in this particular class.

Observations of features of quality: the field of discourse

The teacher's job is not just to maximise equality of participation but to monitor and promote quality of talk. There is little evidence of this happening in the first two episodes. Particularly in Episode one, there is a preoccupation with local and longer-term control tactics and strategies and a relative neglect of the need to listen to what is being said substantively and to invite from students, not simply additions but clarification and expansion of argument. Several students show that they are ready to create a critical community. Victoria, Hanna and Carlos offer turns of extended discourse which honour some of the key principles of constative speech, as they give warrants for points of view, and refer to the classroom community. However my own discourse, especially in early lessons, provides little of the kind of shared reflection which can promote higher quality discussion.

By Episode three, while there is a greater degree of reciprocity in the mutual expansion of points between me and Victoria, this is not reflected in support for each other's arguments on the parts of the other students nor in the other exchanges between teacher and students. Franco, for instance, interprets the mode of discourse more as transmission style teaching and responds to me by merely listing the instances of direct and indirect speech in the *Childminder* text. When he acknowledges uncertainty, it is with a request for clarification from the teacher. It is left to myself to do the exploratory talk around the text. Franco is thereby denied the opportunity both for more extended talk and to learn through talk. On the other hand, other students are beginning to use constative discourse to explain their thinking to others. Moreover, some of them, such as Victoria and Yuko, offer quite complex expansion of argument and are prepared to acknowledge uncertainty and ambivalence in the interpretation of texts, a key aspect, I have argued, of critical talk and critical literacy.

A further major principle in the development of critical talk is that students should incorporate the arguments of others within their own, either to dissent or to support. There is little evidence of this here, although in Episode two Victoria points the way by acknowledging her partner Estelle's observation and then elaborating on it. It is likely that my own over-zealous intervention worked against the students' building the kind of mutually supportive critical community which we see them poised to develop at certain moments in these classroom episodes.

Conclusion

To take a metaphor from the the text studied in the first episode, we need as teachers to aim for control rather than power, if we take power to mean domination solely by virtue of being in authority rather than an authority and control to mean the judicious use of means in the teacher's gift which ensure equality of access to learning. The teacher necessarily exerts two kinds of authority, one based on her institutionally ascribed role as teacher – as principal in Goffman's terms; another on her superior knowledge and experience. Both however are negotiable to some degree, especially in the case of a small group of adults where possibilities exist for considerable loosening of framing. We might imagine a version of critical pedagogy which involved the radical dismantling of all forms of teacher control with no inherent superiority of rights to talk. Pragmatically this would bring us closer to conversation and would in principle also bring one closer to the ideal speech situation characterised by Habermas. I do not embrace such a version in this book, on the grounds that a supposed egalitarianism, which falsely assumes that students have equal rights to teachers is disempowering rather than liberating. Nonetheless, within the constraints of classroom convention, there is potential to reshape the genre. If we as teachers shift footing, asserting authorship of our materials, views of teaching and views of the world, we can offer students too the space to become authors rather than just animators of classroom discourse.

Finally what did the students learn from the course? Because I am not working with baseline classroom data which might show what good discussion or good critical talk looks like, any claims as to growth in awareness in the case of this particular class are necessarily tentative. However, in looking in some depth at classroom interaction, it is possible to observe moments when the students appear to be moving towards differently focused ways of looking at texts in the larger sociocultural contexts in which they circulate. As the classroom teacher I cannot claim disinterested retrospection. Nonetheless, my aim in revisiting the classroom interaction data has been to locate both fulfilled and missed opportunities for developing a CLA which evolves not just through the scrutiny of texts but through classroom talk. We may be able to get closer to a sense of what has been learned by asking the students themselves. In the next chapter, I shall look at data which offers greater insight into the students' own perspective on their development as critical readers.

7
Critical Reading Revisited: Diaries, Reading Protocols and Interviews

This chapter aims to take the students' perspective. I shall explore the manner in which the narratives of selected students, as they emerge in different spoken and written modes, work together to offer insight into their constructions of critical reading, at a distance from the original classroom setting. What sense do students make of CLA study? How do they interpret it in the context of their own lives and future study as language learners? Do they see its claimed transformative potential in comparable kinds of ways to CDA theorists or teachers?

With these questions in mind, I shall look at some of the major themes in samples of students' talk and writing in diary entries, protocols which show students thinking aloud through texts, and relatively unstructured interviews which feature extended stretches of talk. I shall use the term 'narrative' generically to describe these various forms of student-generated texts.

While bringing in illustrative comment relating to the other students in the group, I shall focus on two students in some depth: Victoria and Yuko. I chose them because they both attended regularly throughout the class, although Yuko missed one session. They came to the class with rather different cultural perspectives, educational backgrounds and goals. Victoria was an undergraduate student at a university in Spain, doing one year of her studies at Thames Valley University (TVU). As becomes clear in her texts, she had already studied linguistics, though not systemic-functional linguistics. Yuko was doing a B.Tech degree at TVU, specialising in marketing. She had no background in linguistic study, and had lived for several years in West London with her English boyfriend, whom, when I last met her, she was planning to marry and settle with in Japan. At the time, her main concern was to pass the Cambridge Proficiency examination, which she had failed on two previous occasions. These were their respective answers to key questions in the initial questionnaire:

Victoria's responses to questions:
1. *Why did you choose to enrol for the 'Critical Reading' course?*
   Because I thought it would be a good way to improve not only my English but my knowledge of English culture. I think that written texts can say a lot about a society and I would like to get to understand them well.
2. *What do you understand Critical Reading to be? How, for example, do you think it differs from the kind of reading you usually do in your language classes?*
   The rest of my classes deal with classical texts (poetry, plays) but I think that this course is going to focus on contemporary sources and therefore will help me make my own opinion (being useful not only in my learning of English but also in my analysis of texts in my own language).

To the same two questions Yuko responded:

1. Because I wanted to improve my reading ability, especially in terms of speed and accuracy and double meaning.
2. To understand what the writer really meant, what made him to write a particular article.

It will be seen that Victoria at the outset has a notion of critical reading, which meshes quite well with the overall goals of the Critical Reading course, and some of her key words, such as 'culture', 'society' and 'analysis' reverberate through the student narratives produced both during and after the end of the course. Not surprisingly both students talk of improvement. And it needs to be remembered that, whatever wider, more ambitious goals might be at stake, for Yuko and Victoria the important thing was to feel they had made progress as language students.

At the same time as focusing on these two students, I shall concentrate on three sources of data: diaries, reading protocols and interviews. What these media offer are opportunities for critical reflection on texts and language practices at some distance, spatially and temporally, from the classroom setting described in Chapter 6. A different perspective can also be brought to bear on the interpretations which have been offered within the classroom community, allowing students to shift from direct critical commentary on texts, on the spot so to speak, to metacritical awareness. Indeed it is this kind of metalevel knowledge which is a defining feature of CLA and can only come to the fore when texts, practices and readings are judged from some distance.

The aim then is to see how far these narratives taken together offer a picture of students' understandings, both of what it means to be a critical reader in a foreign language, and their own sense of development and change through the experience of attending the Critical Reading course.

Diaries

Recent studies have drawn on diaries – *journals* is sometimes the preferred term – as consciousness raising (cf. Norton 2000), influenced by feminist studies which are concerned less specifically with academic matters than wider complexities of the lives of new immigrants to English-speaking countries, such as Canada in the case of Norton's study. Others who use diaries within a more specifically critical perspective, such as Janks (1999), are also concerned less with language or subject learning than with identity – how the discourse within the journals charts the changing student identities in terms of, for instance: identity as a learner, identity as a practitioner, identity as a journal writer, identities in conflict, identity under threat (Janks 1999). Here I want to present the diaries not just as personal or intimate responses to the issues raised in class or as testaments to changing identities as language learners and language users, but as opportunities for continuing the debate around texts which we had embarked on in class, especially as I undertook to respond to the student entries.

The students interpreted the diary task in different ways. No one produced a full set of entries, week by week, some preferring to produce long accounts over several weeks. This was the case of Pierre, who from the beginning considered wider cultural implications of the discourses addressed, using the texts surveyed in class more as codes in the Freirean sense, on which to hook some of the wider social commentary he wished to engage in. Pierre was a student whose address of myself as his interlocutor was very specific; at the same time his own text moved far beyond the particular issues raised by the texts he alluded to:

> Catherine, I've been thinking about the letter you wrote to the *Daily Mail* and the answer you received. The text was overtly biased against Spain and its aim was probably to reassure the English people about the viability of the English traditional moral values. I think this simplistic representation of Britain as being the country of the Good is one of the basic styles of the working class ideology – And that's probably the reason why you disliked it, because, as far as I can see, you're no member of the working class – You've probably made long studies and there is no way of fooling you. In other words, the text was not made for you

(Pierre is referring to the fact that I had described how an earlier Critical Reading class had written a letter to *The Daily Mail*, complaining about 'The Blame That Spain Must Share' which is partly reproduced on pages 159–60)

Pierre also acknowledges changes of position. An example is in Pierre's second diary entry, following the one quoted above, where he reconsiders an earlier point of view with the words:

Kathy, You may remember I had claimed previously that each social class had its own ideology – Well, I'd like to question that assumption now

Questions which seemed to emerge from an examination of a number of the student diary entries related first to the way the writer locates herself in interaction with a reader and within her own text, through such features as the use of mood and modality, very strongly signalled in Pierre's text above; secondly to the expository quality of the discourse, which I link to the expansion of argument – the preparedness to offer warrants for points of view. A third feature which repays investigation is, how far the students reveal awareness of language effects in texts and at what level of generality. I will focus on Yuko and Victoria in one sample diary entry for each student, and organise the discussion around three questions:

* How does the writer locate herself in the discussion?
* What warrants are offered for points of view?
* What awareness of language is displayed?

Victoria
Below is the opening part of the text which Victoria refers to. It is headlined: 'The Blame That Spain Must Share'. The discourse covers familiar territory in the UK in that each summer there are reports of 'lager loutism' among young British tourists in popular European resorts.

EXPLOITATION THAT TURNED THE LAGER LOUT PROBLEM INTO
A CRISIS

THE BLAME THAT SPAIN MUST SHARE

Robbie is not really a lager lout. He has been turned into one. He lives at home with his parents in a rather sleepy market town in Somerset. He's neat, quiet. He's got a job.

He's an enthusiastic supporter of his cricket club and his idea of a night out is a dance with his girlfriend, who was a bit upset he'd gone on holiday without her.

All of which makes the sight of him crumpled in a drunken heap among the cigarette ends on the floor of the Casa Padri Bar at 2.30 am so depressing.

How many people back home in Frome would have recognised that livid face, reddened by the sun and an excess of alcohol?........The yellow singlet his mother had ironed before packing for him, torn and stained with beer?

Why is it you English behave like this? Asked the bar's proprietor Paco Munoz as we dragged Robbie out on to the pavement, spewing curses at everyone, before he recovered enough to lurch into the nearest disco.

A hypocritical question for a Spaniard to ask. The Spanish wring their hands and rightfully complain about the shameless excesses of British youth: excesses which have not gone away, despite their disappearance from the news, excesses that this week in San Antonio, Ibiza caused the murder of young waiter Jesus Moreno (extracted from 'The Blame That Spain Must Share', Richard Kay *The Daily Mail*, 3 August 1989)

Victoria: sample diary entry

From the last two weeks, the texts that have struck me most are, by chance, both written by the same journalist (the well-known Richard Kay). It is interesting how his usage of language produces effects in the readers that they can hardly evaluate. What I mean by this is that our reactions as readers can be measured not only by quite recognisable resources, such as vocabulary, headings or pictures. There are more subtle resources that we unconsciously perceive. In these lines, I would like to focus on one of them that appears to be of vital importance, from my point of view.....the device I would like to draw attention to is the use of 'participants'.

Let us observe, first, the text on 'Robbie'. We can draw a line between those participants that can be grouped under the label of 'English' and those that could be labelled as 'Spanish'. Since the main aim of the text is to prove how the responsibility on the part of English youngsters should be 'shared' by the Spaniards and their way of living (although we can notice how, bit by bit, the blame is put on Spanish themselves).

Those participants (nouns) that are on the English part are, for instance, 'Robbie'. 'excesses', 'the talk', 'the other objectives'. The last three examples I consider part of the English group, since they clearly refer to things and acts carried out by British people, although strikingly the ergativeness, the agency of the actions disappears. Thus, for instance, 'the talk was of home, of finding a girl: where talk is a deverbal noun (it comes from 'they talked about') that enables the writer to avoid the explicit mention of who was the ergative agent (the responsible) for the action of talking. Therefore, as it is used in a different sentence, throughout the text, the acts implied by those nouns are left without a performer (explicit). See for instance: 'Excesses that caused the murder of'.

The same analysis would serve for those nouns belonging to the 'Spanish' group but here the effect is the opposite. Spaniards are exemplified in the 'girls', 'the runners of the bars', and a 'worried Mayor' and '...of drunken men and women'. The actions they perform are always aimed at becoming a temptation for those English participants.

I also noticed one very small, maybe insignificant and unimportant detail: Kay refers to those participants that will serve him to embody the British spirit only by their first name (no English surnames are mentioned). On the other hand, he provides the complete names of the Spanish people. In what sense is this important or relevant in the final message?

Comment

How does the writer locate herself in the discussion?

This is a public rather than intimate discourse, the diary task being interpreted as an exercise in exposition and argument rather than personal response. This is suggested by the way in which Victoria positions herself in her text in the opening paragraphs and, in particular, through advance organisers such as: 'The texts I will refer to' and 'I would like to draw attention to' and 'Let us observe'. A reader is clearly envisaged here, though not specifically addressed. At the same time, the discourse is quite strongly opinionated through first person use which offers personal opinion in unequivocal ways, as in 'the texts that have struck me most' and 'what I mean by this'; 'I consider'. When Victoria moves on to the analysis in paragraph 2, she locates herself within a reading community, as suggested by the shift to the more formal and more authoritative *we*, in 'we can draw a line' and 'we can notice' – which I see as an exclusive use of we (to mean *we* as the community of critical analysts), as opposed to the earlier use of first person plural pronoun in 'our reactions as readers' which refers inclusively to *all* readers. She occasionally signals some distancing in the manner in which she relates to the material she is describing, for instance in modal or qualifying phrases such as 'appears to be'; 'from my point of view' and 'we may infer'. However, in general her authorship of this text is confidently maintained with strong adverbs of evaluation such as: 'strikingly the ergativeness disappears' and 'they clearly refer to'. Overall, there is relatively little modulation of truth claims; in other words, there is strong affirmation, as in 'throughout the text.....the acts implied are left without a performer' and 'The actions they perform are always aimed at....'. She concludes apparently tentatively with 'I noticed one very small maybe insignificant and unimportant detail'. However, as argued in Chapter 6, tentativeness can be seen as a feature of a critically aware stance, a preparedness to tolerate ambiguity and uncertainty. Her concluding interrogative seems more to raise a possibility worth further consideration than to demand a reply to the specific question from me. It is exploratory in this sense.

What warrants for points of view are given?

Victoria's identity is at stake as a Spanish person and the other Spanish students in the group offered a more affective response: Franco, for instance, writes in his diary, of 'The Blame That Spain Must Share': 'In the last class I said the text was offensive for me...what is really offensive is the way in which the text was written, because the writer was focusing on surrounding ideas and subsidiary information (Spanish taxes, Robbie, etc.) when the starting point should have been the murder of a waiter.' Although Franco elaborates his argument, aiming for some critical distance, his own identity as Spanish is salient. In Victoria's text this is not apparent; effects are not discussed in terms of her own personal reaction. The verbs are mental processes, which signal largely cognitive rather than affective or very personal responses. She elaborates her own argument in dialogic mode; for example 'It is interesting/what I mean by this'. This is typical of the manner in which skilled writers conduct a continuing imaginary dialogue with a supposed reader. In presenting her comments on the theme she has selected to deal with: 'participants', she continually enhances, elaborates and extends her argument. For example:

1. 'The last three I consider..since they clearly refer' (enhancement)
2. 'What I mean by this' and 'See for instance' (elaboration)
3. 'The same analysis would serve for those nouns belonging to the Spanish group' (extension)

What awareness of language is displayed?

Victoria offers detailed commentary on textual features, and this is accompanied by metalanguage, most of which has been introduced throughout the course, such as *participant*, *agency*, *copula*, though not *deverbal* and *ergative*, likely to be drawn from her earlier linguistic training. She also attributes effects to the use of grammatical choices: she notes, for instance, the writer's differential treatment of the key participants, how the agency of actors disappears in the case of the British participants. At a wider cultural/contextual level Victoria talks both about the context of reception and production, imputing motivation for discriminatory treatment of participants: 'Kay refers to those participants that will serve him to embody the British spirit only by their first name.' However, Victoria attends more to effect than intention, noting, for instance 'effects in the readers that they can hardly evaluate', a claim she then goes on to elaborate. There is a distancing between her own particular reading and 'the reader' or readership more widely considered. Finally though, what is missing from Victoria's text, skilful as it is, is any discussion of the wider socio/political significance of *this kind of text*, the way in which, as Wodak says, 'discourses are always connected to other discourses which were produced earlier' (Wodak 1996: 19). This may be related to

Victoria's lack of access to intertextuality, the history of texts and discourses. Yuko refers to this dilemma in her sample diary entry, which I turn to next.

Yuko: sample diary entry
When I was reading the articles of different newspapers (i.e. quality and tabloids) on the same topic, I found it was much easier to read quickly and understand the quality papers one, than the tabloid's one.

The vocabulary used in the quality paper is the one I have come across before when I was studying English at school. Tabloid's vocabulary is quite difficult to understand even with the help of dictionary. That is because I think they use double meaning, play on words or use particular words referring to former event, some one's quote, history and so on. Therefore, learning history of British might help critical reading of English texts for overseas students, but living in Britain and having lots of contacts with native people are much more crucial. And also it is going to be long-term plan. I wish I could spend more time looking into English Culture, history and people. I suppose not many people are able to do so, though.

By the way, on the other day, I was reading the interview article in Japanese magazine, and came across to the sentence saying 'I (meant writer) felt this woman was...because I don't have a courage nor money etc...' This "I" must have meant the writer of the article (i.e. interviewer) and suddenly started talking about the writer's way of life. At first, I was rather confused what "I" meant, naturally. Moreover, there was not mention of the name of the writer. Since then, I noticed that most of the articles in most of the Japanese magazine, they don't put the names of the writers. It seemed to me as if writers or even publishers are saying that they don't take any responsibilities for what they say in the articles. What do you think?

Comment

How does the writer locate herself in the discussion?

The diary extract is strongly opinionated, more so than Victoria's; there is extensive use of first person, accompanied by mental state verbs, of varying nuance. as in : 'I found..it can'; 'I think'....; 'I suppose...not'; 'I was rather confused'; 'I noticed' 'it seemed to me'. Modality is used both as tentative proposal, as in : 'learning history of British might help critical reading of English texts' and to offer strong opinion, as in 'This "I" must have meant the writer of the article (i.e. interviewer)'. As Halliday notes (1994: 89), however, even a high value modal as in 'must have' is less certain than a polar form. In other words, Yuko is maintaining, through her interpersonal choices, the exploratory, tentative tenor of exposition, the language of enquiry.

Yuko then changes footing. The third paragraph opens with a feature typical of informal conversation where we have a clear addressee in mind: 'by the way' would be unlikely to appear in a personal diary with no envisaged addressee other than the writer. Also it is solidarity rather than status marked. This effect is reinforced by the concluding question which appears to be specifically addressed to me 'What do you think?'. Overall, Yuko interprets the diary task more personally than Victoria, although she limits her account of personal desires and experiences to those related to learning – that is, the wish to learn more about culture, and the experience of difficulty with the popular press, which she mentions again in her interview.

What warrants for points of view are given?

Yuko begins metacognitively with an observation of the relative ease of reading some kinds of material. She then elaborates in the second paragraph with both implied causality (I have come across quality papers at school) and overt enhancement in 'because..they use double meaning'. She then goes on to draw consequences, with a further enhancement in 'Therefore, learning history of British might help critical reading of English texts.' Initially Yuko fails to expand on the statement with which she begins the third paragraph: 'This "I" must have meant the writer of the article.' However, the logical connector 'Moreover', indicating extension, fulfils this function. In the following sentence, 'Since then' offers further extension to her argument. Yuko's penultimate sentence beginning 'It seemed to me' functions as enhancement in that it is presented as a consequence of her observation, even though it is not explicitly signalled as such. The overall effect is of a fairly tightly constructed argument which moves beyond observation to a consideration of implications.

What awareness of language is displayed?

While Yuko discusses the language and content features of a specific set of texts, her language awareness is also more broadly exercised in metacognitive accounts of her own difficulties with texts. She alludes to features of language to exemplify these difficulties such as double meanings, and play on words. She also refers to the principle of intertextuality, without using the term, in noting how writers (of tabloids particularly) bring in reference to former events, quotes and history. She then goes on to draw on her reading of a particular text, and indeed a specific sentence within that, in order to speculate on wider cultural practices. In doing so, she is beginning to respond at a metacritical level, commenting retrospectively on her own responses to texts and drawing implications from these: her awareness of a specific micro-level response is linked to her observation of a wider literacy practice – namely, the absence of obvious referents to 'I' in some genres of Japanese. Thus the work with English language texts appears to have helped enhance awareness, by contrast, with Japanese texts. While Yuko, unlike

Victoria, resists the use of metalanguage, her explanation suggests that scrutiny of grammatical choices has made her aware of what might motivate presences or absences in texts.

Reading protocols

As noted in Chapter 1, the reader's processing of text has typically been researched in terms firstly of identifying the use of specific strategies and secondly has been concerned with comprehension, conventionally understood as the apprehension of writer meaning (cf. e.g. Block 1986; Anderson and Vandergrift 1996). Here my interest was less in comprehension, than in the nature of the stance adopted in the communicative reading event, that is in critical and metacritical responses rather than cognitive and metacognitive ones – less the response to *what* is said, than to the *how* and *why* of textual wordings. Finally I wished to observe how the students' readings might relate to wider societal interpretations, what I have called the 'implications' of texts.

Typically, if asked either to write about or talk their way through a text as in a protocol, students respond to texts unproblematically, as we saw in the case of William, the native speaker reader described in Chapter 1. Thus reading protocols may be competent convergent readings, where textual claims are not met with resistance, where by and large the reader is animating rather than authoring the text. As Koo notes, 'animating will involve close paraphrasing, priority being placed on a relatively non-analytic accessing of the writer's...ideas, and an assumed agreement with the ideological position of the writer (if any is discerned)' (Koo 1998: 116). But we can see readers, not as animators but as creators or authors, constructing texts which are not reproductions of the original text so much as new texts, engaged with the meanings of the original but not merely parasitic on it. It must be acknowledged however, that the genre and topic of the text play a major part in activating a critical stance, or footing in Goffman's terms. As Yuko notes in her interview: 'for example if someone talk about engineering or something like that I have no idea what it's talking about so I just believe what the text's saying but things like marketing or travel things I'll be very critical'.

A critical reading will be characterised by resistance to not just the logic or argument of a text but its underlying ideological premises. The problematising process operates not at the level of the issues explicitly announced for us by the text, but at omissions and distortions. Underlying what is in fact written are versions of what could have been written. And at the same time as different writings are imagined, so are alternative readings.

In looking at reader responses qualitatively, it is clear that we are talking about orientations rather than polar opposites, expressed, for instance, as a bald dichotomy between 'critical' and 'uncritical' reading. Nonetheless

I argue here that it is possible to describe responses as more or less critical. Below I present verbal protocols of Victoria and Yuko as they 'think aloud' through texts which, though they have been introduced during the course fairly briefly, have not been studied in depth. Additionally, to offer a useful point of reference, a verbal protocol of Carlos is presented, as he offers a commentary on the same text as Yuko (in each case the students were presented with a small set of texts to choose from). Extrapolating from this discussion I shall pose three questions to underpin the analysis of the students' protocols

* How does the reader align herself with the text?

A key question is how far the reader responds at an affective, associative level without further qualification. A critically oriented interpersonal stance permits one to see how one's own reader position may be one of several possible ones and that there is a preferred reading; to be aware, that is, of the difference between the reading the writer intends and one's personal reading. In other words, how does the respondent situate herself within the account she offers in the reading protocol, by, for instance, simply stating what the text is about, or by indicating how far and in what ways she aligns herself with the preferred reading? Our reading, commentary and meta-commentary, is made more powerful not simply, as Clark and Ivanic (1997) claim, by the presence of greater voice or sense of personal identity, important though this is, but by the ability to locate ourselves within other possible voices. Moreover this location of the self within other voices and views becomes clearer – more explicit to ourselves and others – if it is articulated through extension, elaboration or enhancement of the position taken. This links to the second question. What warrants are offered for interpretation?

* What warrants for interpretation are offered?

This question relates to the degree to which the reader leaves judgements unqualified or, conversely, makes some attempt to mitigate, illustrate or offer an explanation for the claims made, by way of making them more transparent and deniable. Of course the inclusion of these markers of expansion are also interpersonal and dialogic in the sense that they anti-cipate or pre-empt challenges, queries or objections from an imagined interlocutor.

* How does the reader link text to context?

This question is concerned with the degree to which the reader provides textual detail in the commentary, with or without the accompaniment of particular kinds of metalanguage. In addition, does the reader show any awareness of factors such as source or genre of the text, the processes of production and the immediate circumstances of its appearance? Finally, is the reader able to link awareness of textual features with wider cultural knowledge of practices, phenomena and beliefs? It is here that issues related to racism and gender – the macro issues of social justice which were the wider concern of the Critical Reading course – might emerge. In short, is there any evidence that the student is able to make links between the world of the text and her own cultural background as well as knowledge of the target culture?

Note on transcription: * As might be expected, there are considerable pauses, filled by the students actually reading the text, silently or subvocalising. Only long pauses over a minute in length are indicated. The students read and comment in English, with no translation, apart from the brief exchange in Spanish between Victoria and Carlos

Protocols: Victoria, Carlos and Yuko

The opening part of the text to which Victoria is responding is reproduced here

---

MASKED MOB STONE POLICE

100 HURT AS RIOT ERUPTS ON MARCH

Vicious scenes of violence not seen since the Poll Tax riots broke out on the streets of Britain yesterday as a thousand anti-Nazi demonstrators clashed with police.

More than 100 people were hurt including 12 officers – one suffering serious head injuries – as the 25,000 protesters, a number of whom were masked, confronted 7000 riot police at Welling in South East London. They threw everything they could lay their hands on – bricks, bottles and smoke bombs. They even tried to uproot a road-sign.

The trouble had flared when the marchers – some as young as eight – were prevented from passing the target of their hatred – the British National Party book shop in the town. Each time the riot police, including mounted officers, charged they were forced back by a barrage of missiles. (From *The Daily Mail* October 1993)

Victoria

1   From the very beginning, as you start reading the text the first thing you notice that they're talking about the violent events and it's reflected not only by what they say, the contents of the headlines, the article itself but also the language. Because the fact of saying 'Masked Mob Stone Police'

5   they're making reference to a crowd of people, a big amount of people (?) or
      facing or hurting the police itself. In the headline the language, the device
      of language by which you could use a noun such as 'crowd' or 'flock' or er
      common nouns that include several several members of the same group
      maybe 'people' or 'birds in flock' or whatever, you could use them in plural
10   or singular. You can see in the headline how 'Mob Stone Police' instead of
      'Mob <u>Stones</u> Police' and they are they are emphasising the size and the
      number of people confronting the police. That's what...? for the head-
      line. The pictures, you can see the pictures also alluding to violence – the
      police, the back of the police and the faces of the rioter really shouting
15   with angry faces and then erm..? describing the effects of these rioters of
      this rioting using again words that emphasise the violence such as 'erupts'
      'scenes of violence – that had not been seen for a long time'. Erm 'anti-
      Nazi demonstrators' – just the use of 'anti-Nazi' for me it's interesting
      because the contradictory thing about this article I mean the whole event
20   is that I mean what they're criticising. I mean the demonstration is against
      violence and against bad behaviour with people from another races and
      all those things, but they're behaving in the same way. That is why it's so
      so striking this news. This is what makes this news a news: not only the
      violence that you could see in the demonstration but the demonstration
25   was against violence. They threw everything they could to the police
      they..what did they do? Some of them were masked. This is funny this
      is important because among all the protestors a number of them were
      masked but in the headline they say: 'Masked Mob Stone Police'. It means,
      what it's doing is trans transporting what happens to a part of the crowd
30   to the whole mob. Maybe its attributing more violence than it was or
      more – in fact not all of them were masked. So this is a kind of manipul-
      ation in the headline (PAUSE).
      But I would also stress that its the language used maybe is over – giving more
      importance to the violence that it could have itself um..I don't know..
35   maybe using too many words that themselves can imply violence –
      is making the reader feel this violence and just by reading another paper
      maybe with another ideology or with less – well it depends sometimes on
      the party that the newspaper takes. It can show different a different way
      I mean show the news, the same facts in a very different way, not even
40   justifying them but just, instead of saying 'mob' or 'masked' or – in fact
      'masked' is what Nazis do, what skinheads do. Most of the times they
      cover their head – their faces so that nobody can recognise them. This
      is very – it links again this anti-Nazi movement to the Nazis themselves.
      But I mean that maybe in another newspaper – I think we saw some
45   newspapers and some headlines before – they don't really show as much
      violence as here and it can depend also on the opinion on the on the
      manipulation of the events that some newspapers do – well not some – all
      (PAUSE).

50

Another thing that strikes me is when they say 'the trouble that had flared when the marchers, some as young as 8, were prevented from passing' it's its its people so young – people – they were children – they were involved in this violence. It makes you think that in fact the members of the crowd were not violent themselves maybe there was something more (PAUSE).

55

And the way the word 'vicious' is resulted 'vicious scenes of violence not seen since the Poll Tax riots'. I wonder why they choose this word (PAUSE).

Well I think that in summary, as a summary the language is used as as a means to stress the violence that had in fact taken place in the demonstration and words like 'children' contrasted well I mean not 'children' the

60

word 'children' but..stressing the youth of the members of the demonstration and their being masked when in fact they later say that just a number of them were masked, and classifying them as anti-Nazi and all these things whereas in fact the stressing is the contradiction – what you shouldn't expect from these people has in fact occurred – what they

65

are fighting against has become against them and just (?) remarking how language supports what is reporting to the reader.

Comment

Alignment with the text

Victoria begins with the impersonal 'you' as the subject of her text: for example, 'you notice that' (lines 1–2). Later, however, she shifts more frequently to the use of the first person and appears more willing to assert a point of view, indicated for instance by: 'Just the use of anti-Nazi for me its interesting. (line 18) and 'I would also stress' (line 33) and 'another thing that strikes me' (line 48). These are modalising expressions, making clear that they are matters of opinion and judgement, not fact. She thematises, through fronting, words like 'important' and 'striking' which allows her to highlight aspects of the text she judges as particularly significant (this may be an influence from Spanish which more regularly thematises in this way). Thus instead of saying 'X is funny', she says 'This is funny, this is important' (line 26–27). Victoria's lexical choices and emphatic thematising lend her discourse confidence but expressions of uncertainty, accompanied by modalisation, convey an exploratory tenor. For example, 'I wonder why they choose this word (vicious)? (line 55) and frequent statements with 'maybe', such as 'Maybe it's attributing more violence than it was' (line 30) [I take Victoria to be saying here: the newspaper exaggerated the extent of the violence.]. Mood choices are less affirmative than in the diary, as one might expect in the absence of the opportunity either to study the text in depth, or to monitor or adjust her own responses.

Warrants for interpretation

Victoria offers a number of expanding statements indicating that although the mode of discourse is quite novel to her – she had not been asked to 'talk aloud' through a text before – she interprets the task in similar ways to earlier critiques. As this is unplanned discourse, there are more instances of extension than in the other media; a greater accumulation of points, more typical of spontaneous spoken language. But there is also elaboration, signalled on several occasions by 'I mean' as in 'I mean, show the news..the same facts in a different way', (line 39) and enhancement with clauses of cause and condition. An example is: 'Just the use of 'anti-Nazi' for me it's interesting because the contradictory thing about this article – I mean the whole event – is that the demonstration is against violence and against bad behaviour but they're behaving in the same way.' (lines 18–22). In fact throughout her 'think aloud', Victoria is restating, elaborating, and attempting to clarify for herself her interpretation of the text. Such tentative elaborations, accompanied as they are by modal expressions, which continually restate or refine earlier judgements reinforce the exploratory tenor of Victoria's monologue.

From text to context

Victoria focuses quite closely on linguistic choices and, in doing so, she follows the Hallidayan principle that grammatical choices are not arbitrary but motivated. One might wish to question whether she is right to conclude as she does that 'Masked mob stone police' creates an effect of a larger crowd – a greater number – than if the alternative form, 'Masked mob stones police', were selected. What is significant is, nonetheless, the raising of the question itself; the underlying premise that the grammar allows us to exploit meaning in different ways and that the resultant effects are ideologically significant. She later talks of showing 'the same facts in a different way' (line 39). Finally, Victoria's close reading of the text around the issue of 'masked mob' allows her to see an inconsistency or disjuncture between the headline and the body of the text, namely that not all 'the mob' wore masks, as the headline implies.

Victoria refers to the context of reception in terms of readership, providing distance between her personal reader identity and the model or idealised reader in referring to 'the reader' as a construct in '..is making the reader feel this violence' (line 36). She further shifts from the 'here and now' reading and text, to discuss more widely the genre of newspaper reports when she claims that no reports are neutral, in: 'the manipulation of events that some newspapers do – well not some – all' (line 47). She also makes more specific reference to the occasion when other headlines describing the same event were discussed in class (though the accompanying reports were not analysed). In doing so she acknowledges the role of the classroom community, in 'We saw some newspapers and some headlines before' (lines 44–45).

Key items of cultural knowledge which Victoria brings from her existing knowledge of the world relate to the connotation of 'Nazi' and 'mask'. This allows her to note resonances and contradictions. The peace-loving crowd (as anti Nazi) behave like Nazis (violently). The masks are typically associated with right wing groups, such as Nazis or Neo-Nazis (who Victoria probably has in mind here) and skinheads.

The opening part of the text to which Carlos and Yuko are responding is reproduced here (it was also introduced in Chapter 2)

SINGAPORE

WHERE THE STATE CHOOSES YOUR PARTNER

Singapore's citizens are so law-abiding that many of them participate in state-run matchmaking schemes, which encourage intellectual equals to marry each other. Sophie Campbell reports from the country where failing to flush a toilet can be an offence.

Welcome to Singapore. 'Death to Drug Traffickers' reads the immigration card on arrival at Changi Airport. Driving down a palm-bordered highway to the cluster of futuristic buildings that is downtown Singapore, you find yourself on an island the size of the Isle of Wight inhabited by three million of the most obedient people on earth.

Carlos
1   Well, the first thing is the title which is quite striking. It says 'Singapore
    where the State chooses your partner' – something that the individual
    should do and er amazingly is done by the State, so it's really surprising..
    seems that everything's under control in this place. Now after a very quick
5   reading I find the beginning of the article quite ironic when it says:
    'Welcome to Singapore' – welcome to this state-controlled – to this place
    controlled by the State'... 'Death to drug traffickers' is quite violent, the
    beginning. 'It's the immigration (?) arrival of Changi airport'. 'Futuristic
    buildings' suggests, I don't know – reminds me of novels such as
10 *Brave New World* and all those utopic places.. 'Island the size of the Isle of
    Wight' – it suggests being enclosed in a place. 'Most obedient people on
    earth' I don't know – it reminds me of *1984* by George Orwell as well.
    'Draconian laws', it seems that all the pleasures are banned – gambling
    or smoking or – My God, what a place to live! (PAUSE) 'Singapore is
15 76 per cent Chinese, 15 per cent Malay and 6 per cent Indian.. a tiny
    infidel dot in a sea of Muslim countries.' This 'a tiny infidel dot' provokes
    maybe a humorous effect... it seems the government is involved in all the
    details of the everyday life. My God! 'multiracial society that helps those
    that help themselves'.

(At this point Victoria enters and the following conversation, in both Spanish and English, mediates in Carlos's 'think aloud'.)

20 C: Come in. I'm talking to this thing (the tape recorder). I'm supposed to be reading this article and so..just hold on a second. She'll be coming soon. *Viene ahora...que viene ella ahora (inaudible)....He hecho mucho*
V: *por donde vas?*
C: *Por aqui*

(Carlos carries on reading, subvocalising 'style of leadership exemplified by the recent chewing gum laws'.)

25 V: if you throw a chewing gum to the ground you can go [to prison
C: [even to jail. The government is involved in all the details of the every-day life. My God!
V: But it's one of the most developed places in Asia.

(Carlos: carries on subvocalising....)

V: It's the most prosperous economy in Asia.

(Carlos: carries on subvocalising)

30 V: I have a friend from Singapore and she can speak four languages – four (PAUSE)
C: It's quite amazing when the government gets involved in the private life of the people, as matching them in order to get married. It's quite I don't know – worrying..The whole text is full of words such as 'perfect' and others but I think they're used ironically by the author in some way or
35 another..just amazing. They pay...they're training...they teach you how to be with a girl and all that – I don't know (laughs). Well there's some-thing similar I think in Europe with all these private companies that now are very fashionable that they match people as well, but of course they are not rules by the government and the purpose is not to obtain benefits
40 for the State.

Yuko

1 So I chose the article about Singapore. 'Singapore where the State chooses your partner' (PAUSE). I like the beginning of the text saying 'Welcome to Singapore' which indicates what's this text is about – it's about Singapore. I don't know particularly what it's going to talk about.
5 Then the next one – next sentence starts: 'Death to traffickers'. Now I'm not so sure about this beginning of the sentence because 'death' and 'traffickers' are very strong words to me and then..if people normally say 'Singapore' I don't think of death or drug. I don't imagine these things from the word 'Singapore'. The word..image I can get from the
10 word 'Singapore' is more like..clean, sunshine and say..interesting country (PAUSE).

Now I read on and I can understand why they talk about 'death' and 'drug
traffickers' because of the very strict draconian laws in Singapore. I know
Singapore has very strict laws on many things like throwing the rubbish
15   in the streets. You have to pay lots of fines, I know (PAUSE). And then this
um writer carry on describing what kind of laws and what – how much
fine you have to pay and then.. I found this way of listing these laws is
quite interesting – I think someone would certainly carry on reading this
article because this way of writing this article suggests that Singapore
20   law is very unusual to British people because you don't have to pay a fine
for spitting or littering or failing to flush a public toilet.. but I don't really
like talking about these fines too much because it sounds like the writer
is making fun of Singapore (PAUSE).
And then... this text moves on to the structure of the population, I mean
25   the ethnic origins like Chinese, Malay, Indian um Muslim countries. um.
When they talking about – generally speaking – about South East Asia
they always talking about how good they're doing in the economy and
then they always say it will be a rich country in ten or twenty years time
and then well as I imagine, it says here as well, it says 'with Hong Kong
30   to be the third most prosperous economy in Asia'. I don't like this kind
of introducing South East Asian because this economic growth always
associated with lots of problems like high inflation and the long distance
between...

(another student enters and they greet each other)

I can't remember what I was talking about – oh yes about economic growth
35   and then these things always involve the problem of high inflation and
destroying the nature and erm.. there will be a how do you say – erm
between rich people and poor people.. the difference is just getting
bigger and bigger, never smaller. And when you're talking – when people
talking – about these economic growth they're always looking in the bright
40   side but they don't look at the negative side and they just encourage this
economic growth happening but I don't really appreciate that because
as I said... PAUSE
And then as I read on I don't know which magazine or newspaper this
article was actually put – appeared but I guess it's more or less like a
45   woman's magazine like *Marie Claire* (PAUSE). It says here: 'the creation of
a national ideology may seem excessive, even comical to a Western
observer' and then they carry on talking about encouraging educated
people to marry each other and produce children. Well probably that's
what actually happening in Singapore but I think what they talked about
50   here.. well, in my opinion, is really extreme case um maybe because I just
can't believe this story is usual. If it just extreme case they introducing in
this text, I can understand it, but.. (said emphatically) I don't *like* this
article so much because I think in this kind of text, generally speaking,

I think the British people I mean, and other European people, seem like
55   seem that they looking at Far East people in some different way, I think
it's like they're..as if looking at some completely strangers, like people
who's mad or who act beyond their comprehension. I don't like..well
I don't think um..I know these articles appear in British magazines but
I just don't like the way of introducing these things.
60   The reason why I said it's probably appeared in a woman's magazine is
because the word like 'worried' by the tendency of male graduates to 'marry
down' and leave 'well-educated women unwed' – these word like 'well-
educated'..'marry down' these things might draw some women's attention when they're reading these things (PAUSE). I think this article is very –
65   not very but maybe rather critical about this government's practice of
matching male and female graduates because these things doesn't happen
in this country, in England, which is very unusual and as if the writer is
saying these things <u>shouldn't</u> be happening. That's the impression I get.
They use the example of William and his wife Chew Mei Lian. I think the
70   writer put these examples in order to make the article more enjoyable
to read, because it's more or less like gossip of people because generally
speaking, people like reading someone's personal life. I don't think this
article has got any – how'd you say – any informative aspect: it's more like
they took a very unusual, strange story for this particular space and then
75   they just put this article for fun, for entertaining reading.

Comment

Alignment with the text

Carlos apparently accepts the propositions of the text at face value, as when
he says: '"Futuristic buildings" suggests – I don't know – reminds me of novels
such as "Brave new World" and all those utopic places'. He offers his own
personal response but does not speculate either on what kind of response
the text invites, or countenance the possibility of readings other than his
own. Carlos's responses remain largely at the affective level as signalled by
the use of adjectives and adverbs such as 'striking, amazingly, surprising'.
When Victoria enters, she conducts a kind of counterpoint commentary
on that offered by Carlos, almost playing devil's advocate, in the spirit of
'well hang on a minute, Singapore has a successful economy you know; its
citizens are multilingual. In other words, don't believe everything you read'
(Interestingly too, she shifts to English, after the first few exchanges in
Spanish). However Carlos, having initially greeted his fellow student, and
picked up her point about the chewing gum laws, does not acknowledge her
interventions, instead maintaining a very consistent stance to the text.

Yuko, on the other hand, while her initial responses are descriptive and
affective, shifts fairly quickly to a stance of reflective uncertainty: 'Now I'm
not so sure.' This negation was characteristic of her problematising stance

in the classroom interaction, in particular, as we noted, in the *Childminder* episode and is absent in Carlos's protocol, where negation is limited to fillers such as 'I don't know'. Yuko's unease later becomes firmed up into dislike of some aspects of the discourse. For, although Yuko eschews words like 'discourse', it is clear that she is responding not to *what* is said but *how* things are talked about. She does not dispute the factuality of information but the motive for taking what she suspects is not a typical case: 'Well probably that's what actually happening in Singapore but I think what they talked about here..well..in my opinion, is really extreme case..' (line 50)

There are many instances, as in the above sentence, of statements of belief and opinion, with frequent use of first person pronoun. What one notices in Yuko's narrative much more than in Carlos's is the accompanying modulation and hedging: as in *probably* and *in my opinion* including ongoing modification of assertions, as when Yuko says: 'I think this article is very – not very but rather critical about this' (lines 64–65). Moreover the mental state verbs which introduce these assertions are used not just as fillers but substantively, to mean 'I believe X to be the case'.

Warrants for interpretation

While Carlos fails to expand on his responses to the text, Yuko, beyond the opening remarks, expands each point she makes with elaboration, enhancement or extension, sometimes in great detail. For example, she offers an enhancement in: 'Now I'm not so sure about this beginning of the sentence because "death" and "traffickers" are very strong words to me' (line 5). She then appears to extend this with an additional point, although arguably it functions as an elaboration, a clarification of the preceding point: 'and then..if people normally say "Singapore" I don't think of..' (lines 7–8).

In short, Yuko does not merely respond to the text; she offers expansions on those responses, with a justification for the response in every case, as we see in further examples taken from across the protocol

'But I don't really like talking about these fines too much because it sounds like the writer is making fun of Singapore.'

'It says here as well, it says "with Hong Kong to be the third most prosperous economy in Asia" I don't like this kind of introducing South East Asia because this economic growth always associated with lots of problems like high inflation and the long distance between..rich people and poor people.'

In 'Now I read on and I can understand why they talk about "death" and "drug traffickers" because of the very strict draconian laws in Singapore'. Yuko also shows a preparedness to modify her previous response as she processes more of the text. She is willing to give the writer the benefit of the doubt by acknowledging for the moment the appropriateness of the lexical choices made. She concedes, however only to reassert her unease with the text at a later point, importantly, though, offering a reason for her discomfort: 'because it sounds like the writer is making fun of Singapore' (lines 22–23).

From text to context

In orthodox terms Carlos's protocol is more sophisticated. He notes the presence of irony and literary allusions, either implicit or intended by the author, as in 'Reminds me of *Brave New World*'. However, he does not pursue this point to consider why the text producers might first have contrived this intertextual reference, if indeed it is calculated, and whether it might be open to challenge. Carlos makes no mention of point of view and the writer's claims seem to be accepted at face value, as in 'My God what a place to live!' (line 14). At the same time there is no mention of the reader, to mean the model or ideal reader, such as we noted in Victoria's protocol. Yuko too makes reference to the notion of readerships, though more obliquely, for example, 'I know these articles appear in British magazines but I just don't like the way of introducing these things' and more specifically in: 'these word like "well – educated".. "marry down" these things might draw some women's attention when they're reading these things'. Yuko is able to see her own responses in the context of what she feels to be other likely responses: she puts some distance between her own reactions and those of 'some women'.

In short, Yuko makes reference to a wider context of production and reception than does Carlos, who limits contextual commentary to the title, and intertextually to *1984* and *Brave New World*. Yuko, unlike Carlos, is reading text in context, context understood moreover, as complex and layered; she is aware of both immediate context – why for instance the text might be 'filling this particular space' – and wider sociocultural contexts. For instance, we see her generalising from the particular Singapore situation to touch on discourses of economic prosperity in South East Asia which she appears to find cliched and suspect.

Yuko does not demonstrate metacritical awareness here, that is she does not expand on *reasons* for her difference of stance to that of the model readership. Nonetheless, it is clear that she is aware of her own outsider reading, and the principles of intertextuality, even in the absence of the use of metalanguage. Without using terms such as 'genre' and 'intertextuality', she moves beyond a critique of this particular text to comment on texts *of this kind*, texts which she has come across before. She is able to offer a cogent account of the common features of the genre, as observed from other exemplars. This is evident for instance in the section:

> I think in this kind of text, generally speaking, I think the British people I mean, and other European people, seem like seem that they looking at Far East people in some different way (lines 53–55).

Yuko is here simultaneously commenting on genre (this kind of text) and the producers and receivers of the text as they collude in a shared unanalysed view of the world (the British people and other European people). This is against the backdrop of her own outsider reading as someone from the Far East, though not from Singapore. In doing so, she is challenging what Said has called the 'discourse of orientalism' by which the 'Other' is exoticised in a relationship between the West and its object of knowledge which is fundamentally a relationship of power and domination (Said 1978). In this way, Yuko is moving from the immediate contextual circumstances of the text's production to consider the wider implications of cultural stereotyping.

Finally, it must be acknowledged that in aligning himself with the text's model reader, Carlos would, in orthodox, convergent terms, be counted the better reader. Yuko does not offer such a close paraphrase of the text as she processes it; rather she expands on the wider implications, as she sees it, of what has motivated the discourse choices. Yuko's divergent reading, creating a parallel new text, would be judged in orthodox comprehension terms to be 'off task': indeed that she is, in Block's (1986) terms, excessively reflexive, concerned more to develop a personal line of enquiry than build on the author's intentions.

Interviews

The interviews selected here took place three months after the end of the course. I wished to get a sense of how the students, through the interview narrative, recreated the classroom experience in their own terms.

I aimed to analyse the interviews holistically in terms of the major purpose they served, which was to reach some judgement about the degree to which the students had developed critical awareness of ways of reading, the nature of texts and their place in wider cultural contexts; in particular, too, to gain greater insight into the classroom context itself and the degree to which pedagogic choices had facilitated or frustrated the students' development, from their own point of view. In short, how did the students see the role of the texts surveyed, their own reading of those texts and the classroom context itself as empowering them as readers, language learners and citizens in the world?

With these questions in mind the commentary will consider (1) the texts, to include awareness both of features of texts as products and ways of processing texts as readers, (2) the classroom community, and (3) the wider political/social context, under the headings:

- Looking at texts in different ways
- The classroom
- The wider context.

Although my questions were calculated to draw responses around these concerns, Victoria and Yuko took the interaction in slightly different directions. However, in each case it is possible to see, as interwoven strands, some reference to the ideology of texts, the classroom setting with its own power relations and finally, links being made to broader social and political implications of genres and their accompanying discourses.

As the interviews were very long, selected excerpts, largely relating to discussion of texts and the classroom environment, are given here. Transcription is more broad-brush than in the classroom interaction sections, with hesitations and overlaps not represented, as this is largely a content analysis. I was here more concerned with the *what* rather than the *how* – substantive content than the evolving construction of the interviews as social interaction.

Victoria

Looking at texts in different ways

1 CW: I was wondering if you looked at texts in different ways?
Victoria: My interest in newspapers grew with this course because I didn't really pay attention to the language in the papers. At least in Spain it isn't very good language at all. I don't think you can take one of these texts in
5 newspapers and show it as a model. It's very interesting whether you imply – you have several levels of meaning apart from the most obvious one and the language tells you – if you use passive, you use this determiner or article or you don't use it or you use this pronoun or you don't use it – it conveys a lot more meaning than the text itself. Do you under-
10 stand what I mean? So I look at the text in that way as well. I don't really read the news to get the idea of the facts that they are reporting but also the way they are given. Also in the news – in the TV I pay attention to it......
CW: So you think that doing this course helped you think a little bit more
15 about..erm
V: I stop to think – I stop and think about it and previously I didn't.

Comment

Probably, because we had discussed newspaper texts in some detail, Victoria draws on them to exemplify the point about layers or levels of meaning within texts. Victoria's responses indicate some awareness of the principle of syntactic options which had informed the course, for example 'You use this pronoun or you don't use it, this determiner or you don't use it.' She offers this account as an elaboration, offered in advance, of her claim that what matters is not the factual verifiability of what is reported but the manner in which facts are reported: 'I don't really read the news – to get the idea of the facts that they are reporting but also the way they are given.' She indicates awareness of how meaning may be more or less salient within texts, that significant meaning may be discoverable beneath the surface, for example, 'you have several levels of meaning apart from the most obvious one' (lines 6–7) and 'it conveys a lot more meaning than the text itself' (line 9). After that, she quickly changes footing from interviewee/student to more of a co-participant in discussion by spontaneously introducing the wider implications. She brings in the new topic of the TV news, in: 'also in the news – in the TV'. At the same time she comments, metacritically, on her own stance to texts, not just written texts but, extending the notion of text more widely, to all media: 'I stop and think and previously I didn't.'

The classroom

CW: I asked Carlos whether when he's talking English he's more articulate

V: I think it was a very good practice for me to be in a class and at first I felt very scared by the micro (the microphone) but then I forgot about it. You
20   start thinking your opinion is important. I'm not used to participating in the lessons. Sometimes it's more important to get the meaning across than to utter a perfect sentence. You have to forget about being perfect.

CW: And do you think the class helped you to become more fluent?

V: And to believe in my own opinions, to defend what I thought was right
25   and by the discussion you see other points of view and people convince you of their points of view. And then you say OK they are right and I was wrong and you look at things in different ways...........

CW: So did you feel you quite liked the group work and learned from it?

V: More than the group work the the – what we did afterwards which
30   was the debate itself... and then some people disagreed and you had to think again what you had said and defend it or just withdraw.........

CW: How was the course different? Do you want to say how it's different from courses you do in small groups here in this college?

V: This is the same class (i.e. classroom) where we do translation and the
35   teacher sits here and then she starts pointing out the students and says 'you do this sentence'. People never give suggestions or discuss what is better. It's more teacher centralised.
    In literature it's the other way round. I think they want the people to talk too much so that you miss the point. You start taking notes on what the
40   students say and maybe it's wrong what they are saying but they give your opinion a great importance. In literature you really have to take into consideration the subjectivity, you cannot be objective, you have to be open and accept all the different impressions but sometimes the teachers just shut up – just close their mouth, doesn't say anything at all. The students
45   start talking and talking and talking and sometimes they talk nonsense. It's not what you should be learning.

CW: It's not constructive talk
V: No
CW: Didn't you feel there was a danger of that happening in our class
50   because there could have been?
V: But we had this pattern – we had to follow a pattern in our commentaries
   and then, following that, we disagreed in many things but we agreed in
   many others. But you had your scheme.
CW: Framework.
55 V: Your framework yes but in the literature lessons we were asked I don't
   know what, a very broad question and you never get the feeling that you
   have learned something because you have listened to everybody talking
   about it, everybody with different opinions but the teacher never gives
   the last word.
60 CW: So you want something to bring it together some kind of...
V: cohesion
CW: To make the connection
CW: Was there anything else about any text we discussed? Any moment in
   the class that you found interesting?
65 V: There was an advert of a car talking about Lenin and I had my point of
   view and for the first time I wanted to make it clear. I think I felt I wanted
   my opinion to be heard and as I said Spanish students are not very used
   to that.
CW: How did you feel about working in the group?
70 V: I felt very comfortable. We were all different and as we're all different you
   don't feel strange. I don't know how it would have been if there had been
   any English native speakers. The English (if the group was a mixture of
   native and non native speakers) would get to know different points of
   view from different countries – they would be able to know about different
75   cultures and we would be able to know why things are like this here
   because one of the readers to which those texts are aimed would be there
   to explain us why.
CW: I mean I'm there but I'm not representative. I'm there as the
   teacher.
80 V: Yes many of times you were giving your own opinion but it's true your
   point of view's different – you were an example but you're the teacher as
   well.

Comment

Victoria claims that the feedback episodes, in particular, offered her the
opportunity to find her own voice, especially on occasions when she felt
strongly that she wished to offer an opinion (e.g. about the 'Lenin' text). She
appears to have had no difficulty with negotiating interpretations around
texts, acknowledging the value of testing one's own opinion against those

of others, and of finally conceding one might be wrong. Moreover, she critiques options regarding pedagogy, by comparing different modes of classroom discourse with which she is familiar: one where turns are clearly and predictably allocated (the translation class); one where students are given considerable freedom, on a reader-response model, to take and hold the floor (the literature class) and the class under consideration here, which was, certainly compared to the literature class, tightly framed, with rights to speak allocated, in general, by the teacher, as noted in Chapter 6. Interestingly, Victoria does not appear to share my unease with what I judged to be excessively structured episodes and where invariably I claimed final turns for myself. Indeed, she emphasises the value, for her, of the teacher's summarising turn, the teacher having the last word.

A missing dimension in the class, we both agree, was the presence of native speaker readers who would have offered their own perspectives, as model readers of the texts we critiqued as well as gaining in turn from a diversity of culturally inflected meanings in a class such as this one. Importantly, Victoria sees the role of the native speaker not as expert but as complementary resource, a participant who would both contribute to but also in turn gain from discussion which included non-native learners of English. One is not talking of inherently privileged positions here.

The wider context (this section of the interview is a continuation of our earlier discussion about news reporting, both in the press and other media)

V: because it's a very very funny way of reporting news that you have here in England. You always look for a very specific example – a person
85   who is suffering, like when they were talking about the killing bug (the killer bug) they look for a person with that problem and inter-viewed him and they had number and surname and age and job and they always look for specific examples and you don't find that in Spain. They give you the news but from a very erm detached point of view..
90   and I did not realise until I started thinking of the way the news are reported.
CW: So it's not just written texts but erm...
V: In general yes. It's like it talks about the English – the British character and I compare it to the Spanish and there are huge differences.
95 CW: What do you think it suggests about the British character?
V: The importance of the individual. Do you remember the Spanish text talking about the waiter – the text of the tourist – English man who went to Spain – the one we were discussing? (Victoria here alludes to the text: 'The Blame That Spain Must Share')..The first lines of the article were the
100   description of the guy and his mother and what he did on Saturdays and his girlfriend and then once you have presented and introduced the person then you can tell the story. It's very personalised very – they

always look for an example, and he and he and he and he did that and
something happened to him and it's everywhere in the news..in the
105   radio.
CW: I hadn't thought of that until you mentioned it. Well now you
mention it I think of course...
V: You think it's natural but it was new for me. It drew my attention. You
need proofs in general – in British newspapers everything's got its name
110   and surname and age and everything. Even when they go to Rwanda...
and they interview a person and they always give the name and – who
cares what's the name, the important thing is the opinion...they become
aware of the importance of the event when they've got someone who has
suffered the event and is telling it. It's because it's very important indi-
115   vidualism here.

Comment

Victoria has moved from the scrutiny of particular texts to observation of
their location in a wider social/political context. In this sense she might be
said to have drawn on her access to specific texts in order, in Lankshear's
(1994: 10) terms to 'make critical readings of wider social practices'. So in
the discussion of 'The Blame That Spain Must Share' she is less interested, at
this point, to attribute blame to individual writers or even particular newspapers, such as *The Daily Mail*, than to look beyond specific discourses to
wider patterns and implications. She generalises from the particular instance
to offer the related observation about what she claims is a cultural tendency
in the British media to favour the personal and the individual. She states
this categorically, with no modalisation: 'It's because it's very important
individualism here.' Fairclough (1995: 39) talks too of 'our contemporary
culture's focus on individualism'. This preoccupation, claims Victoria, is one
which is emphasised far more in Britain than through Spanish media texts.
It is likely too that this media discourse, reflects a tendency in British contemporary culture to follow a more individualistic ideology in a wide range
of affairs than in other European countries.

We see then that Victoria uses texts intertextually and interdiscoursally,
not merely to read off the effects from specific texts, nor to attribute specific
intentionality. Thus she makes the connection with the discourses in a
specific text, 'The Blame That Spain Must Share' to note that the personalised manner of presenting a social issue, here the lager loutism of young
British tourists in Spain, is mirrored across different media and genres,
evidenced in the way in which news, in the United Kingdom of both
domestic and international affairs is presented. It's important to add too,
that in the process of noticing phenomena in the target culture Victoria
becomes more aware of aspects of her familiar cultural environment – the
'way we do things back home'.

Yuko

Looking at texts in different ways

1 CW: I just thought I'd ask you a few questions about the reading course particularly. I mean one question I wanted to ask – I looked through your diaries and you commented a lot on you know how you read things in different ways. Do you think, now three months later, do you look
5   at texts in a different way?

   Y: Yes, yes I think so. Well because I haven't got much time to read the newspapers these days. I can't be how d'you say be analytical to read the texts but yeh I think so, specially because I read all the Japanese papers as well to just to keep up..yeh sometimes I really think what actually does it
10   mean this word, why the writer wrote this article, used this particular word because it doesn't really make sense in the context.

   CW: Are you saying that even when you read Japanese you perhaps look at texts or notice things that you didn't notice before?

   Y: Yes ahah Yes

15 CW: Can you think of any examples?

   Y: Reading Japanese texts is bit different from reading English texts because they use lots of words which implying something – something else and sometimes you've got to read it back again and again to understand the meaning. It's so irritating to me. Once I thought – I read the particular part –
20   and I thought I understood the meaning and when I moved on to the next I realised I hadn't understood the meaning of the previous one and I just have to come back to it. I don't know. It's more straightforward English texts.

   CW: You find it easier to read English texts?

   Y: Sometimes yes, not the tabloids but the quality papers.

25 CW: Do you think the course improved your reading?

   Y: I think so. I've become more – a bit more critical about reading things. Before when I was reading any text and (it said) A is B, I thought OK it's B. I believed it – well, now I think, well it could be C......the reason why I said that may be based on the knowledge or the experience I've got pre-
30   viously so sometimes if I don't have any of this erm knowledge of one particular thing, I just believe.

   CW: You mean you do now, or you did before?

   Y: Yeh, for example if someone talk about engineering or something like that I have no idea what it's talking about so I just believe what the text's
35   saying but things like marketing or travel things I'll be very critical.

   CW: More than you were before?

   Y: I think I'll be very..more suspicious about what the text is saying – become more critical I think – not always (laughs) sometimes I do enjoy reading rubbish things.

40 CW: Of course we all do. You can't be critical all the time. It would be tedious and boring.

Comment

Yuko makes a distinction between reading analytically, which she links with critical reading, and 'reading rubbish things'. We agree the need to 'take time out', that we cannot have our critical antennae out all the time. In this, Yuko seems to have accepted that critical reading is a stance which one moves in and out of, depending on need, context and inclination. Yuko reinforces the impression gained from other sources, such as the diaries, that she is not particularly interested in the level of detail, already much modified and simplified, offered by the Hallidayan framework. Her initial remarks here refer to texts in very general ways, with terms such as 'article', 'context' and 'text' itself. Later in the interview, she shows that she is able to draw on some of the metalanguage used during the course, albeit at a rather general level, for example, in 'what kind of verb is this – is it a passive or action verb' (lines 93–94). She acknowledges the importance for critical reading, in principle, of fine-tuned analysis, for example, when she says 'I thought it's really important to say that.. who's saying that and why, where and what implication its got', (lines 88–90) but claims that for her own current purposes such close analysis is too time-consuming. On the other hand, Yuko is able to elaborate at some length on ways in which her own reading strategies have shifted as a result of the course. This kind of awareness is evidenced in this first part of the interview in comments such as:

1. 'Reading Japanese texts is a bit different from reading English texts', a point she then goes on to elaborate with a specific example: 'once.. I read the particular part, and I thought I understood the meaning and when I moved on to the next (part) I realised I hadn't understood the meaning of the previous one' (lines 19–21) and
2. 'before when I was reading a text and (it said) A is B, I thought OK it's B, – I believed it – well now I think well it could be C' (lines 27–28). Yuko goes on to qualify this point, emphasising that it depends on her existing background knowledge of the subject matter.

Statement 2 is of greater interest for the purposes of this study in that it arguably represents a development from a metacognitive statement, typified in example 1, to a metacritical one. In other words, Yuko shows a metalevel awareness of her own critical stance towards texts in general.

The Classroom

CW: Do you feel that the class helped you become more articulate in giving an opinion...In the group work for instance there was quite a lot of talk and discussion?

45 Y: I think I think it did help to improve my English actually because I don't
    think – if I didn't – if I hadn't taken that class I don't think I would have
    passed Cambridge Proficiency.......
    CW: More particularly what did you find helpful about the course and what
    did you not like?
50 Y: I like the analysing things like adverts and travel brochures. It was quite
    good fun to do but maybe analysing with other people sometimes I had
    completely different opinion from – than my partner and sometimes he
    annoyed me really. Sometimes I feel like I want to be dominant if I can't
    express myself or if I can't agree with other people. I find this very diffi-
55 cult and quite annoying to be honest, especially with the Spanish people.
    They've got a strong opinion about particular things and sometimes
    I can't agree with it, but they are so how do you say so persuasive, they
    got a kind of a power to tell someone, to persuade.
    CW: Are you saying they imposed their point of view?
60 Y: Well sometimes yes, if I may say so. I know I'm a stubborn person because
    I can't change my mind either. Probably what they say might be right, but
    I just can't admit it.
    CW: But what I tried to suggest in the class that there wasn't a right or
    wrong but that people needed to support their point of view.
65 Y: Yes that's true that's true and I think sometimes I thought well hang on
    a minute maybe what the other person's saying may be right I thought.

    (we continue discussing who Yuko worked with in the class)

    Y: I rather did it on my own to be honest so that I can say well what
    I want to say but if it's in a group someone from the group – I don't
    know – representative just represent a view how do you say the overall
70 view of the group but sometimes I think, oh that's not what I think.
    CW: You should have said. So when we had the feedback and people were
    supposed to represent the group, they didn't really, you're saying – not to
    your satisfaction?
    Y: Not always but sometimes I'd rather study on my own.
75 CW: Did you find the framework – the Hallidayan framework that talked
    about *field tenor and mode* – Did you find that helpful or not?
    Y: I wasn't so interested in it to be honest. I didn't use that handout not
    so much. Maybe..if I were studying language maybe I was more inter-
    ested but erm not so much.......Well I am personally I like it. I like
80 analysing language. Otherwise I wouldn't study English at all in the first
    place. I wasn't so interested in being so – how d'you say – analyse so
    deeply the one particular text.
    CW: Did you find any of the features, like we looked at pronouns and modal
    verbs and subjects and objects, participants. Did you did you find some of
85 those categories more useful than others? Did you find it useful to have
    some labels?

Y: You always saying like use of nouns or pronouns like why is it used here, what's the background of it, why is it used. I thought it's really important to say that why – erm who's saying that and why, where and what impli-
90   cation it's got, things like that, I think it's quite important and interesting.
CW: But what you didn't find so useful was the detail?
Y: If I had more time maybe......I could have done a more detailed – analysed more – like what kind of verb is this, is it a passive or action verb, things like that. If I had more time I didn't mind to do that.

Comment

Yuko found the work with a partner on texts (usually just one other person) frustrating. In this she was not alone. Carlos announced on one occasion that he 'hated group work', that he was 'an individualist'. Yuko felt that her partner – they will have varied from week to week – occasionally dominated, that in any case she was not always open to persuasion ('what they say might be right, but I just can't admit it' [lines 61–62) and that the represen-tative did not always adequately represent the views of his or her co-discus-sants in the feedback episodes ('but sometimes I think, oh that's not what I think' [line 70]). Yuko's comments clearly raise doubts about the whole prin-ciple of intersubjectively reached consensus. On the other hand, while she resisted some of its processes and outcomes, Yuko seems to have understood the intention of the pair work and subsequent feedback episode, pedagogi-cally speaking, which was to argue through cases for one interpretation or point of view rather than another, to be prepared to abandon existing views in the face of certain kinds of evidence and, in the role of spokesperson for the feedback sessions, to represent a consensual view – or at least specify areas of disagreement – rather than one's own individual position. Indeed it was the group spokesperson's failure to do this in a fully representative way, which had irritated her.

The wider context

95 *CW*: Do you remember any particular class or text that..particularly you like? Is there any class or text or moment that was memorable?
Y: There are quite a few actually, to be honest. First of all I remember the Chinese women carry the stones. I remember that text very well actually. I think I told you in the diary I was not interested in the text at first but
100   now..I remember it well and then you said something like as well the erm long-neck...?
CW: Oh yes, the long-necked – the giraffe-necked women of Burma.
Y: And then you said something like it might be – it sounds very strange to <u>us</u> but for them it might sound strange why we wear high-heeled shoes or
105   why we do our face lift, things like that and then I thought yes, that's true. And then I thought probably if that particular article was published in

that country then I think it was just nothing, just ordinary article but here it attracts peoples' attention......I can't remember the country. Was it Singapore?

110 *CW*: It was Burma.

Y: Burma yes. If, I don't know, if in Burma there was article about European people – women doing face lift, things like that, they will be very interested in I think..I know it's a cultural difference but I find it's very interesting, particularly when you said that.

115 *CW*: You remembered that? It sticks in your mind?

Y: Yeh yeh.

CW: Was this something that you hadn't thought of before?

Y: Not really no and it all depends your how'd you say you your concept of valuable things and not valuable things as well. For example in Japan like
120 buying flashing cars is a really important thing to show the status, but here people don't care if their car is covered with mud or not cleaned for a year (laughs) or rusty, but for Japanese its unbearable really. Since what you said I thought these other things as well. You got different concept completely.

125 *CW*: Different cultural perspectives.

Y: Yeh yeh aha

CW: Is there any other moment in the class or..a text or discussion we had perhaps?

Y: Yes, yes I remember I think it was Monica and she brought a text
130 about Germany, yes she found it in an English paper – talking about, well speaking ill about German people. She was so angry and I can tell from what she said and things like that, I could tell it's probably for English people. It's just article and just one opinion but she took it so seriously.

135 *CW*: Could you understand when she explained?

Y: Yes yes I understand that she was saying something like it's all misunderstanding.......I was surprised how angry she can be.

CW: Do you feel – have you felt angry? Reading any of the texts?

Y: Reading a text? Yes yes I am especially about Japanese things, if an English
140 paper is criticising something about Japanese things I would find it quite offensive and feel angry I think yes – but not like Monica (laughs).

CW: Can you remember any other occasion or was there any moment that you felt was embarrassing or difficult in the class – because sometimes we discussed perhaps sensitive issues in the class? We talked about race,
145 women – you know, gender.

Y: Yes I remember once you saying something about 'butterfly girls' – Japanese girls – yes well I must admit that I wanted to protest. I mean I was trying to say something like: Japanese women treated like second citizens in Japanese society but that's not what they want to be.

150 *CW*: Japanese women don't want that?

Y: Don't want to be. I think well inside of them I think. In a way they have
to behave like that because otherwise it's not acceptable. Something like
that I wanted to say but it was difficult to explain.
CW: Do you think it was interesting having people from different back-
155   grounds?
Y: It was quite interesting I think. You've got different cultural backgrounds
and they've got different opinions. But sometimes at the same time it
was annoying as well because you can't agree with them at all. But at
the end of the day I thought they just human beings......when you get
160   down to the bottom line it's just the same thing we're saying, like human
rights, about racism, things like that. I thought we shared our opinion
I thought. But – I can't explain to you well but it does – we did have
cultural differences I think yes.
CW: There was a cultural difference but also there was some kind of shared...
165 *Y*: Yes aha I think so, for example, I think it was the French girl – I can't
remember her name – but she was studying British...
CW: British National Party.
Y: National Party yes BNP BNP. It wasn't about her country because she
was from France I think but she was so against it.......and then for
170   example for me, Japanese, I do understand Nazism and things like that
but it wasn't so, how d'you say, close to me at all so – until she showed
her consideration and she take it so seriously...
CW: her concern
Y: it's not even about her country I thought..I thought if I was asked
175   my opinion I thought I can't say anything because I never thought of it.
I never experienced it...
CW: that kind of racism
Y: yes but I can understand what they're saying yes, but I didn't have my
particular opinion.
180 *CW*: Did you feel at the end of the course you were more aware about some
of these issues?
Y: Yes yes I thought now – but before I didn't I just didn't care at all.
I felt a bit ashamed of it because you should be aware of these kind of
things.

Comment

It is at the macro level of awareness that Yuko seems to have been most
prepared to engage with texts and to reflect upon them. Her commentary is
intertextual in the sense that the texts that she quotes as memorable formed
part of a set which, all taken from the magazine *Marie Claire* over a period
of several months, presented women of the East. Yuko has recalled the
vivid image, in the first of these texts, of women in a remote part of China
carrying heavy stones as part of the manual work expected of them, with
which she then connects a later one in this series, the 'Giraffe-necked

women of Burma'. She draws on this second text, as we did in the class, to gain some critical distance from the discourse represented, by hypothesising comparable kinds of representation which might be made of the ways in which Western women adorn or mutilate their bodies. She sees the text as encoding and problematising the position of women in different societies, an observation which she builds on in her discussion of the 'butterfly' metaphor repeated, as a way of describing Eastern women, in two of the texts we examined.

Yuko has appeared to gain in cross-cultural awareness from her engagement with texts and her peers in the classroom. Both the texts and the talk have allowed her to notice what has previously been taken for granted, to look at the familiar with fresh eyes. Evidence for such growth of awareness emerges both in enhanced awareness of different cultural values and practices ('it all depends your concept of valuable things and not valuable'), and in the need to look beyond the local and parochial to reflect on issues of social justice and equity which have universal applications and implications. This would seem to be indicated by Yuko's words: 'when you get down to the bottom line, it's just the same thing we're saying like human rights, about racism, things like that'.

Conclusion

How do the student narratives illuminate the overall research question, namely 'what are the distinguishing features of critical reading in the language classroom?'. In this chapter, I have investigated the question from the students' point of view. What is salient for them? Revisiting these narratives once again, I find it is the issue of point of view itself, of opinion which echoes across these texts, in three major ways. First, the students all offer opinions and judgement using mental process verbs in different kinds of ways. They make extensive use of the language of enquiry and judgement, which brings in 'I think', 'as far as I can see' and 'what I find striking'. Secondly, they comment metacognitively on their own opinion forming and reflection as in for example: 'I've been thinking about' and 'I'd like to question that (i.e. my own) assumption now' (Pierre); and 'I noticed' and 'I found it was easier' (Yuko). And finally and most importantly, for the purposes of critical language study, the students refer directly to the value of having opinions and of being able to articulate them effectively. For Victoria, this was one of her stated goals in attending the Critical Reading course, that it 'will help me make my own opinion (being useful not only in my learning of English but also in my analysis of texts in my own language)' (questionnaire data: page 157). In the interview narrative, it is clear that this remained a central theme of the value of the Critical Reading class for her: 'I wanted my opinion to be heard', she says. Carlos too, while sceptical of the role of a Critical Reading course, sees 'giving my opinion' as a central part of what it means to be a critical reader. Yuko had, as she frankly acknowledges, simply not considered some issues, prior to the course : 'I didn't have my particular opinion', she says.

It is clear that for the students, trying out their voice, defending and arguing through what they wanted to say, was as important as the professed major goal of the course, which was to develop a critical stance to text. Finally the two objectives are complementary in that, being a critical reader, as I have argued the case here, does not involve us merely in individual private scrutiny of the logic or ideology of specific texts. Textual critique is part of public life – or should be, if dominant discourses are to be challenged. The students are therefore right to feel that having the linguistic and critical resources to express their opinion in constative talk gives them a place in an English speaking critical discourse community which extends beyond the language classroom. Critical reading is as much social, to do with negotiations around texts, as it is personal and private. Both the analysis and the interpretation of texts were socially shared in the classroom, against the background of first glance, 'response' readings done privately, in preparation for the class. This links to a second major theme of the book, relating to the classroom community itself. How were views sought, acknowledged, listened to and defended within the smaller groups or the whole class? Did the Critical Reading class offer significant support both in the formation and articulation of opinion?

Yuko was ambivalent. On the one hand, she was frustrated at not having her personal view represented by the group leader. This confirms my own observation that communicatively negotiated interpretations, while idealistically aspired to, were in reality much compromised. However, as noted in the comment on her interview, the classroom talk around text, was in itself opinion forming for Yuko. It seems that she learned from her peers in the classroom something about the kind of social and political issues which would inspire strong views, as when she says: 'I thought if I was asked my opinion, I thought I can't say anything because I never thought of it. I never experienced it.' It becomes clear in Yuko's comment at this point, that opinion is being seen as related to issues of equity, of social justice, as she goes on to acknowledge the need for awareness of such matters: 'you should be aware of these kind of things'. The desirability of having opinions is seen not in an individualistic, self-interested spirit but one of empathy. Difference is acknowledged: as in 'we did have cultural differences I think yes', but is seen within a context where matters of social justice are everyone's business: 'It wasn't about her country because she was from France. I think but she was so against it.......and then for example for me, Japanese, I do understand Nazism and things like that but it wasn't so, how d'you say, close to me at all so-until she showed her consideration and she take it so seriously.'

Finally, what progress did the students make as readers or language learners? Is it enough that the students felt – or so they claimed – to have changed ways of reading, to notice what before was less readily accessible to consciousness? It is difficult to make claims for the role of this particular course in enhancing students' critical awareness, as they were following a number of other courses concurrent with this one, and were living and studying in an English-speaking environment, where they were exposed to many cultural influences and diverse kinds of language input. Nonetheless it is possible to argue, if we refer back to the key principles claimed for critical pedagogy in Chapter 3, that the students were beginning to notice, at varying levels of specificity, features of texts and literacy practices, located in contextual and cultural settings, in ways which had hitherto eluded them. So, at least Victoria claims when she says at one point in her interview: 'I stop and think and previously I didn't.' The evidence of diaries, reading protocols and interviews suggests, that, for some students at least, their own voices became clearer to them by locating them within other voices in a multicultural classroom community.

A Postscript

Let us return to the overall question with which I began this book: what does it mean to be a critical reader in a foreign language? I noted at the outset that I aimed for a two-layered kind of analysis: the analysis of texts, and the analysis of the classroom interaction in which students critique text. Within the classroom, I wanted to explore the materials and procedures which might promote critical reading, to embrace not just the approach to specific texts but, eventually, ways of relating those readings to wider social and cultural practices.

It may seem presumptuous to make claims about the value of critical reading pedagogy on the basis of one class and, moreover, a handful of students within that class. Nonetheless, it seems important in principle to ground some of the grand narratives of critical pedagogy within more local and specific kinds of engagements between participants in a particular setting, the language classroom in my case; also to gain a sense of the students' own views of the Critical Reading course.

Most of the students appeared to welcome opportunities to express opinion in extended talk and they engaged enthusiastically with the texts, which they had a hand in choosing. However, one is bound to ask whether they made progress as language learners or as readers. Having made a – rather unfashionable – plea for the notion of progress throughout this book, how do my claims stack up, if we look for evidence of the students' development of knowledge and understanding? For, in arguing against a relativist position, it is clear that I think progress matters. Nonetheless, conclusions as to what the students gained from the Critical Reading course can only be very tentative for a number of reasons. One is that no test was carried out to establish how critically aware students were on embarking on the course, other than through a very open 'commentary on text' task with which the course began. Indeed it would be difficult to offer conclusive proof as to development, in a case such as this, which eschewed assessment by quantitative methods and was in any case more concerned with longer-term effects. All of which begs the question whether one can teach criticality at

192

all, and also leads me to the first of the set of objections to critical reading which I posed early in my book, in Chapter 2. It will be recalled that there were three: namely, that critical reading cannot, should not or need not be taught. In other words that it is unfeasible, unethical and unnecessary. I shall discuss each point in turn. At the same time I shall take the opportunity to revisit these issues with reference to some of the key themes of this book.

Feasibility

As discussed at the start of this book, a major dilemma about the feasibility of CLA for L2 learners relates to their knowledge of the language they are analysing for ideological effect. If they have not fully mastered the core features of the language, how might they know what are significant lexical or syntactic departures from textual norms? Is it not like offering cake before the bread and butter? Thus a methodology which might be effective for fully proficient first language learners, who have acquired the language system, cannot operate with foreign and L2 learners. They need texts for *learning*, not for critical use. My answer to this objection is that I believe that language for learning and language for analysis need not be antithetical: learning about language arises in the course of analysis. That is, language awareness and language development can occur in tandem in that both the analytic reading of texts and critical talk around texts constitute learning opportunities. When we argue through a point of view or defend a position or 'think aloud' through a written text, in that process we gain a clearer understanding of what we ourselves mean as well as a fuller understanding of the meaning potential of English.

Equally, when it comes to reading, conventional and critical stances are not mutually exclusive. On the contrary, critical interpretation of text needs to be grounded and supported by adequate understanding of the language system, as conventionally understood. Moreover, provisional submission to the text may be necessary in the first instance, before any kind of resistance can become meaningful or sensible. As noted in Chapter 1, texts cannot mean anything one wishes them to; both text qua text and authorial intention, must be respected: hence the characterisation of reading as a three-way interaction between the author, the text and the reader. However, one does not need to wait for the achievement of some kind of perfect or full competence in text comprehension to be achieved (not in any case realisable, I would argue) before the work of critique is begun.

In the case of the Critical Reading class, the first phase of reading was done prior to the class through surveying the texts at home. As language proficiency levels varied, for some students this experience would consist of a 'reader-response' approach, where, especially with some texts, a fairly quick read would establish their initial impression of what the text was about; with other students some work with dictionaries might be needed.

This was the ground work, the personal preparation on texts done by students in advance of the class, before the move into shared analysis and interpretation which the lessons themselves centred on. However, the 'noticing' aspects of language analysis can also work in favour of orthodox comprehension. For, in critical reading, students are inevitably forced to scrutinise core, unexceptional textual features as well as those which might be claimed to carry ideological significance. Both are defined by reference to each other. In this way critical awareness may develop in tandem with a growth of understanding, more generally about the nature of texts and features of the English language.

A second objection to critical reading, as defined here, centres around the inevitable partiality of analysis – in both senses of the word – as incomplete and as biased. First, as Fowler (1996) notes, the fundamental concepts of systemic functional grammar are abstract and difficult for students. One can attempt only to provide some key terms and concepts in the hope that one can get as high a mileage as possible out of such tools to illuminate aspects of texts which are otherwise opaque. Moreover, while in Chapter 2, I set out reasons which favour systemic-functional grammar as a tool for CLA, it may be that traditional grammatical terms, already known or partly known by students, can serve the purpose equally well. Hudson (forthcoming) argues the pragmatic case, by proposing that the teacher's role is not necessarily to teach new sets of terms but to 'guide the pupils through the grammar they know already, providing established ideas and terminology as required' (p. 7). The fact, that students on the Critical Reading course drew in highly selective ways on the very schematic framework I provided, suggests that the terminology was cumbersome. Nonetheless, students claimed in general to welcome the framework as a guide or heuristic, a point of reference regarding what it might be worth attending to within texts. Finally, as Widdowson (2000), strongly critical of CDA, concedes, all analysis is necessarily selective. I aimed to address this dilemma by locating text analysis and interpretation within an interpretative community, such as a classroom, whose members could bring different insights, resources and linguistic knowledge to the task in hand. The second meaning of 'partial', that is bias, is also at least partly addressed by locating the analysis and discussion within an interpretative community where participants, taking their bearings against the principles of an ideal speech situation, debate in a manner which is as unconstrained as possible.

What about the gains in language awareness, specifically CLA, which it was the aim of the course to promote? At the micro level, there is some evidence towards the end of the course that students are drawing to a greater degree on conventional grammatical terms, which some students were already familiar with, as well as some of the Hallidayan terminology. However, it is noticeable that students produce the systemic-functional terminology to order, that is, on request, rather than draw on it in ways which significantly enhance insight, either for themselves or for the group. Some terms, such as 'participant' are readily taken on board by most students while a fuller range of terms are used only by a few. This clearly raises the issue of what kind and degree of metalinguistic scaffolding supports CLA. As noted in Chapter 2, research in SLA (cf. Ellis 1997) raises doubts of the value of metalanguage in itself – at least as supporting language development. This issue has arisen recently once again in the United Kingdom in connection with the National Literacy Strategy which introduces a considerable amount of metalanguage to very young children. The assumption has been that explicit teaching of terminology makes aspects of literacy and texts more transparent to young learners, and by the same token gives them more control over learning to read and write. Research, which I have carried out with young bilingual ten-year-olds (Wallace 2001), suggests that this assumption is doubtful. However, this does not mean that metalinguistic terminology, either more generally or specifically based around systemic-functional grammar, is worthless for reasons I set out next.

Even if the students themselves may not make active use of a wide set of grammatical terms, it is useful for the teacher to use metalanguage as a way of making ideas more explicit and transparent. That is, it may support students' understanding of language practices, products and processes, provided that it is conceptually well grounded and not presented in merely mechanistic fashion. Secondly, while the grammar may not be immediately taken into active use by learners, it serves as a longer term resource, possibly to be drawn on in future. This was certainly suggested in the Critical Reading class by Yuko, who did not challenge the usefulness of a grammatical framework for aiding focus of analysis; merely that it did not serve her present purposes. Moreover, salient features of language, significant in identifying ideology, as I have suggested, can still be pointed to, in the absence of terminological specificity. For the students in the present study, while metalanguage was sparingly used, textual phenomena were, nonetheless, pointed to, sometimes in quite fine-grained ways. That is, the ideological effects of language use were noted, even in the absence of specific systemic-functional terminology. Yuko was able to see, for instance, how the use of quoted material enabled *The Times* newspaper to offer opinion without taking direct responsibility for it. She notices the ideology of text, while avoiding the metalinguistic baggage. It must be remembered too that language awareness, critical or otherwise, is open-ended. There is no finite end point to textual critique, merely greater depth of exploration into what I have called, following Halliday (1987), 'hidden grammar'. It was largely for this reason that I aimed to discuss processes rather than products or specific outcomes through the classroom analyses and student narratives.

A third problem around feasibility is more fundamental than the facilitating role, or otherwise, of a grammatical framework. For, critical language study is located within critical pedagogy as I argued in Chapter 3, and critical pedagogy has greater ambitions than merely providing tools for the analysis of particular texts in immediate contexts. This is nothing less than to change the world. Pennycook (2001), in his comprehensive overview of the field, even though he challenges enlightenment modernist views of progress, states the need for a notion of preferred futures, an educational vision that is 'capable of narrating stories of possibility' (Simon 1992 in Pennycook 2001: 172). In what way can critical language study, whether seen as critical reading, or CLA more widely, be emancipatory for students in meaningful ways? I have argued against an individualist interpretation of emancipation and change. However, the social and the individual are mutually defining, if we take Habermas's (1992) notion of 'individuation', by which the individual emerges from the social. It follows that both students and teachers will look for ways, as individuals, to use critique productively in their lives, a notion which seems to me to be captured in ideas such as preferred futures, stories of possibility, and, a term used by Kress (2000a) 'design for social futures'.

Kress suggests that critique is backward looking, that 'it looks at the present through the means of past production' (Kress 2000a: 160); we therefore need some notion of design to take us forward. Kress sees such designs as making use of a wide range of textual forms, in music, dance and the new technologies. But even in pedagogy which relies on print sources, as in the cases drawn on in this book, unless there is some resolution, some sense of a way forward, students can feel unsettled that their worlds and, in some cases, deeply held values have been challenged to leave them, as McKinney (2002) puts it, 'stranded in critique'. This was the case with her students. Trapped in the guilt of an apartheid past in which their lives and identities were deeply interwoven, they were looking for a discourse to take them forward. McKinney's class which specifically confronted issues of continuing racism in South African society led in the short term to resentment and opposition. Coming from a context of recent social upheaval, students felt that they had already embraced change. While this was not at all necessarily the case, McKinney acknowledges that these particular students needed, not just to acknowledge the past, but to engage actively in some kind of transformation for the future.

In short then, critical pedagogies need to find some way of taking their project forward so that participants, both teachers and learners, are not stranded in critique, powerless rather than empowered. In the Critical Reading class we did not adequately address the issue of how one might take CLA forward in constructive ways. The final question which I had posed: what other 'ways of writing about the topic are there?' might be applied not just to texts but to the formation of alternative discourses. In other words, although the question is posited around a specific text, it has wider implications. How can we reshape dominant discourses so that, collectively and socially, we take part in reshaping social life? On the Critical Reading course, we remained centred around texts as currently realised; we needed to think more creatively of reshaping texts, imagining new discourses, even new genres and modes. In a concrete way, this can involve various kinds of rewriting or other forms of textual adaptation and production. More ambitiously it might involve challenging and changing social arrangements in classrooms and in education more widely. We did not make these imaginative projections.

Nonetheless, I would also argue that critique is itself creative; that social change and design cannot be separated from critique but is inseparably part of it. Even in preparing designs they should be open to continuing critique. Also we can defend talk as social action in its own right. This is very much in the spirit of Habermas's use of the term 'communicative action'. As Pusey, commentating on Habermas, notes: 'we are born with the potential to use (universal skills of communication) to create a better society' (Pusey 1987: 73). Talk can change the world; it can make war and make peace. More generally, ways of talking and ways of reading are part of social life. Working on language then is not just preliminary to change but is an inherent part of social change. In particular, critical talk and critical literacy, in standing back from everyday social life, offer the potential for change and challenge to dominant ways with words.

Desirability

A more fundamental criticism of CLA and its satellite pedagogies is that not only is CLA not feasible in any significant way, but it is positively damaging. There is a danger that one is promoting not enhanced critical – and therefore independent – thinkers but 'instruction in ideological partiality' especially, the argument goes, as most critical pedagogy teachers would see themselves as politically on the left. As I note in Wallace (1995: 347), there is a whiff of missionary zeal around projects with audacious, not to say arrogant, ambitions to change the world. There is no doubt that, because CLA is a pedagogy which makes no claims to disinterestedness but is committed to the pursuit of change towards a better world, the teacher's own ideological role necessarily comes to the fore. We may (cf. Wallace *op. cit.*: 347) be replacing the tyranny of the conventional classroom texts with the tyranny of the most powerful interpretative voice in the classroom, that of the teacher.

Clearly, where the stakes are higher, the risks are greater and the consequences worse, when the project fails. It is for this reason that careful thought needs to be given to the place of a critical pedagogy within wider social and institutional structures. For various reasons, I was able to offer a very specific kind of course to students who enrolled. It was an optional course, not seen as part of mainstream language teaching, in the way that the literature class and the translation class were, which Victoria describes.

This has its advantages. However, it also creates problems. For CLA to be meaningful in a wider sense and for the longer term, both for foreign language and native speaker students, it needs to be not a marginalised project but one which commands the respect and commitment, if not of the mainstream, then of significant numbers of co-operating teachers and learners. While there are then dangers of a somewhat attenuated critical curriculum, it would seem important that critical reading should be, not something, done as a discrete kind of activity from time to time, or as a distinctive set of procedures, but ultimately a way of reading which cuts across curriculum areas and circumstances in daily life, an available 'stance' or perspective on texts of all kinds and in all contexts.

In terms of the charge regarding the supposed left wing bias of critically oriented teachers (for I have never heard it claimed that critical pedagogues are in any way of the political right), the first point to make is the obvious one that all teaching, including language teaching is political, as are all texts, a point I made at the start of the book. However, there is the undoubted danger that critical reading can slip into the demonising of texts and, more particularly, of writers. The pursuit of specific, individual targets is often conducted more strategically than rationally. It is important to acknowledge and respect a range of views within the texts critiqued in the classroom and offered by classroom members. We might aim for a negoti-ated understanding that the contributions of all participants will be valued and carefully considered and that strategic interventions will be ruled out of court; that is, contributions are to be intended as co-operating in the pursuit of greater understanding, not as persuading others to one's particular point of view. The presence of a critical stance, in its sense of preparedness to resist, must be balanced against the essentially collaborative nature of class-room enquiry if it is to be conducted as a rational pursuit of greater truth and truthfulness.

Ethical dilemmas arise, I would argue, not in decisions about overall values of respect for others – these are non-negotiable – but at more local specific levels. It is clearly very difficult to make judgements about what kinds of statement in which written or spoken context are prejudicial to certain groups of people. On many occasions, a teacher needs to make finely tuned judgements as to whether to pursue debate, or to allow a personal opinion to stand unchallenged by oneself or by fellow class participants. I recall Carlos, in the context of our discussion on the 'butterfly' metaphor, to describe oriental women, and which Yuko had found offensive, saying defiantly: 'Well they *are* like butterflies'! What is important is that, judge-ments about equity and discrimination should be negotiated by the students themselves in constative talk, though clearly this will be steered, with varying degrees of control, by the teacher, as I noted in Chapter 6.

I would argue that ethical assumptions operate in any class. They are simply aired more explicitly in a critical pedagogy, in the sense that issues related to inequality and social disadvantage are on the agenda. It is important to add, too, that such issues need not be presented as 'topics' to be talked about; they may emerge from the discourses embedded within any texts which are brought into the class by teacher and student and which might concern a whole range of subject matter, not at first sight contentious. However, I believe that the educational value of attention to social justice issues can be defended in principle, if we recall Yuko's words in her interview, relating to her enhanced awareness of the experience of racism, her sense of shame that such issues had not previously exercised her, and her expression of empathy with some of her class mates.

Necessity

The final caveat relates to the need for critical language study for foreign language students in particular. Yes, one might say, people need to read critically in their first language, but surely not in a foreign language. We read, it might be said, for a whole range of quite different purposes in a foreign language. In answer to this I would say, firstly, that language awareness and ways of reading are linguistically interdependent. Both Yuko and Victoria talk at various points of how their understanding of Spanish and Japanese, respectively, has grown and changed, in the light of the Critical Reading course. Critical ways of reading, whether of specific texts or of language and literacy practices, will cross language boundaries. Second, I would argue that a CLA pedagogy supports foreign language learners in two further ways: first, although the focus is not on formal language development, opportunities to engage in discussion around texts allow students to draw more fully on their existing linguistic resources and to stretch them at the same time. What's more, grammatical accuracy, as well as general fluency, can, ultimately, be extended in the search for precision, in wishing to be clear and co-operative in argument. These abilities are better promoted by CLA than by most versions of CLT, encapsulated in what I have called the *how many calories has an orange* school of teaching.

Finally, I would like to restate the case for the special role of *English*: unlike any other current language, and however much we might deplore its hegemony in terms of the health of world languages, for the foreseeable future English is the language of globalisation. I wanted my learners to acquire a powerful English, not to empower them as individuals for the here and now, but as members of the widest possible community of English language users. My argument is that the development of critical talk and critical literacy, mutually supportive as I have claimed, allows foreign language learners to function in a wider arena than the local, the specific and the immediately relevant. In spite of the likely presence of formal inaccuracies and infelicities in their language production, learners of English as a foreign or second language can be highly effective users of English as a world language, as it embraces a range of settings. My point has been indeed that they are potentially more advantaged on this kind of territory than in day-to-day, informal interaction. A critically nuanced, elaborated English offers learners a potentially powerful identity outside the classroom, as well as within it.

My final plea, then on the necessity of critical work with second and foreign language learners of English, is that it is in fact discriminatory not to provide the tools and resources which allow them access to powerful uses of language and literacy. It is irresponsible to teach students the domesticating discourses of CLT and task-based learning. We need to reposition our students both as readers of English language texts and as students of language more generally. They happen to be foreign language learners. In some ways this is irrelevant in the context of English as a global language. As I started this book by saying, following Rampton (1990), it is becoming less relevant to talk about 'native speaker' English. We should be thinking in terms of producing expert readers and expert talkers around text, whether they are first or second language users of English. But this should not be taken to mean a relativistic notion that all are equally effective users of English, or of any other language. Constative speech and analytical forms of reading need working on. What it does mean is that native speakers have no premium here. For, while the speech of the students in this study displays what are conventionally viewed as non-native features, it nonetheless exemplifies what I have called (Wallace 2002) literate English, talk which is mediated by access to written texts, and is effectively elaborated for public use and for public critique.

As noted earlier, the question of what to do about English as critical educators is complex. I have chosen to take one stance on this. Learners in many parts of the world need English both for personal empowerment, but more relevant for my purposes here, to be part of a world community which will necessarily, for the immediate future, use English. This need emerged strongly through the students' own narratives: they want their voices to be heard. And specifically they want them to be heard in English. They are not alone: demonstrators round the world use English, knowing they will thereby get world TV and press coverage. This is even more the case since 1989, when I taught my first Critical Reading class. My aim in the Critical Reading course was that my students should feel part of this world and ultimately be able to contribute to and reshape its dominant discourses. This is what I mean by being powerful users of language and literacy – to be active questioners not just of texts nor of their own reality, but of wider social and political iniquities.

Finally, the whole concept of what might be meant by critical pedagogy, dealt with very partially in this book, needs to be more fully explored. The classroom study at the centre of this thesis can only serve to raise questions about the nature of texts and methodology, and classroom methodology which might form the basis of a pedagogy which is differently focused, designed to serve different ends, from language teaching programmes inspired by the Communicative Movement. Finally, this study is presented, as argued throughout, not as a definitive model of good practice but as a tentative step towards the development of materials and classroom procedures which can help learners to notice language phenomena, and to articulate their observations in unaccustomed ways. It is inspired by the view that change and progress are possible and that seemingly intractable unjust social arrangements can be challenged. In this spirit, I conclude with words by Raymond Williams:

It is only in a shared belief and insistence that there are practical alternatives that the balance of forces and chances begins to alter. Once the inevitabilities are challenged, we begin gathering our resources for a journey of hope. If there are no easy answers there are still available discoverable hard answers, and it is these that we can now learn to make and share. This has been, from the beginning, the sense and the impulse of the long revolution (Williams, 1983: 268–69).

Bibliography

Adams, M. J. *Beginning to Read* (Cambridge, MA: MIT Press, 1990).

Adjer, C. and Hoyle, S. *Strategic Language Use in Later Childhood* (Oxford: Oxford University Press, 1998).

Alderson, C. 'Models of language? Whose? What for? What use? BAAL 1996 Pit Corder Memorial Lecture', in A. Ryan and A. Wray (eds) *Evolving Models of Language*. British Association for Applied Linguistics in association with Clevedon (Multilingual Matters, 1997).

Alderson, C., Clapham, C. and Steel, D. *Metalinguistic Knowledge, Language Aptitude and Language Proficiency*, Mimeograph (University of Lancaster, 1995).

Alexander, R. *Culture and Pedagogy: International Comparisons in Primary* Education (Oxford: Blackwell, 2000).

Andersen, R. *The Power and the Word* (London: Paladin, 1988).

Anderson, N. and Vandergrift, L. 'Increasing metacognitive awareness in the L2 classroom by using think-aloud protocols and other verbal report formats', in R. Oxford (ed.) *Language Learning Strategies Around the World: Cross Cultural Perspectives* (Honolulu: University of Hawaii Press, 1996).

Apple, M. *Ideology and Curriculum*, 2nd edition (New York and London: Routledge, 1990).

Archer, D. and Cottingham, S. *The Reflect Mother Manual: A New Approach to Adult Literacy* (London: Actionaid, 1996).

Arizpe, E., Coulthard, K. and Styles, M. 'Visual literacy and children's books' paper presented at 19th World Congress on Reading, Edinburgh, 2002.

Atkinson, D. 'A Critical approach to critical thinking in TESOL', *TESOL Quarterly* 31(1): 71–94 (1997).

Auerbach, E. and Wallerstein, N. *English for the Workplace. ESL for Action: Problem Posing at Work* (Wokingham: Addison Wesley, 1987).

Bachman, L. 'The development and use of criterion-referenced tests of language ability in language program evaluation', in R. K. Johnson (ed.) *The Second Language Curriculum* (Cambridge: Cambridge University Press, 1992).

Baker, C. and Freebody, P. 'The crediting of literate competence in classroom talk' in, H. Fehring and P. Green (eds) *Critical Literacy* (Delaware: International Reading Association, 2001).

Bakhtin, M. *Speech Genres and Other Late Essays* (Austin: University of Texas Press, 1986).

Barro, A., Byram, M., Grimm, H., Morgan, C. and Roberts, C. 'Cultural studies for advanced language learners', in D. Graddol, L. Thompson and M. Byram (eds) *Language and Culture*. (British Studies in Applied Linguistics 7 in association with Clevedon: Multilingual Matters, 1993).

Barthes, R. *Image-Music-Text* (Glasgow: Fontana, 1977).

Bartlett, F. C. *Remembering: A Study in Experimental and Social Psychology* (Cambridge: Cambridge University Press, 1932).

Barton, D. *Literacy* (Oxford: Blackwell, 1994).

Barton, D. and Hamilton, M. *Local Literacies* (London: Routledge, 1998).

Barton, D., Hamilton, M. and Ivanic, R. *Situated Literacies* (London: Routledge, 2000).

Bauman, Z. *Intimations of Post-modernity* (London: Routledge, 1992).

Baynham, M. *Literacy Practices: Investigating Literacy in Social Contexts* (London: Longman, 1995).

Berger, P. and Luckman, T. *The Social Construction of Reality* (London: Penguin, 1966).
Bernstein, B. *The Structuring of Pedagogic Discourse Class, Codes and Control*, Vol. 4 (London: Routledge, 1990).
Bernstein, B. *Pedagogy, Symbolic Control and Identity: Theory, Research, Critique* (London: Taylor & Francis, 1996).
Best, S. and Kellner, D. *Postmodern Theory* (Basingstoke: Macmillan, 1991).
Block, E. 'The comprehension strategies of second language readers', *TESOL Quarterly* 20(3): 463–94 (1986).
Blum-Kulka, S. and Peled-Elhanen, N. 'Child-directed ulpanit: language and ideology in Israeli second language classrooms for children', in *Kognitive Aspeckte des Lehrens und Lernens voc Fremdsprachen Festschrift fur*. Willis J. Edmondson sum 60. Geburtstag (Gunter Narr Verlag Tubingen 1998).
Blything, M. 'An Enquiry into the Theory and Practice of Critical Discourse Analysis', Unpublished dissertation submitted for the degree of MA by the Modular Master's method (University of Salford, 1994).
Brice-Heath, S. *Ways with Words* (Cambridge: Cambridge University Press, 1983).
Brown, R. and Gillman, A. 'The pronouns of power and solidarity', in P. P. Giglioli (ed.) *Language and Social Context* (Harmondsworth: Penguin, 1972).
Brumfit, C. *Communicative Methodology in Language Teaching: The Roles of Fluency and Accuracy* (Cambridge: Cambridge University Press, 1984).
Brumfit, C. 'Teacher professionalism and research', in G. Gook and B. Seidlhofer (eds) *Principle and Practice in Applied Linguistics Studies in Honour of H.G. Widdowson* (Oxford: Oxford University Press, 1995).
Callinicos, A. *Social Theory a Historical Introduction* (Oxford: Polity Press, 1999).
Canagarajah, S. *Resisting Linguistic Imperialism in English Teaching* (Oxford: Oxford University Press, 1999).
Canagarajah, S. 'Globalization, methods and practice in periphery classrooms', in D. Block and D. Cameron (eds) *Globalization and Language Teaching* (London: Routledge, 2002).
Carter, R. 'The new grammar teaching', in R. Carter (ed.) *Knowledge about Language and the Curriculum* (London: Hodder and Stoughton, 1990).
Carter, R. and Walker, R. *Literature and the Learner: Introduction to Literature and the Learner: Methodological Approaches* (Modern English Publications in association with the British Council, 1989).
Cassell, P. (ed.) *The Giddens Reader* (Basingstoke: Macmillan, 1993).
Cavalcanti, M. 'Investigating FL reading performance through pause protocols', in C. Faerch and G. Kasper (eds) *Introspection in Second Language Research* (Clevedon: Multilingual Matters, 1987).
Cazden, C. *Classroom Discourse: The Language of Teaching and Learning*, 2nd edition (Portsmouth NH: Heinmann, 2001).
Cazden, C. Seminar on 'Classroom Discourse' at Institute of Education, University of London, 2002.
Chouliaraki, L. and Fairclough, N. *Discourse in Late Modernity: Rethinking Critical Discourse Analysis* (Edinburgh: Edinburgh University Press, 1999).
Clark, R., Fairclough, N., Ivanic, R. and Martin-Jones, M. 'A Critical review of three current approaches to language awareness', *Language and Education* 4(4): 249–60 (1990).
Clark, R., Fairclough, N., Ivanic, R. and Martin-Jones, M. 'Critical language awareness part 2: towards critical alternatives', *Language and Education* 5(1): 41–54 (1991).
Clark, R. and Ivanic, R. *The Politics of Writing* (London: Routledge, 1997).

Clark, R. and Ivanic, R. 'Raising critical awareness of language: a curriculum aim for the new millennium', *Language Awareness* **8**: 63–70 (1999).

Clayton, M. 'Visual and Verbal Texts and Language Teaching', Unpublished Ph.D. thesis (University of London, 1995).

Clegg, J. 'The cognitive value of literate talk in small-group classroom discourse', in P. Skehan and C. Wallace (eds) *Thames Valley University Working Papers* **1**: 1–22 (1992).

Collini, S. *Introduction: Interpretation Terminable and Interminable in Umberto Eco; Interpretation and Overinterpretation with Richard Rorty, Jonathan Culler and Christine Brooke-Rose* (Cambridge: Cambridge University Press, 1992).

Comber, B. 'Classroom explorations in critical literacy', *Australian Journal of Language and Literacy* **16**: 73–82 (1993).

Cook, G. *Discourse Analysis* (Oxford: Oxford University Press, 1989).

Cook, G. *Discourse and Literature* (Oxford: Oxford University Press, 1994).

Cooper, D. 'Missing Manchester values', *The Guardian*, 22 December, 2000.

Cope, B. and Kalantzis, M. (ed.) *Multiliteracies* (London: Routledge, 2000).

Culler, J. *On Deconstruction* (London: Routledge and Kegan Paul, 1983).

D'Andrade, R. and Strauss, C. (eds) *Human Motives and Cultural Models* (Cambridge: Cambridge University Press, 1992).

Davies, F. *Introducing Reading* (London: Penguin, 1995).

Deriawianka, B. *Exploring How Texts Work* (Newtown, Australia: Primary English Teaching Association, 1990).

Dictionary of English Language and Culture (London and Harlow: Longman, 1992).

Eagleton, T. *Ideology* (London and New York: Verso, 1991).

Eagleton, T. 'Capitalism, modernism and postmodernism', in D. Lodge (ed.) *Modern Criticism and Theory: A Reader* (Harlow: Longman, 1988).

Easthope, A. and Mcgowan, K. *A Critical and Cultural Theory Reader* (Buckingham: Open University Press, 1992).

Eco, U. *The Role of the Reader* (London: Hutchinson, 1979).

Eco, U. 'Between author and text', in S. Collini (ed.) *Interpretation and Overinterpretation* (New York: Cambridge, 1992).

Edwards, D. and Mercer, N. *Common Knowledge: The Development of Understanding in the Classroom* (London: Routledge, 1987).

Ellis, R. *Second Language Acquisition* (Oxford: Oxford University Press, 1996).

Ellis, R. 'Explicit knowledge and second language pedagogy in knowledge about language', in L. Van Lier and D. Corson (eds) *Encyclopedia of Language and Education*, Vol. 6, pp. 109–18 (Dordrecht: Kluwer, 1997).

Ellsworth, E. 'Why doesn't this feel empowering? Working through the repressive myths of critical pedagogy', *Harvard Educational Review* **59**: 297–324 (1989).

Fairclough, N. *Language and Power* (London: Longman, 1989).

Fairclough, N. (ed.) *Critical Language Awareness* (London: Longman, 1992a).

Fairclough, N. *Discourse and Social Change* (Cambridge: Polity Press, 1992b).

Fairclough, N. *Media Discourse* (Bristol: Edward Arnold, 1995).

Fairclough, N. 'The discourse of new labour: critical discourse analysis', in M. Wetherell, S. Taylor and S. Yates (eds) *Discourse as Data* (Milton Keynes: The Open University, 2001).

Fish, S. *Is there a Text in this Class? The Authority of Interpretative Communities* (Bost Ion, MA: Harvard University Press, 1980).

Foucault, M. *The Archaeology of Knowledge* (New York: Tavistock Publications, 1972).

Fowler, R. 'On critical linguistics in texts and practices', in C. Caldas-Coulthard and M. Coulthard (eds) *Readings in Critical Discourse Analysis* (London and New York: Routledge, 1996).

Fowler, R., Hodge, R., Kress, G. and Trew, A. *Language and Control* (London: Routledge and Kegan Paul, 1979).

Freeman, A. 'Eye Movement Study of Biliterate Spanish/English Fourth Graders', Paper presented at 19th World Congress on Reading, Edinburgh, 2002.

Freire, P. *The Pedagogy of the Oppressed* (London: Penguin, 1972a).

Freire, P. *Cultural Action for Freedom* (London: Penguin, 1972b).

Gee, J. *Social Linguistics and Literacies* (Basingstoke: Falmer, 1990).

Gieve, S. 'Response to Atkinson: a critical approach to critical thinking', *TESOL Quarterley* 32: 123–29 (1998).

Giroux, H. 'Theory of reproduction and resistance in the new sociology of education: A critical analysis', *Harvard Educational Review* 3(53): 257–93 (1983).

Giroux, H. 'Literacy and the politics of difference', in C. Lankshear and P. McLaren (eds) *Critical Literacy: Politics, Praxis and the Postmodern* (Albany, NY: State University of New York Press, 1993).

Goodman, K. *On Reading* (Portsmouth: Heinemann, 1996).

Goodman, Y. 'The development of initial literacy', in H. Goelman, A. Oberg and F. Smith (eds) *Awakening to Literacy* (Exeter: Heinemann Educational Books, 1984).

Goffman, I. *Forms of Talk* (Philadelphia: University of Pennsylvania Press, 1981).

Gough, P. 'The new literacy: caveat emptor', *Journal of Research in Reading Special Issue*: *The contribution of psychological research* 18(2): 79–86 (1995).

Gramsci, A. in Q. Hoare and G. Nowell Smith (eds) *Selections from prison notebooks* (London: Lawrence and Wishart, 1971).

Grabe, W. 'Current developments in second language reading research', *TESOL Quarterly* 25: 375–406 (1991).

Graves, D. *Writing: Teachers and Children at Work* (Exeter: N. H. Heninmann Educational, 1983).

Gray, J. 'The global coursebook in English Language Teaching', in D. Block and D. Cameron (eds) (2002).

Greaney, V. Keynote Lecture on the global textbook: 19th World Congress of Reading, Edinburgh, 2002.

Gregory, E. *Making Sense of a New World: Learning to Read in a Second Language* (London: Chapman, 1996).

Gregory, E. and Williams, A. *City Literacies: Learning to Read Across Generations and Cultures* (London: Routledge, 2000).

Grice, H. P. 'Logic and conversation', in P. Cole and J. L. Morgan (eds) *Syntax and Semantics*, Vol. 3 Speech Acts pp. 41–58 (Academic Press, 1975).

Habermas, J. 'Towards a Theory of Communicative Competence', *Inquiry* 13, 360–75 (1970).

Habermas, J. *Communication and the Evolution of Society* (London: Heinemann, 1979).

Habermas, J. *Theory of Communicative Action*, Vol. 1. Reason and the Rationalization of Society, translated by Thomas McCarthy (London: Heinemann, 1984).

Habermas, J. *Postmetaphysical Thinking* (Oxford: Blackwell, 1992).

Hall, S. 'New ethnicities', in J. Donald and Rattansi (eds) *Race, Culture and Difference* (London: Sage, 1992).

Halliday, M. A. K. 'Language structure and language function', in J. Lyons (ed.) *New Horizons in Linguistics* (London: Penguin, 1970).

Halliday, M. A. K. *Learning How to Mean: Explorations in the Development of Language* (New York: Edward Arnold, 1977).

Halliday, M. A. K. 'Language and the order of nature', in N. Fabb, D. Attridge, A. Durant and C. MacCabe (eds) *The Linguistics of Writing* (Manchester: Manchester University Press, 1987).

Halliday, M. A. K. 'New ways of meaning: a challenge to applied linguistics', *Journal of Applied Linguistics* 6, 7–36 (Annual Publication of the Greek Applied Linguistics Association Thessaloniki, 1990).

Halliday, M. A. K. *An introduction to Functional Grammar*, 2nd edition (London: Edward Arnold, 1994).

Halliday, M. A. K. 'Literacy and linguistics: a functional perspective', in R. Hasan and G. Williams (eds) *Literacy in Society* (Harlow: Addison Wesley Longman, 1996).

Halliday, M. A. K. and Hasan, R. *Language, Context and Text: Aspects of Language in a Social-semiotic Perspective* (Victoria: Deakin University Press, 1985).

Hammersley, M. Lecture on 'Value Neutrality' at Institute of Education, University of London, 1996.

Hargreaves, A. *Changing Teachers, Changing Times: Teachers' Work and Culture in the Postmodern Age* (London: Cassell, 1994).

Harrison, C. 'The reading process and learning to read: what a teacher using a "real books" approach needs to know', in C. Harrison and M. Coles (eds) *The Reading for Real Handbook* (London: Routledge, 1992).

Held, D. *Introduction to Critical Theory Horkheimer to Habermas* (Cambridge: Polity Texts and Practices, 1990).

Hesse, H. *Steppenwolf* (London: Penguin, 1965).

Hewitt, R. Lecture on 'Discourse of racism' given at inaugural meeting of Applied Linguistics Centre, Thames Valley University, 1996.

Hoggart, R. *The Way We Live Now* (London: Chatto and Windus, 1995).

Holborow, M. *The Politics of English* (London: Sage Publications, 1999).

Hosenfield, C. 'A preliminary investigation of the reading strategies of successful and unsuccessful second language learners', *System* 5, 110–123 (1977).

Hosenfield, C. 'Case studies of ninth grade readers', in C. Alderson and S. Urquhart (eds) *Reading in a Foreign Language* (London: Longman, 1984).

Hoy, D. and McCarthy, T. *Critical Theory* (Oxford: Blackwell, 1994).

Hudson, D. 'Grammar teaching is dead NOT' to appear, in R. Wheeler (ed.) *Language Alive in the Classroom* (Westport CT: Greenwood forth coming).

Iser, W. *The Act of Reading: A Theory of Aesthetic Response* (London: Routledge & Kegan Paul, 1978).

James, C. L. R. Interview with Kenan Malik, *The New Statesman* July, 2001.

Janks, H. and Ivanic, R. 'Critical Language Awareness and Emancipatory Discourse' in N. Fairclough (ed.) (1992).

Janks, H. (ed.) *Critical Language Awareness series* (London: Hodder and Stoughton in association with Witwatersrand University Press Johannesburg S. Africa, 1994).

Janks, H. 'Closed meanings in open schools' in *Literacy for the New Millennium Conference Papers* (Australian Reading Association, 1993).

Janks, H. 'Critical language Awareness Journals and Student Identities', *Language Awareness* 8(2): 111–22 (1999).

Janks, H. 'Domination, access, diversity and design: a synthesis model for critical literacy education', *Education Review* 52: 175–86 (2000).

Janks, H. 'Identity and conflict in the critical literacy classroom', in B. Comber and A. Simpson (eds) *Negotiating Critical Literacies in Classrooms* (New Jersey: Lawrence Erlbaum Associates, 2001a).

Janks, H. 'Critical literacy: beyond reason', paper presented at *Applied Language Studies into the Millennium* Conference, Cape Town, 9–11 December, 2001b.

Just, M. A. and Carpenter, P. A. *Cognitive Processes in Comprehension* (Hillsdale, NJ: Erlabaum, 1977).

Kalantzis, M., Cope, B., Noble, G. and Poynting, S. *Cultures of Schooling:Pedagogies for Cultural Difference and Social Access* (London: Falmer Press, 1990).

Kletzien, S. B. 'Strategy use by good and poor comprehenders reading expository text of differing level', *Reading Research Quarterly* **26**(1): 67–85 (1991).

Koo Yew Lie *Submissive and Assertive Reading: A case study of variable reader roles in a Multicultural Society* Ph.D. thesis (University of London, 1998).

Kourilova, M. Lecture on 'Medical English' at Institute of Education, University of London, 1995.

Kramsch, C. *Context and Culture in Language Teaching* (Oxford: Oxford University Press, 1993).

Kramsch, C. 'The applied linguist and the foreign language teacher: can they talk to each other?', in G. Cook and B. Seidlhofer (eds) *Principle and Practice in Applied Linguistics* (Oxford: Oxford University Press, 1995).

Krashen, S. and Terrell, T. *The Natural approach: Language Acquisition in the Classroom* (Oxford: Pergamon, 1983).

Kress, G. *Learning to Write* (London: Routledge & Kegan Paul, 1982).

Kress, G. *Linguistic Processes in Sociocultural Practice* (Victoria: Deakin University Press, 1985).

Kress, G. 'Against arbitrariness: the social production of the sign as a foundational issue in critical discourse analysis', *Discourse and Society* **4**(2): 169–191 (1993).

Kress, G. 'Representational resources and the production of subjectivity: questions for the theoretical development of critical discourse analysis in a multicultural society', in C. Caldas-Coulthard and M. Coulthard (eds) *Texts and Practices: Readings in Critical Discourse Analysis* (London: Routledge, 1996).

Kress, G. 'Design and transformation: new theories of meaning', in B. Cope and M. Kalantzis (ed.) (2000a).

Kress, G. 'Multimodality', in B. Cope and M. Kalantzis (ed.), (2000b).

Kristeva, J. 'The Kristeva Reader', in T. Moi (ed.) (Oxford: Blackwell, 1986).

Lankshear, C. and Lawler, M. *Literacy, Schooling and Revolution* (London: Falmer, 1989).

Lankshear, C. 'Critical Literacy', Occasional Paper No. 3, Australian Curriculum Studies Association, 1994.

Lankshear, C. (with James Paul Gee, Michele Knobel and Chris Searle) *Changing Literacies* (Milton Keynes: Open University Press, 1997).

Lather, P. *Getting Smart: Feminist Research With/in the Postmodern* (London and New York: Routledge, 1991).

Littlejohn, A. 'The analysis of language teaching materials: inside the Trojan House', in B. Tomlinson (ed.) *Materials Development* (Cambridge: Cambridge University Press, 1998).

Lodge, D. 'After Bakhtin', in N. Fabb, D. Attridge, A. Durant and C. McCabe (eds) (1987).

Luke, A. 'Genres of power? Literacy education and the production of capital', in R. Hasan and G. Williams (eds) *Literacy in Society* (London: Longman, 1996).

Luke, A., O'Brien, J. and Comber, B. 'Making community texts objects of study', in H. Fehring and P. Green (eds) *Critical Literacy* (Delaware: International Reading Association, 2001).

Lunzer, E. and Gardner, K. *The Effective Use of Reading* (Heinemann Educational Books for the Schools Council, 1979).

McKinney, C. 'Critical Reading in a Bridging Programme for Afrikaans Speaking Programme', Unpublished paper presented at BALEAP, Glasgow, 1998.

McKinney, C. (forthcoming) Ph.D., thesis on 'Student Identity in post apartheid South Africa', University of London.

McKinney, C. and van Pletzien, E. 'Student identity and critical language study', Paper presented at *Applied Language Studies into the Millennium* Conference, Cape Town, 9–11 December, 2001.

Martin, J. *Factual Writing: Exploring and Challenging Social Reality* (Oxford: Oxford University Press, 1989).

Martin, J., Christie, F. and Rothery, J. 'Social processes in education: a reply to Sawyer and Watson (and others)', in I. Reid (ed.) *The Place of Genre in Learning: Current Debates* (Centre for Studies in Education Deakin University, 1987).

Meek, M. *How Texts Teach What Readers Learn* (Stroud: Thimble Press, 1988).

Meijer, M. *Intekst gevat inleiding tot een kritiek van representat* (Amsterdam: Amsterdam University Press, 1996).

Mellor, B., Hemming, J. and Leggett, J. *Changing Stories* (London: The English and Media Centre, 1984).

Mellor, B. and Patterson, A. 'Teaching Readings', in B. Comber and A. Simpson (eds) 2001.

Mercer, N. 'Language and the guided construction of knowledge', in G. Blue and R. Mitchell (eds) *Language and Education* (British Association for Applied linguistics in association with Clevedon: Multilingual Matters, 1995a).

Mercer, N. *The Guided Construction of Knowledge: Talk amongst Teachers and Learners* (Clevedon: Multilingual Matters, 1995b).

Mercer, M. 'The educational value of "dialogic talk" in "whole class dialogue"', Paper presented at *New Perspectives on Spoken English in the Classroom*, conference organised by Qualifications and Curriculum Authority, London, 27 June, 2002.

Mills, S. 'Knowing your place: a Marxist feminist stylistic analysis', in M. Toolan (ed.) *Language, Text and Context* (London and New York: Routledge, 1992).

Montgomery, M., Durant, A., Fabb, N., Furniss, T. and Mills, S. *Ways of Reading: Advanced Reading Skills for Students of English Literature* (London: Routledge, 1992).

Morgan, W. *Critical Literacy in the Classroom* (London and New York: Routledge, 1997).

Morgan, C. and Cain, A. *Foreign Language and Culture Learning from a Dialogic Perspective* (Clevedon: Multilingual Matters, 2000).

Murata, K. 'The discourses of anti- and pro-whaling in the British and the Japanese press: an intercultural perspective', Unpublished paper.

The New London Group. 'A Pedagogy of Multiliteracies: designing social futures', in B. Cope and M. Kalantzis (eds) (2000).

Norton, B. *Identity in Language Learning: Gender, Ethnicity and Educational Change* (London: Longman, 2000).

Nuttall, C. *Teaching Reading Skills in a Foreign Language* (revised edition) (London: Heinemann Educational, 1996).

O'Malley, J. and Chamot, A. *Learning Strategies in Second Language Acquisition* (Cambridge: Cambridge University Press, 1990).

Olson, D. 'From utterance to text: the bias of language in speech and writing', *Harvard Educational Review* **47**(3): 257–81 (1977).

Olson, D. 'When a learner attempts to become literate in a second language, what is he or she attempting?' The Forum in *TESL TALK* **20**(1): 18–22 (1990).

Olson, D. *The World on Paper* (London, Routledge, 1994).

O'Regan, J. (forthcoming) Ph.D. thesis on 'Post critical perspectives in Critical Discourse Analysis', University of London.

Paran, A. 'Reading in EFL: facts and fictions', *ELT Journal* 50: 25–34 (1996).

Peirce, B. 'Towards a Pedagogy of Possibility in the Teaching of English Internationally', *TESOL Quarterly* 23(3): 401–20 (1989).

Peled-Elhanan, N. and Blum-Kulka, S. 'Dialogue in the Israeli classroom', Xelkat Lashon 24 Seminar Levinsky Publishers, 70–84 (1998).

Peled-Elhanan, N. Keynote speech at 'Peace in the Middle East', a day of dialogue at the Institute of Contemporary Arts, London, 2002.

Pennycook, A. 'Incommensurable discourses', *Applied Linguistics* 15(2): 115–38 (1994a).

Pennycook, A. *The Cultural Politics of English as an International Language* (London: Longman, 1994b).

Pennycook, A. 'Borrowing others' words: text, ownership, memory and plagiarism', in V. Zamel and R. Spack (eds) *Negotiating Academic Literacies Teaching and Learning Across Languages and Cultures* (New Jersey: Erlbaum, 1998).

Pennycook, A. *Critical Applied Linguistics* (New Jersey: Erlbaum, 2001).

Phillipson, R. *Linguistic Imperialism* (Oxford: Oxford 1992).

Pusey, M. *Jurgen Habermas* (London: Routledge, 1987).

Quist, G. 'Culture in the university foreign language classroom: some theoretical considerations', *Dutch Crossing Journal of Low Countries Studies* 24(1): 3–28 (2000).

Rampton, B. 'Displacing the native speaker', *English Language Teaching Journal* 44 (1990).

Reynolds, M. 'Classroom power: some dynamics of classroom talk', in R. Clark, N. Fairclough, R. Ivanic, N. McLeod, J. Thomas and P. Meara (eds) *Language and Power* (Clevedon: Multilingual Matters, 1990).

Richardson, P. 'Human motives, cultural models and literacy', *The Australian Journal of Language and Literacy* 18: 76–80 (1995).

Roderick, R. *Habermas and the Foundations of Critical Theory* (London: Macmillan, 1986).

Said, E. *Orientalism* (London: Penguin, 1978).

Said, E. *Culture and Imperialism* (London: Vintage, 1994).

Sarangi, S. 'I actually turn my back on (some) students: the metacommunicative role of talk in classroom discourse', in *Language Awareness* 7: 90–108 (1998).

Sarwar, S. 'Veiling and Identity: Implications for English Language Teaching', Unpublished M.A. thesis Institute of Education, University of London, 2002.

Searle, J. *Speech Acts* (Cambridge: Cambridge University Press, 1969).

Shor, I. *Freire for the Classrom: Crisis in Teacher Education* (Portsmouth New Hampshire Boyton Cook, 1987).

Silverman, D. *Interpreting Qualitative Data: Methods of Analyzing Talk, Text and Interaction* (London: Sage, 2001).

Simon, R. *Teaching Against the Grain: Essays towards a Pedagogy of Possibility* (London: Bergin and Garvey, 1992).

Sinclair, J. and Coulthard, M. *Towards an Analysis of Discourse* (Cambridge: Cambridge University Press, 1975).

Smith, F. 'The promise and threat of microcomputers for language learners', *On TESOL '83 The Question of Control*. Selected papers from the Seventeenth Annual Convention of Teachers of English to Speakers of other languages, Toronto, Canada, 1983.

Street, B. *Literacy in Theory and Practice* (Cambridge: Cambridge University press, 1984).

Street, B. *Social Literacies* (London: Longman, 1995).

Stubbs, M. *Knowledge about Language: Grammar, Ignorance and Society* (University of London, Institute of Education: London, 1990).

Stubbs, M. 'Grammar, text and ideology: computer-assisted methods in the linguistics of representation', *Applied Linguistics* 15(2): 201–23 (1994).

Stubbs, M. 'Whorf's children: critical comments on critical discourse analysis', in *Evolving Models of Language*. British Studies in Applied Linguistics 12 (British Association for Applied Linguistics in association with Clevedon: Multilingual Matters, 1997).

Swales, J. *Genre Analysis* (Cambridge: Cambridge University Press, 1990).

Taylor, S. 'Locating and conducting discourse analytic research', in Wetherell *et al.* (eds) (Milton Keynes: Open University, 2001).

Thompson, J. 'Universal Pragmatics', in B. John, Thompson and D. Held (eds) *Habermas: Critical Debates* (London: Macmillan, 1982).

Trew, T. 'What the papers say: linguistic variation and ideological difference', in R. Fowler *et al.* (eds) 1979.

Urquhart, S. 'Identifying the good reader' in To read in a foreign language TRIANGLE 14 Goethe Institute/the British Council/ENS-CREDIF, 1996.

Urquhart, S. and Weir, C. *Reading in a Second Language: Process, Product and Practice* (London: Longman, 1998).

Van Dijk, T. 'Semantic Macro-Structures and Knowledge frames in Discourse Comprehension in Cognitive Processes in Comprehension', in M. A. Just and P. Carpenter (eds) (New Jersey: Lawerence Erlbaum, 1977).

Van Dijk, T. 'Discourse, power and access' in C. Caldas-Coulthard and M. Coulthard (eds) *Texts and Practices: Readings in Critical Discourse Analysis* (London and New York: Routledge, 1996).

Van Lier, L. *The Classroom and the Language Learner* (London: Longman, 1988).

Vygotsky, L. *Thought and Language* (Cambridge, MA: Harvard University Press, 1986).

Wallace, C. 'Critical literacy awareness in the ESL Classroom', in N. Fairclough (ed.) (London: Longman, 1992a).

Wallace, C. *Reading* (Oxford: Oxford University Press 1992b).

Wallace, C. 'Reading with a suspicious eye: critical reading in the foreign language classroom', in G. Cook and B. Seidlhofer (eds) (1995).

Wallace, C. 'Critical Language Awareness in the Foreign Language Classroom', Unpublished Ph.D. thesis, 1998.

Wallace, C. 'Critical language awareness: key principles for a course in critical reading', *Critical Language Awareness Special Issue of Language Awareness* **8**: 98–110 (1999).

Wallace, C. 'Conversations around the Literacy Hour: A Case Study of the responses of four bilingual children to the British National Literacy Strategy', Paper presented at *Applied Language Studies into the Millennium* Conference, Cape Town, 9–11 December, 2001.

Wallace, C. 'Local literacies and global literacy', in D. Block and D. Cameron (eds) (2002).

Wells, G. 'Apprenticeship in literacy', in C. Walsh (ed.) *Literacy as Praxis: Culture, Language and Pedagogy* (Norwood, New Jersey: Ablex, 1991).

Whorf, B. 'Grammatical categories', in J. B. Carroll (ed.) *Language, Thought and Reality: Selected Writings of Benjamin Lee Whorf* (first published in 1956) (Cambridge, MA: MIT Press, 1971).

Widdowson, H. 'Discourse and Text', Paper given at Ealing College of Higher Education Conference on the Reading Skill, 1979.

Widdowson, H. *Learning Purpose and Language Use* (Oxford: Oxford University Press, 1983).

Widdowson, H. 'Reading and communication', in C. Alderson and A. Urquhart (eds) *Reading in a Foreign Language* (London: Longman, 1984).

Widdowson, H. *Practical Stylistics* (Oxford: Oxford University Press, 1992).

Widdowson, H. G. 'Discourse analysis: a critical view', *Language and Literature* 4(3): 157–72 (1995).

Widdowson, H. G. 'On the limitations of linguistics applied', *Applied Linguistics* 21(1): 3–25 (2000).

Williams, R. *The Year 2000* (New York: Pantheon Books, 1983).

Willis, P. *Learning to Labour: How Working Class Kids Get Working Class Jobs* (Farnborough: Saxon House, 1977).

Wineburg, S. S. 'On the Reading of Historical texts: Notes on the breach between school and academy', *American Educational Research Journal* 28(3): 495–519 (1991).

Worsthorne, P. On the Regime of General Pinochet in 'Blueprint for Britain' by A. Beckett *The Guardian* 4 May, 2002.

Young, R. *Critical Theory and Classroom Talk* (Clevedon: Multilingual Matters, 1992).

Index